T0392278

EVERYDAY BELIEVER

LIVING OUT THE GREAT COMMISSION

Book and Study Guide

MICHAEL S. COOLEY SR.

WESTBOW
PRESS®
A DIVISION OF THOMAS NELSON
& ZONDERVAN

WestBow Press books may be ordered through booksellers or by contacting:

WestBow Press
A Division of Thomas Nelson & Zondervan
1663 Liberty Drive
Bloomington, IN 47403
www.westbowpress.com
844-714-3454

ISBN: 979-8-3850-3344-7 (sc)
ISBN: 979-8-3850-3345-4 (e)

Library of Congress Control Number: 2024918990

Print information available on the last page.

WestBow Press rev. date: 09/28/2024

CONTENTS

DEDICATION

This book is written and dedicated to you, the Everyday Believer.

The Everyday Believer typically has no theological degrees, but a servant's heart, in stepping forth to help, love, serve, and pray for others. Above all, sharing the good news of Jesus Christ.

It challenges you to step out of your familiar territory and fully embrace the divine moments God has designed for you, urging you to cast aside all fears and insecurities. It invites you to live the life that Christ has uniquely tailored for your journey and purpose.

In the pages of this book, you will not find embellished stories for mere entertainment purposes. Instead, you will encounter authentic and genuine accounts that aim to deeply engage you in understanding the profound truth that already belongs to you. It unveils that the gifts of the Holy Spirit are not limited to a select few but are available to all who seek God.

As I reflect on the content of this book, we serve a God of limitless possibilities, unconfined by what our eyes see or what we have understood through religious traditions. Rather, I am captivated by the knowledge that God holds divine appointments, meticulously designed for His perfect timing, and meant for everyone to experience through a personal relationship with Him.

This book invites you to embark on a transforming journey, where boldness intertwines with sensitivity, strength harmonizes with the tenderness of a caring heart, and where unwavering faith prevails in every circumstance. It is a testament to the abundant blessings that God has given us. Our Father lavished upon His children who diligently seek Him and know this-He loves every one of us.

This book emphasizes that obedience to God's will is not about earning recognition, but about humbly serving and loving others. Overall, it offers a perspective on living a faith life and surrendering to God's plan.

This book will open your eyes to a realm of possibilities that surpasses human comprehension and inspire you to live a life characterized by unwavering faith. The relentless pursuit of God, and a more profound sense of purpose can be realized.

The faith walk is indeed a journey full of wonder and purpose. Remarkably, God chooses each one of us to play a part in fulfilling His plan. Being used by God to impact someone's life and witnessing their transformation is a truly incredible and fulfilling experience. It is a testament to the power of faith and God's love for His children. One of the greatest messages you can share with others is the life you live, and your character revealed.

ENDORSEMENTS

Those seeking to deepen their relationship with God and to find true joy and impact in their service will find *"Everyday Believer"* filled with powerful and inspiring testimonies. Listening to God's prompting and acting upon it results in incredible acts of service and love. Michael's stories are inspiring but provide practical insights into discerning God's voice and responding with a servant's heart. This book has the potential to transform your faith and perspective on serving others, and I believe it is a valuable resource for anyone seeking to live out their faith in a meaningful way.

David A. Murphy,
former Xerox executive
and nutraceutical entrepreneur,

"Everyday Believer" is a must-read! We have enjoyed having Mike take us through his life-long ministry of helping and praying for people while following the lead of the Holy Spirit. Some were in crisis and life-threatening situations, and others needed someone to listen to them and pray with them. Some experiences even took years of praying for them to help them find their way to Christ. Seeing how God uses ordinary people to accomplish extraordinary things is awe-inspiring. It reminds us of His sovereignty and the power of His love to transform lives and bring hope amid difficult circumstances. We can indeed be grateful for how God's timing and intervention have impacted my life and those around us.

As "everyday believers", we can all make a difference in the lives of others by learning, listening, and being obedient to the leading of the Holy Spirit. Through our willingness to be open to His guidance, we can effectively minister to those around us in our everyday lives. The Holy Spirit equips us with the wisdom, discernment, and compassion we need to offer support, prayer, and comfort to those in need. It's a beautiful reminder that ministry is not limited to a specific profession or title but a calling we can embrace.

It's incredible how the power of prayer can work in someone's life over an extended period. The prayers of our neighbor and contractor friend have undoubtedly played a significant role in our journey out of a cult and into a personal relationship with Jesus Christ. Prayer is a powerful tool that connects us with God and invites His intervention and guidance in our lives. It demonstrates the faithfulness and persistence of those who intercede on behalf of others, and it's a testament to the transformative power of God's love and grace. We will always be thankful for those who have spent years praying for us. Prayer truly is a remarkable gift that can bring about profound change and healing.

Dean and Norine Kasten

We Love the Lord with all our hearts. Mike's book has helped me boldly share the news of Christ's love for everyone. I am a quiet person who leans more into helping and serving others. Mike's book will help believers stand out in faith, speak to the lost about the love of Jesus, and then turn the new believers into ambassadors for Christ. Mike and his wife, Robin, are lovely friends and great examples of how to live a life serving God and mankind. I believe Mike's book will help Christians become bold in speaking to others about Jesus and making them doers of the Lord.

Sandy has spent 34 years in the telecommunications industry and has a bachelor's degree in Christian Ministry and Bible study from the International School of Ministry. John is a Trial Attorney of more than 50 years and a Graduate of Michigan State University and Denver Law School.
Sandy Engman & John Engman

The *Everyday Believer* book is a real adventure to read. I enjoyed all the stories and real-life applications. While reading the book, I was encouraged to listen to the Holy Spirit's prompting in the Marketplace. Opportunities to encourage and bless people are all around us.

Mike's last book, *Power of Forgiveness*, was amazing. I gave away many books to hurting people. For many people, forgiveness is the gateway to their healing.

I love how your wife, Robin, is behind the scenes covering you in prayer. What a team.

After more than 30 years of real estate service and 4,500 happy clients, I still enjoy helping people buy and sell real estate. Our whole family is involved. Our mission is to serve people through love, dedication, and honesty.

Larry Martin
Jewels Martin
Larry Martin Realty Group
Grand Rapids, MI

Mike has chronicled his life-long journey with the Holy Spirit through poignant, real-life accounts. *EveryDay* Believer gives step by step insight into the Holy Spirit's leading and protection so one can grow deeper in their relationship with Him through true stories and study guide questions that can be used for personal growth or in a small group setting. You will enjoy this opportunity to grow closer to the Holy Spirit as it is written for people at every level in their faith walk.

The book's title *Everyday Believer* reflects the transformative journey you'll read about. Inside, you'll explore the pivotal moments that shaped Mike's spiritual path with God. Through trials, Mike emerged stronger, guided by Jesus Christ. The narratives illustrate the Savior's presence, reassuring Mike—and you, the reader—that you are never alone.

Remember, your story isn't finished. As an *"Everyday Believer,"* you can trust that the Lord, who is close to the brokenhearted, oversees all for His glory and your blessing.

Mindy Rentfrow/Tim Rentfrow
Medical Insurance/Billing Specialist
MBA, Global Account Manager

God has gifted Mike with the ability to highlight relatable insights to propel any individual to a vibrant, fruitful life of purpose and ministry. Mike's overwhelming number of personal examples of overcoming challenges, dealing with grief, extending forgiveness, and staying responsive to the Holy Spirit's leading is wonderfully inspirational. The thoughts and examples shared are instructive and applicable for every individual wherever they find themselves in their faith journey.

Jim Kregel
Kregel Parable Christian Stores – Grand Rapids

Thank you for trusting me to pre-read your book. I believe it is what you intended it to be, reflections of your walk of faith and listening and obeying the Holy Spirit's voice, while encouraging others to do the same. It felt as though personal stories came alive. I pray this book will be a blessing to everyone who has the opportunity to read it.

Having served in ministry as a youth pastor and evangelist for over four decades, I have read the Bible, and continue to study and research the Holy Spirit. I believe this book is a testimony of the person of the Holy Spirit, hearing His voice, and walking in obedience. Mike has done an outstanding job sharing personal story of ministry in this book, which I hope will touch your heart and inspire your faith as it has mine. I endorse this book wholeheartedly.

Randy & Lori DonGiovanni
RandyDon Ministries

Mike Cooley invites you to experience the adventure of a life lived in obedience and faith. His relationship with Father God through Jesus Christ shows us God's intention for any and every Christian.

Mike inspires us to live a life of power and fulfillment led by the Holy Spirit. After reading this book, you will be encouraged to continue choosing to partner with God in a life of spontaneous personal ministry every day!

Pastor and small business owner- Randy and Tammy Ritsema

Everyday Believer- Inspiring, Faith-filled, and Reflective!

Mike Cooley has opened his heart fully and completely to the prompting of the Holy Spirit in ways that few people rarely do. He is solidly grounded by the biblical principles and scriptural references found throughout his book, *Everyday Believer*. His daily prayer life is a beautiful testament to his dedication to God, family, and friends.

The critical importance of LISTENING to God for wisdom and direction has served Mike and Robin so very well on their journey to bring glory to God and genuine love and encouragement to others. How refreshing to see a couple so deeply and sincerely secure in their convictions that God is always with us, always faithful and desires to be in a loving relationship with all his children.

Through the years, Mike shares how he has become emboldened in his faith by being ready and willing to share the love of Christ with those in whom he comes in contact daily. He shares that he is watchful and "on the lookout"-just like any good hunter would be!

Mike's God-given abilities, talents, and testimonies align with God's will for his life as he discovers his purpose and continues to heed the "Word" from above. Be encouraged in your own faith-walk as you reflect and gain insight from this honest and heartfelt book. *Everyday Believer*. Our prayer is that God continues to use Mike and Robin in powerful, miraculous ways bringing joy to others and glory to God.

Martha Ann Riggs, MMIN Chaplain
Biblical Counselor & Mental Health Coach, Ordained
Member of Clergy, Teacher of Biblical Studies
Eugene Riggs
Co-Founder & CEO – Selleio LLC – A National Real Estate Company
CEO and Founder – West Michigan Notary Services

FOREWORD

By David A. Murphy
Men's Ministry leader, Bible Study facilitator, Entrepreneur,
and former Senior Account Executive Xerox Corp.,

I have been privileged to know Michael and his wife Robin through a variety of meaningful interactions, from serving together in the inner city of Grand Rapids to engaging in Men's ministries, Bible studies, social events, and heartfelt dinner conversations.

Michael and wife Robin embody a true partnership in faith, exemplifying a genuine love for serving others while always seeking to give God the glory. The experiences in sharing the Gospel throughout the book are not only engaging and encouraging but also of real value to the spiritual journey of the "Everyday Believer".

The summary message is crystal clear:

THE GREAT COMMISSION
IS YOUR COMMISSION!

As Christians, we are bearers of a unique hope in a world often overshadowed by darkness and despair. Our faith in Christ empowers us to carry the message of good news and share it with others. By humbly expressing the love and teachings of Jesus, we can bring hope and fulfillment to our divine purpose.

Hope stands as an indispensable facet of our existence, providing sustenance during times of adversity. In a landscape where hope may appear scarce, our duty as Christians is to offer the hope that stems from a relationship with Christ. This hope transcends temporary, worldly solutions and serves as a steadfast foundation for a better present, future, and eternity.

Just as we require food, water, and air for physical survival, hope is essential for the health of our emotional, mental, and spiritual well-being. It serves as a powerful force that motivates and inspires us to persevere through challenges. By extending our hope in Christ to others, we provide them with the strength and resilience necessary to navigate life's complexities.

David A. Murphy

PREFACE

Mark 5:19 (NIV)
"Jesus did not let him, but said, "Go home to your
own people and tell them how much the Lord has done
for you, and how he has had mercy on you."

Someone somewhere needs to hear your story. It gives them the courage to keep going and share their story. A strong testimony brings comfort and confidence that God will fulfill His promises. With Him, we can conquer any obstacle that comes our way. This encourages us to share with others the incredible works of God in our lives. Together, this reminds us of the power of testimony and the importance of sharing God's goodness with others. Your testimony is one of the most powerful tools you have in sharing the gospel.

Michael Cooley

ACKNOWLEDGMENTS

Many years ago, I would come from a work trip and share how God moved and used me to share my faith with those I had met throughout the week. Robin suggested that I start writing these moments down. These stories and testimonies will make an exciting book.

These were humble beginnings as we began to look at how God uses every one of us in His time to share, pray, or sometimes in just simple acts of kindness for others. These were divine appointments set forth by the Holy Spirit. The act of obedience can have its challenges primarily because of fear, mostly of rejection from others.

A special note of thanks to Sharon Brothers, who understands the vision of the Everyday Believer. Sharon edited and polished my writing so that each story lives with the precise accuracy needed. Sharon could see the power in testimonial stories, the backbone of our faith walk; everyone wants to hear the stories of answered prayers, divine appointments, and what God has done.

Rarely can a person be so blessed to have friends since early grade school. Today, in our mid-sixties, we still talk regularly, fish, and hunt together. I am thankful for my friend Dan Hughes as we have journeyed life together. Dan, my friend Rick Heath, and my brother Phil helped recall some essential details and contributed their editing expertise.

Lastly, my review team includes Skip Longcore, Dave Murphy, John and Sandy Engman, Randy and Tammy Ritsema, Larry and Jewels Martin, Randy and Lori DonGiovanni, Dean and Norine Kasten, Chuck Bedinger, Tim and Mindy Rentfrow, Scott Smith. Doug and Sandy Payne, and Don and Lisa Hannel.

A special thank you to Gregg Glutting, Sandy Engman, and Julie Kaiser for their contributing comments on The Power of Prayer.

With their friendship and professional help, each person brought unique talents to improve this writing and bring this book to life.

I wanted to express my gratitude to Martha Riggs, my Senior Editor, for your invaluable editing expertise in bringing my book, *"Everyday Believer"* to life. Your keen insight and attention to detail have truly captured the essence of the everyday believer within the body of Christ, highlighting how we can all be used through the unique gifts we've been given. Thank you for your dedication and for helping me convey this message so effectively. I appreciate your support and guidance throughout this process.

Lastly, I want to thank my wife, Robin, for her love for our family, children, and grandsons and continued support for my writing and our ministries. Couples that work together model the very best in marriage but also for a very happy and blessed home.

Truly, I could not have done this without your help. Thank you from the bottom of my heart.

Michael Cooley Sr.

INTRODUCTION

To God be the glory for everything that is written. None of this could have been made possible without the leading of God the Father, Jesus the Son, and the Holy Spirit.

My friend Dan wrote this...

"The greatest thing you can do in this life is to lead people closer to Christ, primarily through your words and by your example."

I have prayed for years to understand the Holy Spirit. On my early morning drives across the country, my prayers sometimes went on for hours. In many of those prayers, I asked God to make me into the man He created me to be. I prayed to be used and to be a blessing to others wherever and whenever I was in private and public places. I desired to hear His voice, go forth in obedience, and be used in His mission.

God sets up divine appointments in which we meet people in unique circumstances. Most of my stories in this book are about meeting people at critical times in their lives. I am a believer that all things are possible. I'll pray if it aligns with the word of God. Some of the prayers went on for decades before the Lord moved. I'll pray until the Lord releases me from that burden. Sometimes, that's a "one-and-done", and other times the prayers go on for years.

I don't believe in coincidences. I believe in God, His power, and His plan. My sensitivity to the Holy Spirit bears witness to this. God has developed me from a quiet, shy teenager to someone who speaks love and kindness to strangers.

Here is a recent example of this and the perspective of this book:

A few weeks ago, my wife and I were at a restaurant in central Florida. We were dining with friends Dave and Sara. While looking at the menu and deciding on my meal, the waitress asked me what I would like to have. The Holy Spirit spoke to me somewhere between ordering the chicken salad and a side of baked beans. His voice was clear and concise. This all happened in a normal dinner-time conversation in a busy restaurant.

He said, "I want you to pray with Matthew.' That was it, and I asked what He wanted me to pray for with Matthew. He said, "I want you to pray with Matthew." I responded, "Yes, Lord, I will call." In the morning, I asked a few prayer partners to pray for me so that God would lead me into this conversation and prayer.

I didn't really know Matthew. I only said "hello" in passing six months before. My meeting Matthew was nothing more than a one-time casual acquaintance. I prayed and sought out clarity. I learned that Matthew was very sick with a disease that was overtaking his body, and that he was doing poorly.

Through my efforts, it took a few days to make the connection. I called and introduced myself, and as we spoke, Matthew shared about his health. I asked him about his relationship with God. Matthew said, "I believe in God, but have not been to church since I was a child".

I shared the gospel through our conversation, and Matthew gave his heart to Jesus. He repented and prayed a prayer of salvation. That was a modern-day miracle made possible by the Holy Spirit speaking to me during a dinner with some friends. Nothing can compare to seeing God work through the obedience of His people!

This moment could only be from the God of the universe bringing one of His children unto Himself. Matthew was in a northern state while I was in Florida. The Holy Spirit transcends miles and time as a regular, everyday occurrence of His goodness.

The Holy Spirit lives inside us when we accept Christ and are born again. I desired to learn more about the gifts of the Holy Spirit and then step forward through acts of obedience to be used by Him.

Sometimes, these are challenging, and others are stepping out in faith, led by the Father. My faith walk is foundational growth, and my development is one step at a time. The more I exercised my faith, the easier it became to hear His voice and then move and speak as He led me; sometimes scary, but never alone! Every time He led the conversations, He used me as the vehicle to bring forth and share His message.

I am a regular midwestern guy, with no theological degrees. God will use ordinary people to do extraordinary things for the kingdom. I attend church, small group studies regularly, and read my Bible. I pray to seek opportunities to be used by God to bless others. I share many of these testimonial stories throughout this book to encourage others to seek God and His will and to be used by Him.

The faith-walk for you and me is a journey much like a long-distance runner running a marathon. When you are weakest, God's grace is vital, for He is our strength. Develop endurance to not only finish the race but also to finish the race strong.

Go and live the message of Jesus.
Then go out and tell the world about Him.

CHAPTER ONE

DREAM

Part One

1:11 Ephesians (NIV)
In Him, we were also chosen, having been predestined
according to the plan of Him who works out everything
in conformity with the purpose of His will.

In my business life, I could see the completed project. I would latch on to that dream before the weeds of life choked out my vision. The plans God has put into your heart - chase them, pursue them, run them down, and most importantly - do not let them get away! In business, I have always been a visionary, sometimes thinking of a project a year to even a decade ahead of the project becoming a reality. That is what I do. This is who I am! That is what dreamers do.

Know your purpose, know what God has created you for, and do it all for God's glory and always for His kingdom.

The dream in my heart and the love for my God are so intense that I trust Him enough to steer me to a destination without me trying to change and manage the outcome. It is nothing more than the submission of my strong will.

I love people who dream. Dreams can happen in several ways. Everyone knows that people dream while asleep. We know lots of people who dream wild and vivid dreams. Some dreams are full of happiness and joy, while others can be scary. Some people dream they are driving and feel themselves driving off a cliff into a steep canyon, and then - You are suddenly jolted awake!

These dreams are so real that our minds can recall the most intricate

MICHAEL S. COOLEY SR.

details. In addition, our minds remember facts about the instances in our sleep that would be impossible to recognize during our waking hours.

We need to tell others what we dream, hoping they understand, but ultimately, it only makes perfect sense to us. Why? Only the dreamer of the dream can tell the dream in detail. Is this a sign of something bigger or of something yet to come?

Numbers 12:6 (NIV)
And he said, "Hear my words: When there are prophets among you, I, the Lord, make myself known to them in visions I speak to them in dreams."

The other kind of dreamer is one I can relate to; this type of dreamer sees the possibilities in everything. This dreamer encourages the hurting, the sick, and the unlovable in society. These kinds of dreamers are also inventors and innovators in this world. Their minds are laser-focused and cannot rest without drawing, writing something out, and figuring out or finding the solutions to multiple problems simultaneously and, sometimes, waking from a sound sleep in the middle of the night to work on and solve problems.

I remember dreaming of having a cottage on a lake or a river. Robin, my wife, and I began discussing owning a second home. We considered the added expense and maintenance of owning a second place. Because our business was hectic and I traveled throughout the week, I wanted a place to rest and relax. Another thought was that it needed to be close to home after week-long travel. I tried to avoid being on the road for hours fighting traffic while trying to get out of town late on a Friday afternoon.

We made lists of properties as being within two hours of our home. We are active in our church, so coming home on Saturday evening would work to keep our church priorities aligned with who we are. We were okay with doing some projects on a cottage, but on the other hand, we did not want to become overburdened with the place, either!

We also wanted a place for families to have getaways and gatherings. I wanted a fireplace to enjoy throughout the long, cold, Michigan winters. Robin and I would pray for these things which were essential to us. But, most of all, we wanted to be where God wanted us to be and where He could use us.

Wherever we are, there is ministry. To understand this better, we are disciples according to His purpose. We pray daily that God sends us and uses us to share Jesus with someone today. The actual prayer goes like this: "Holy Spirit, give me (us) the sensitivity to hear your voice, to understand what you are saying today, and to empower us with boldness to speak your word in love, kindness, and respect."

Colossians 4:17 (NIV)
Tell Archippus: "See to it that you complete the ministry you have received in the Lord."

To understand the previous paragraph better, I can put this into a few simple words: Firstly, we get it. We know and understand who we are in Christ. Our faith-walk is a journey of living out our purpose every day. We do not wait for others to do what God has called us to. We surrender ourselves daily with sensitivity to the Holy Spirit's leadership, which can go in several directions.

Secondly, we are all in for our faith. We are transformed by the word of God and apply the Bible's principles to our daily lives. We are far from perfect humans, and humans make mistakes. However, we discipline ourselves to be the same person in church on Sunday as the same person you see out on a Friday night.

The definition of "Christian" is to be "Christ-like". Therefore, I do my best to represent myself according to who I am in Christ.

We began to dream of the perfect getaway place - This many bedrooms... the setting to look like this... Our dreams then became our prayers. We prayed God-honoring prayers to find a cottage where God would use us and be a place to glorify Him.

So why not hire a realtor to do a home search and let them show us what they have available? That is not who we are. That might seem odd, but because we believe in prayer - there are no deadlines, no hurries, and we trust our instincts while being led by the Spirit. With our list of ideas, we began to dream and to pray big prayers.

In my prayer life, there has been one constant over the years. My love goes deep, very deep, more profound than I can explain, but I will try!

In my extensive travels for my construction company, I spent many years and long hours driving across the Midwest. Many of these were sixteen to eighteen-hour days.

These long drives developed my prayer life generally in the morning and throughout the day. I would spend hours in prayer, looking for and asking for sensitivity to the Holy Spirit, while asking God to shape me into the man, husband, father, and grandfather He wanted me to be. In my prayer life, I pursued the Holy Spirit to better understand who He is.

I WANT TO LIVE EACH DAY IN CONSTANT COMMUNICATION WITH THE HOLY SPIRIT.

I learned from my late friend Brent as he described his walk with the Lord; Brent said, "I live every day in constant communication with the Lord." I looked at him as he explained, "I drive, walk, and work throughout my day in prayer." He continued, "I see that person walking on the street, and I pray for that stranger as I drive by." I learned from Brent a new level of relationship with God in my faith-walk.

As the years passed, I became sensitive to the Holy Spirit's voice. You will read some of my experiences throughout this book. Being in constant communication throughout my days and nights, I began recognizing that I had been given a special gift.

Sometimes I receive a quick and absolute "no" on something; other times, the "doors open." and sometimes I wait.

Throughout the years, I often fished on the Betsie River, about a two-hour drive north of our home. The Betsie River is a tremendous fishery! It has a sizable fall salmon run, and those salmon can grow into the thirty-five-pound range. Following the salmon run, the steelhead and rainbow trout migrate up the river from Lake Michigan in mid-October. Some stay in the river all winter until the main steelhead run begins early each Spring.

As Robin began searching the area for listed properties, we set the budget and picked a date early one Saturday to look at cottages. We drove to the first place with zero expectations. The place was nice, but the river access was hazardous. Years of flooding left the yard with a steep drop- off to the raging river below which was far too dangerous for us to consider for our young grandchildren!

Later, we went into town to get some breakfast and decided to drive along the river on our way home. As we drove, we saw a sign for waterfront property, so we followed the directions to the cottage. We parked the van, and I got out. I looked, and said, "Robin, this is the place." The Holy Spirit had spoken to me. We did not take one step; I knew this cottage was ours.

We contacted the listing agent, and later, she met us and walked through the home and property. We made "an offer" on the property. A few days later, the offer was accepted, and the cottage was ours.

The cottage was relinquished a couple of years earlier in foreclosure. The property was listed repeatedly with no buyers. Finally, the bank owned the property and tried to sell the property on the courthouse steps. Again, no bidders and no buyers were interested. When God has a plan for you, He will not only "open doors" for you, but He will also "pave the way" for you. This was the place – and now, it was ours.

GOD HAD A BIGGER PLAN, MUCH BIGGER THAN WHAT WE COULD HAVE IMAGINED.

I genuinely believe that God has a bigger plan when we dream big. More extensive than our minds can understand, that makes our walk with Christ so special! When we think we know it and understand it, the plan changes. When we are in the center of God's will, what we believe is the plan is only the beginning of His plan. The dream of buying a cottage was a dream come true for us, but the cabin was His. We recognize that we are caretakers and stewards of the land, sometimes for an extended period or simply through a season in life.

We took possession of our little cottage and began cleaning up a couple of years of neglect. Our street had about 14 homes on it. Neighbors stopped by to say "hi" and introduce themselves as we worked to clean up the place. People seemed genuinely happy that the cabin had new owners and that this abandoned house was being cared for.

The Spiritual Gift of FAITH

THOSE WITH THE GIFT OF FAITH TRUST THAT GOD IS SOVEREIGN - AND THAT HE IS GOOD

Those with the gift of faith trust that God is sovereign, and that He is good. They take Him at His word and put the total weight of their lives in His hands. They expect God to move and are unsurprised when He answers a prayer or performs a miracle.

I Corinthians 12:9 (NIV)
"...to another faith by the same Spirit, to another gifts of healing by that one Spirit".

Hebrews 11:1-3 (NIV)
1 Faith is confidence in what we hope for and assurance about what we do not see. 2 This is what the ancients were commended for. 3 By faith, we understand that the universe was formed at God's command so that what is seen was not made out of what was visible.

We had a slight slope from the yard to the river. I would usually cast out a fishing lure or a dry fly from our shore for a few minutes in the morning and evening. When the guys in the neighborhood saw me fishing, they'd come over and we had conversations that led to some lovely friendships. Fred was the oldest full-time resident on our road. Fred had lived there with his wife for nearly thirty-eight years. Fred was the go-to guy for bait when the brown trout would be biting. Fred was also the local neighborhood historian and was a wealth of knowledge in our little community.

Fred was a nice guy. He would be found cutting firewood for a needy family, stopping by to make sure things were okay, and would watch the place in our absence. The neighborhood had connecting yards, so it was an effortless walk along the river to connect over a cup of coffee. Fred was a friend. Fred could be counted on no matter the task or challenge. Fred had a true servant's heart, not out of duty or obligation. I wish everyone could witness, know, and understand this quality in a man. Fred was the "real deal" and a man of his word. I am a relationship guy; I enjoy learning about people's lives and listening to them share their stories. Great friendships were formed and developed over these casual conversations.

One Friday evening, Sig, my chocolate Labrador, and I walked to Fred's house to say hello. Our conversation lasted well over an hour. Fred was explaining that his back was hurting from a tree-cutting injury as I was leaving. Years earlier, I had a spinal fusion in my lower back, so we began to speak the same language. As I left, I said, "Fred, I will pray for you." He gave me the coldest, most hard look and said, "Mike, I'm not religious; I don't even believe in God." But, he continued, "life is like a tomato plant in the garden; the plant grows and gets beautiful yellow flowers, the flower turns into a small green tomato, then it ripens to a tasty red, flavorful tomato over time. The less desirable tomatoes fall to the ground and rot back into the earth." That was Fred's story of "life." According to him, there is no Heaven and no Hell - just the life cycle of the tomato plant rotting back into the soil.

Esther 4:14 (NIV)
For if you remain silent at this time, relief and deliverance for the Jews will arise from another place, but you and your father's family will perish. And who knows but that you have come to your royal position for such a time as this?"

ROBIN REMINDS ME OF THIS
WHEN GOD IS MOVING IN OUR LIVES....

God has created you for such a time as this. Robin knows the right time to speak this into my life, and it is always when I feel inadequate or underqualified for a challenge. I am a confident, mature man; however, her support for me is incredible. Our close marriage partnership ensures we stand together in ministry. As a man and husband, nothing can give me more confidence than knowing that my wife believes in me, prays for me, and stands with me as we minister.

WHEN WE SURRENDER OURSELVES
COMPLETELY TO GOD,
A TRANSFORMATION OCCURS WITHIN US.

The Holy Spirit reminds me of the journey to this place, and it is not by accident or random choice. It is God's design and His Divine appointment for Fred and me. I will honestly say when these moments occur, I am nervous that I do not have the right words to say. I will not rely on my words, but God's words to be spoken through me.

When we surrender ourselves completely to God, a transformation occurs within us. Our dreams and prayers become powerful enough to shape history. God yearns to fill us with His presence and use us as a vehicle to reveal Himself to the world. This is the purpose and the reason for which we were created - To be the light of the world, sharing the good news with those around us.

It is then, and only then that the Holy Spirit reminds me my total reliance is on Him and Him alone. I will open my mouth, and He will give me the necessary words to speak, which bring His love and healing into hurting hearts.

God had used us to minister to other families in our little river community, leading some to Christ and, at other times, giving counsel and praying for those were hurting. God used us throughout our neighborhood and a nearby small town. I am reminded that we are to be the light of the world, to be available to share the love of Christ with kindness, love, and respect wherever we are. The Holy Spirit would prompt me about Fred. Fred was different from the rest. The Holy Spirit drew me to Fred.

I understood that the battle was not flesh and blood; the battle was against the principalities and the powers of darkness. Generations of disbelief had held Fred's family in darkness, held them tightly, and would not let them go. There was an immovable rock between Fred and eternity - an obstacle so big it would take an act of God for him to change.

This is difficult to explain, but I will try! The Holy Spirit will put someone in my life that I will pray for in earnest. I began a six-year prayer journey the day we met, and none of it was easy. Several times a day, Fred would come to mind. I would pray God would use me to speak life and truth into Fred's life, asking the Holy Spirit to soften Fred's heart to at least hear what I have to say. I am not a forceful, preachy person; however, I will pray until I am released from the burden.

As the years passed, there was still no breakthrough. Fred would remind me, saying, "My grandparents were atheists, so were my parents, my uncles, and so on". Knowing what you are up against is a part of the battle; however, the name of Jesus trumps everything else in existence. The demons of hell cringe at the name of Jesus, and the demons of generational unbelief fall at the name of Jesus. It is easy to understand there is a battle for your soul.

THERE IS NOTHING ON EARTH THAT IS AS VALUABLE AS ETERNAL LIFE.

God knows and has perfect timing for you, me, and Fred.

Robin and I were at the cottage one Friday night and went to bed in our upstairs bedroom. After an hour or two, I went downstairs and prayed for Fred as several hours passed in the night. Although this was a battle, I could feel the urgency that the next morning, Saturday, would be the day I would boldly speak the truth about Fred's life. I would confront him with the truth of salvation.

Knowing this was God's timing, I felt at peace with the decision to have a deeper conversation with Fred about where he would spend eternity. I processed my thoughts, rested, and fell asleep in my chair for the rest of the night. Robin arose early, making coffee. She asked, "Was your back hurting so much that you came downstairs?" I said, "No, the Holy Spirit prompted me to pray for Fred. I prayed for hours. Finally, the Holy Spirit said, 'This is Fred's day'. I will go and present the gospel to Fred and pray with him."

Knowing and trusting the Holy Spirit for upcoming conversations are essential moments in our spiritual lives. These are the most intense spiritual warfare battles you will ever face; Eternity is at stake for Fred or someone else you have been praying for and believing in.

Robin and I prayed before I left. We bound the demons of hell in Jesus' name. We prayed that the Holy Spirit would soften Fred's heart and that his heart would be changed. Robin would continue in prayer until I returned from my visit. I can walk confidently, knowing my prayer partner is in battle with me this day and every day!

Sig, my Chocolate Labrador, and I left our cottage and began walking through the connecting lawns along the river. I prayed "in the Spirit" as we walked through the cottage yards toward Fred's house. Sig's personality is a big, lovable, and incredibly loyal friend. He would sniff ahead, always looking back to see me, never venturing more than ten to fifteen yards from me as we walked toward Fred's house. Then, out of nowhere, two stray dogs ran in on him! I had never seen these dogs before. They were biting him from all directions, growling, fangs showing! This was an all-out dog fight! I tried to stop them from the attack, yelling and kicking at them. I yelled, "Be Gone in Jesus' Name!" The dog fight ended instantly, and the two stray dogs ran away crying and whining, sounding like they had been whipped.

Peter 5:8-9 (NIV)
Be alert and of a sober mind. Your enemy, the devil, prowls around like a roaring lion looking for someone to devour. Resist him, standing firm in the faith, because you know that the family of believers throughout the world is undergoing the same kind of sufferings.

The dogfight was proof of the evil forces trying to stop the meeting with Fred. But there is power in the Name of Jesus - powerful enough to call off the attacking dogs or whatever attacks you may face! My pace and resolve increased as I knocked on Fred's door. Fred answered the door, and we shared some small talk. I began to explain what was on my heart and the reason I came to share Jesus with him. Fred said again, "Mike, I am not religious." I replied, "This is not about religion, but about a relationship with Jesus Christ."

In Fred's doorway, we stood face to face for at least three minutes, looking into each other's eyes without saying a word. I prayed for the Holy Spirit for a breakthrough as the minutes passed in unbelievable awkwardness. Finally, Fred broke; he looked down, then up, and said, "Okay." It was then I began to share my testimony about my relationship with Jesus Christ. As I spoke, Fred listened while I shared from my heart. I talked about eternity and knowing that Fred mattered to God and that He knew Fred before he was born. We had a conversation about salvation when Fred said, "Let's pray!" I prayed with Fred as he accepted the Lord and surrendered his life to Christ. I left knowing I had surrendered to the Holy Spirit's call. I was obedient, going where He had sent me to go and fulfilling what He had called me to do. Robin and I rejoiced, praising God for using us to fulfill His promise in Fred's life.

Breaking Down the Strongholds

Ephesians 6:12 (NIV)
12 For our struggle is not against flesh and blood, but against the rulers, against the authorities, against the powers of this dark world and against the spiritual forces of evil in the heavenly realms.

The adversary refuses to let go and will stop at nothing to create confusion and disarray. The enemy's plan is destruction - pure and simple! He is out to discredit testimonies, marriages, families, churches, and lives everywhere. He plans to lay carefully set traps to prey on people's weaknesses, and these attacks can come from a thousand different directions.

A few weeks passed, and I heard from someone who had recently spoken to Fred. It was relayed to me that Fred said, "When I prayed with Mike, I didn't mean it", and that he vowed to go back to his old ways of living and his old way of thinking. I was devastated by hearing this! The evil one had its claws deep into Fred's heart and refused to let go. We began to pray daily that I would have another opportunity to minister to Fred.

GOD USED AN OLD STORY IN A NEW TIME

THE HOLY SPIRIT TAKES OUR LIFE EXPIERENCES AND USES THEM AT HIS APPOINTED TIME FOR SOMEONE WHO NEEDS TO HEAR A WORD OF ENCOURAGEMENT AT THE EXACT TIME IN THEIR LIVES.

Today, I am reminded that my faith life is a journey. It takes each of us on many twists and turns. God uses our story sometimes the same day and other times decades later to reveal His glory. In the valleys of time, struggles and sickness are never wasted for the Everyday Believer, as it is in the valleys of life where actual growth takes place, and our character and faith are made stronger. When we listen to the voice of the Holy

Spirit, He will take the experiences of our lives to share our testimonies with those who need them most. The Holy Spirit takes our life experiences and uses them at His appointed time for someone who needs to hear a word of encouragement at the exact time in their lives. I desire to live a life with sensitivity to the Holy Spirit's voice and having the boldness and discernment to speak those words into a life that is hurting or even to someone who is a stranger to me.

I received a call one day that Fred was extremely sick and in the hospital. Fred refused all visitors except his wife. Fred was then released from the hospital, and a week or so later, I stopped by. I prayerfully felt led by the Holy Spirit to revisit Fred.

YOUR STRUGGLE IS NOT JUST FOR THE HERE AND NOW. IT COULD BE THAT YOU ARE GAINING INSIGHT, AQUIRING SKILLS, AND GETTING READY FOR SOMETHING BIGGER IN THE FUTURE.

I walked down to Fred's house and knocked on the door; he invited me in. Fred was weak from his sickness. We sat at the kitchen table surrounded by pictures of big fish he had caught over the years. I asked him what kind of sickness did he have? Fred said, "Mike, you have never heard of it." I persisted in asking. Finally, Fred said, "I have something wrong with my blood. It is like leukemia, but it is not leukemia." Fred told me they had given him lots of blood transfusions and powerful steroids to help keep him alive.

When I was about thirty years old, I, myself, had developed a rare blood disease where my platelets were attacking themselves and killing off the good blood clotting cells inside my body. The condition was called (ITP). ITP mimics leukemia and is just as fatal. I was extremely sick and near death during this phase of my life, and I had been given many blood transfusions to keep me alive.

NOTE: Your struggle is not just for the here and now. It could be that you're gaining insight, acquiring skills, and getting ready for something bigger in the future. Maybe there's a lesson to be learned that will equip you for what's to come. Overcoming obstacles of the past becomes our story and testimonies in sharing our faith. Our testimonies are one of the most powerful ways to share our faith.

Sometimes, something more profound might unfold within the challenges you face. Your struggles may be serving a greater purpose in your life. They could teach you valuable lessons, prepare you for future endeavors, and equip you with the necessary skills and strength for what lies ahead. God will heal you for His glory and your testimony. In my example, God used my healing of my sickness to witness Fred thirty years later.

I asked Fred again what the name of his sickness was. Fred showed me a piece of paper with Idiopathic Thrombocytopenia Purpura (ITP), saying "You had never heard of it." I then told Fred the story of my journey with (ITP) and that we were "blood brothers." I shared how prayer brought me through my sickness, that I am healed, and that the glory belongs to God.

I also told him that I had heard what others said about him not giving his heart to Christ. Fred said, "Mike, I'm just not sure." As I shared again, Fred listened, and we prayed for salvation in Fred's heart. Finally, we shook hands. That was the last time I saw Fred.

Fred returned to the hospital and was given just a few short hours to live. At this moment, Fred had declined any visitors. Once again, he was wavering on his faith as generations of unbelief were deeply embedded into his soul. The adversary NEVER gives up; he is relentless, bringing up old memories, guilt, self-doubt, and thoughts that run through your mind repeatedly telling you are not good enough.

Luke 15 4-7 (NIV)

"Suppose one of you has a hundred sheep and loses one of them. Doesn't he leave the ninety-nine in the open country and go after the lost sheep until he finds it? And when he finds it, he joyfully puts it on his shoulders and goes home. Then he calls his friends and neighbors together and says, 'Rejoice with me; I have found my lost sheep'. I tell you that in the same way, there will be more rejoicing in heaven over one sinner who repents than over ninety-nine righteous persons who do not need to repent."

WAITING ON GOD IS TRUSTING IN GOD.

God does not move at our will but according to HIS plan and purposes. The prayers had been prayed. I waited patiently on God. Waiting on God is trusting in God. I was not released from praying; however, I waited quietly, praying to God, "please do not let Fred pass without knowing You as his Lord and Savior."

Fred's wife recalled the last hours of Fred's life. She cried at his hospital bedside. Fred was upset seeing her tears and sadness. Fred asked her why she was so sad, and she replied, "I have always been a believer, and you refuse to believe in God, so I won't see you in Heaven." Fred thought momentarily and responded, "If you love Jesus, I want to love him too." Fred's wife led him into another prayer of salvation in his hospital bed, and Fred received Jesus again. there was no going back or changing his mind. Fred was all in. A few short hours later, Fred met Jesus' face to face, his King of Kings, and his Lords of Lords.

Romans 8:28 (NIV)
And we know that in all things God works for the good of those who love him, who have been called according to his purpose.

Throughout the difficulties of life and certainly in the "in-betweens", God is in it. I do not believe God gave me sickness so thirty years later I could witness to Fred about my healing. When I became sick thirty years ago, God used that moment to remove the distractions from my life and rely only on Him and Him alone. During that most challenging time, I began to understand there was no greater place to be than out on a limb with God.

Those moments became divine appointments to minister to Fred, to become "blood brothers", ultimately in Christ. There are no checkmarks for doing good - just walking with God, being sensitive to the Holy Spirit's voice, and then taking bold steps to share the love of Christ with someone. The hardest part of this is having confidence - confidence to speak sometimes to strangers about God's love for them while overcoming the fear of rejection. God honors our obedience even when we feel less than qualified for the task and lets the Holy Spirit lead the conversations.

My relationship with Christ is not about feeling good about church on Sundays but about growing in the truth and knowing who I am in Christ all day. No merit badges to earn, but being a disciple of Christ, being always available to share the love of Jesus with someone today.

In Conclusion

The Right Word
At The Wrong Time
Is The Wrong Word

We will only have the right word at the right time if we listen. HEARING the voice of the Holy Spirit is necessary but WAITING on the Holy Spirit to act or speak in ministry is His perfect timing. Seeking God throughout the six-year prayer journey with Fred was an exercise in patience. Through the years with Fred, we began to understand each other as men. Hurrying through the process with him would have failed. However, as time passes, a relationship's true character is revealed; Fred was a man who wanted to see the "real deal."

Fred was a man that was solid in what he believed in and lived his life with a code of conduct for who Fred thought he was. Throughout his family's generations, Fred lived out what he was taught. Like many men, Fred was strong on the outside and a soft, caring man on the inside. His life was genuinely changing as Christ became the Lord of his life. I prayed for Fred, and the Holy Spirit guided me through the process. Under challenging circumstances, I asked the Lord to work in His timing and that Fred would not perish without knowing Jesus as his Lord and Savior. Patience and trusting the Holy Spirit were vital to walking through these years with Fred.

Our dream was fulfilled in many ways. Where God leads us, He is already there. He knows the lives you will meet before His works move us into action; the Holy Spirit is already at work. Walking out the steps in faith as He leads makes everything fall into place, though rarely easily. The oppressor is also doing everything he can to foil God's plan. There is no greater name than the name of Jesus and to Him all glory, honor, and praise. It is a pure joy to walk it out and be used in this and other situations as He leads!

It is nothing short of a miracle that the Holy Spirit brings lives and helps build relationships together. Men joined by a common interest in fishing for trout and conversations around a campfire were born from the dream of our cottage on the Betsie River. We planned to have our cottage for rest and getaways - which it did for us. Still, the ministry doors that opened were life-changing for some, and for others, they changed their course for eternity.

The Change of Seasons

The cottage was never meant to be exclusively for us but to be used by others. Over the years, the cottage was used as a pastor's retreat for their families. It hosted many events in ministry, cookouts, and gatherings. Time spent with others and campfires made good wholesome family memories. Trout fishing and time with family and friends are memories to be cherished forever!

A few months passed after Fred's funeral service, and so did the season of owning our little cottage. Our time away was becoming more complex, and the desire to be there began to wane. The Lord revealed to Robin six months earlier that He would prompt me to consider selling; Robin said nothing but prayed for me. The decision to sell was a joint decision, we listed it, and it sold in three days.

The friendship with Fred was a journey; I would not trade those memories for anything. The joy of conversation, fishing together, and enjoying a cup of coffee around a campfire are the life and times of the Everyday Believer.

I recognized that I could only say so much to help Fred believe in the Lord. I had lived by example; we had solid conversations about eternity, life, and my relationship with Jesus. I did what I could for Fred, but in the end, Fred had to want it for himself, his life, and the relationship with the Lord that only the Holy Spirit can provide.

It is then, and only then, that the Holy Spirit does what the Holy Spirit does; He ministers to the heart. I continued to pray and trust His leading for Fred. Fred is His child. I did everything I felt led to do. In these moments, the months turned into a year, then the years passed. With the same passion I prayed, never giving up on my call for Fred, I just trusted the process believing Fred's heart would soften.

We will either accept Jesus as our Lord and Savior or reject Him. When our physical bodies die here on earth, our life is over as we know it. Those who believe and accept Jesus as our Lord and Savior will go on to Heaven. Sadly, those who reject Christ will spend eternity separated from God.

Thoughts and footnotes:

The power of your dreams may have greater significance than what you give them credit for. Our dreams may provide us with the subconscious desires of our hearts. Throughout the Bible, God spoke to people in their dreams. What I understand about dreams is - know that you know where God may be leading you throughout your life. We felt confident about wanting a riverfront cottage but left it up to God to direct us to the place where we should go. He knew the people we would interact with through thoughtful heartfelt conversations where we could share our Christian witness.

God knows the bigger picture. So, we can plan, set goals, and line everything up. The daily surrendering of our hearts to God allows us to be used in fulfilling His plan for something we cannot see. You may have heard the statement, "Let go and let God." We learned in our lives to make that a top priority. The journey to the cottage was one of the examples in our lives where we let go. For the greater unseen picture, God knew the plan for our little place.

He knew the gatherings and the people affected, both guests to our cottage home, and the residents, as well. Robin and I went into the 'cottage season' of our lives to be available for Him to use us. We have lived by the belief that where we are, there are ministry opportunities all around us.

I have always been a relationship kind of guy; God used my personality traits to connect with Fred and others throughout my life. I previously stated Fred wanted the "real deal"; anything artificial would have broken the connection we had as friends. Fred's family lineage produced generations of unbelievers. It is what he knew, it is what he believed. To some, understanding of spiritual warfare and the battles that exist for one's soul - are real.

When I shared that I was sick thirty years ago, I could have never in my wildest imagination thought God would use that story as He did. Instead, God knitted the dream in our hearts for a place on the river and prepared the neighborhood's people. This was a complete submission of our will to Him.

The persistence to pray for Fred was a six-year journey. I am glad to have stood in the gap for my friend and been used by God in Fred's journey of faith. There was never a coincidence or an occasion where I thought, "This is how it goes." Every step on this journey was God's divine plan and purpose. To God be the glory, honor, and praise to Him!

Main Takeaway:

The importance of focusing on hearing the Holy Spirit and waiting on His timing for a word in season. "Timing is not our own and seeing success may take years." (Paraphrase, mine.)

The Lord will always provide an opportunity for His children.

Chapter 1 Study Guide Questions

What can happen if you give yourself the possibility to dream?

Starting with the end in sight - and never letting go of the destination, can you trust God to see your dream through to fulfillment without interruption?

Does the all-knowing God of the universe use something like a sickness some thirty years earlier to bring someone like Fred into faith?

Or how do you see it differently?

God will do whatever He can do to bring His children back to Himself. Do you have examples that you experienced in your life?

Where, without question, did you see the hand of God move things in perfect alignment for His will or His purpose?

What does being "all in" - in your faith, mean to you?

Explain what it means to be burdened for someone so much that it changes your life. Can you go far in praying for a friend or a loved one, even if it takes months, years, or even decades?

What drives your determination not to give up when praying for a lost friend or loved one?

In my faith-walk, I believe God can do anything and everything. How can you passionately pray for someone or a situation when it seems impossible in man's eyes?

In my search for our cottage, I explained how God gave us the desires of our hearts. Before I stepped foot in the driveway, God said, "This is the place".

Do you have a testimony of God's faithfulness as you searched for something - a house, a job, a spouse, etc., and the Holy Spirit said, "This is the place?"

Explain your answer.

CHAPTER TWO

MISSION DRIVEN

Part One

Ephesians 1:15 (NIV)
"For this reason, ever since I heard about your faith in the Lord Jesus and your love for all of God's people…"

"People, even more than things, have to be restored, renewed, revived, reclaimed, and redeemed; never throw out anyone".
-Audrey Hepburn

I sometimes think about how to love others when we do not feel like loving them. The word 'feeling' is an emotion; REAL love comes right from the word of God. Wow, that is a powerful statement! We are commanded in the Bible to love one another and all of God's people, even the most difficult people in our lives.

It is easy to love the people who are most like us, those with whom we are drawn, and those with whom we are most comfortable. This is how most friendships and groups establish themselves among people with a common interest. If we stay comfortable within our groups, we will never be all God has called us to be. When we venture into the unknown and love outside of our comfortable circle, to an uncomfortable place where God calls us, we grow in our faith, and our lives are changed forever. People are touched and ministered to. Another unforeseen blessing is that as we follow the Holy Spirit, our obedience will take us to another level in our faith. I never want to be in the same place in my faith for two days in a row, and this desire is refreshing in my walk with God. A new place, new challenges, and 'walking the line' to where you never thought you could do what God calls you to do.

I remember my siblings and me riding with my mother to visit the doctor in the downtown inner city as young children. We would leave our house in the suburbs, the car windows down, the sweltering summer wind blowing on our faces. When we reached a particular neighborhood, Mom would say, "Lock your doors and roll your windows up." The ride would feel tense as groups hung out in the streets, and mom's anxiety quickly transferred to me and my siblings. She drove, staring straight ahead, gripping tightly to the steering wheel while navigating the car to our destination without deviation.

After parking the car, we would cling together, holding hands while quickly crossing the street, only to feel a sense of relief once safely inside the doctor's office building. The scene would play out again in reverse fashion on our way home. The people downtown seemed different from where we lived. This was life as a six-year-old in the early 1960s; we were not taught to hate but were given a healthy dose of fear while in the downtown environment.

The inner city was years or even decades ahead of my mindset. Our life in the suburbs was innocent with our biggest challenges on any given summer day amounting to choosing sides for sandlot baseball games or deciding what section of the creek to go fishing. Almost every home in our neighborhood had two parents, and most mothers stayed home to raise their children. Our view of life was one-dimensional, a linear view of what we were taught, so it was all we knew. We avoided these "unsafe" places when our parents showed us, but we were still inflicted with a broad sense of fear at an early age.

With maturing both in age and in my spiritual walk, I was burdened to do more for the kingdom of God. As the years passed, I grew in my understanding of Christ's limitless love, with an emphasis on those who are hard to love. The Holy Spirit brought me to His awareness of people in their greatest need - which can be anywhere - but my heart ached for the addicted and the homeless community. The homeless community includes the unwanted in society who have either been rejected or have walked away from their families. The thought of being unwanted in and of itself can deepen substance abuse.

It is during this time I began to think to myself. What is it like to be them? Growing up, my childhood was much different having a mother and father who loved me. Others may have never known their father or been victims of abuse. One inevitable thing is that, at some point, things go wrong. Nobody would choose to live under bridges or tarps, especially in brutal wintertime conditions. I remember thinking about how I could help without enabling bad behavior and choices.

I CAN DO SOMETHING, BUT I CANNOT DO EVERYTHING. Am I willing to give time to love, feed, and share Jesus with strangers? What would Jesus do?

During this time, I began volunteering with the Grand Rapids Dream Center. The Dream Center helped me transition into inner-city ministry. It was most rewarding to be involved in serving the needs of others. My men's ministry pastor, Tom, was involved in leadership with the Dream Center and helped form its leadership team.

After a men's ministry meeting, Pastor Tom told me, "Mike, there is an abandoned church in the downtown area. Would your company be interested in volunteering for general cleanup, carpentry, and painting?" I met with pastor Moses, the pastor of Acts Gospel Church - his new church location. I listened to his hopes and dreams for his new building. The building had been left empty for about twenty years. We walked throughout the building and developed a plan.

Our tour of the building ended in the church kitchen, where we enjoyed some conversation. I sensed the Holy Spirit speaking about an old commercial stove against the back wall. The stove was broken and was not up to code. Moses said if the stove could be replaced, the ladies in the church would put together a meal program.

I started pricing out new commercial stoves and started raising money. The new stove was installed shortly thereafter. Years have passed, over two hundred fifty thousand meals served, and over a thousand salvations for Christ was realized because of the 'stove project'. The stove project united a wonderful friendship with Pastor Moses and his wife, Co-Pastor Diane. Our lives began to grow as we became ministry partners.

(Footnote)

The Power of Forgiveness (released August 2017).
Xulon Press, Amazon Books. (Chapter 17, The Power of Prayer)

Casting My Judgment Aside

God was at work in my life. I did not know where I was going or where He was taking me. This was the beginning of my understanding of tough love. As the journey unfolded, I began to understand the term 'loving the unlovable'. Serving the people of the inner city brought lots of opportunities as I began to see homeless people living in challenging situations where addictions and prostitution run rampant. I listened to their stories, noting that a life-defining moment usually led them to this place. Everyone has a story, and everyone wants to be heard, so I listened and offered to pray and believe with them. I encouraged them in Christ.

John 13:34-35 (NIV)
"A new command I give you: Love one another. As I have loved you, so you must love one another. By this, everyone will know that you are my disciples." - Jesus Christ

When God puts a dream in our hearts, we can choose to serve our flesh thinking, "how will people view us when we do this?" We can be too busy, or say, "I am not comfortable with that", or maybe begin to believe "I am not qualified," or "Oh *God, please send someone else!*" Some people will fight the inner fight of complacency. Feeding those fleshly thoughts will not allow personal growth or help anyone. The word given in our hearts and mind may leave God's plan unfulfilled. Will God find another willing vessel to fulfill His plan?

I know who I am in Christ. I know what I am called to do: Serve others and share the gospel with love, kindness, and respect. Most of the time, this comes at inconvenient or inopportune times. I must set aside my agenda and submit myself to Him and His will, answering the call to serve Him. At these times, the harvest is significant, even if it is just one person. When the seeds have been planted, I understand that this is, and is always, the Holy Spirit's job to bring people unto Himself.

Part Two

Cowboys and Bad Guys

We had spent months planning for our Rocky Mountain vacation. Our early morning flight from Michigan touched down at the Denver International Airport. We picked up our rental car and drove to the West. The sky-lined view of the Rocky Mountains is something to behold! Being away from our business and the rest from the responsibilities for the next week was needed. Throughout the day, we drove toward Cheyenne, then West toward Rock Springs in the foothills of Wyoming.

The history of the West has always fascinated me. The Wild West - where the outlaws and bank robbers re-play in my mind and take me back to a child reading paperback novels. The Western United States is a rough and unforgiving country. It makes you wonder where the hide-outs were on the rocky cliffs and ravines for the bad guys staying just ahead of the sheriff's posse. These areas are synonymous with Doc Holliday, Wild Bill Hickok, and many others.

It is hard to believe you can drive fifty miles or more between houses. Our minds find it difficult to grasp the openness of the country and the beauty of creation. With each turn and the gradual elevation climb, we said, "Oh, look at that!" or "That's SO beautiful!" and so on. In my mind, I wished I had my fishing gear to take a few casts as we passed beautiful mountain streams with their clean and pure waters!

Matthew 10:20 (NIV)
"...for it will not be you speaking, but the Spirit of your Father speaking through you." - **Jesus Christ**

In times like this, we pray and listen to biblical teaching as the miles click away. We reflect and slow down and listen to the voice of the Holy Spirit. Many years before, God spoke to me on a trip like this. He said, "Start an in-home Bible study." The message came with such clarity that I shared it with Robin, and we began to develop a plan. Hundreds of Bible study nights later, our relationships grew deeper with Christ and our study friends.

We drove out of Rock Springs, Wyoming, in the morning, heading north towards Jackson, Wyoming. As we drove, I felt the Holy Spirit speak to me from the book -*The Power of Forgiveness,* and about creating a Bible study and teaching each chapter of that book to Moses's inner-city church. The voice of the Holy Spirit was unquestionable as I shared this message with Robin. The book is nineteen chapters long, meaning we would commit ourselves to teaching each chapter for nineteen straight weeks every Tuesday night.

We sat on this 'word' for a few days, continuing to pray about the possibilities. Upon returning home, I met with Pastor Moses to review God's word that was spoken to me. Moses was all in, and I began to write a study guide to go with the book to guide our studies. Months passed, and the study guide began to come together.

A Change of Heart

God has a way of changing your heart. Our home Bible study group suggested a dinner and a movie night at the inner-city church. Each Bible study family would bring a homemade dish, and our group would serve the movie attendees a meal after the movie. We did this on a few Saturday nights with remarkable success. We made popcorn, handed out candy, and created a fun atmosphere for everyone. Some nights, we even had people inquire deeper and give their lives to Christ. This all came from God speaking to our hearts months before in preparation for the people we would meet that would be changed as they gave their lives to Christ.

Other times throughout the year, Robin and I would fill in for Pastor Moses and Diane and preach what was on our hearts. Our hearts began to love the people of this church and this community as our relationships grew closer. Each time we would drive down into the inner city to serve, speak, and minister - our hearts and minds grew in anticipation of our forged partnerships. Gone were the thoughts from my childhood and my mother saying "lock your doors and roll up your windows" as we drove through the inner city. We were growing and developing friendships in the body of Christ.

After several months, *The Power of Forgiveness* study guide was complete. We visited the church one Sunday morning to announce the upcoming Tuesday evening study. We spoke about the book and its impact in hopes of generating excitement and direction for the months ahead.

The Message Is Jesus

3 John 1:4 (NIV):
"I have no greater joy than to hear that my children are walking in the truth."

PEOPLE WANT THE TRUTH - EVEN WHEN IT HURTS PEOPLE ALWAYS WANT THE TRUTH.

The message is always the Word of God. When we speak, we speak the truth in love. Our actions and speaking reflect hearts that have been changed through our relationship with Jesus Christ. We are the world's 'light', and the light transforms the darkness. Today's culture will try to bend and distort God's Word, and we stand on the word as an Absolute Truth and a reference point for our compass to return to no matter the circumstances. The answers people are looking for are in the Word of God.

Soon, the first Tuesday evening came, and I set up two chairs for Robin and me, facing the class at their level. The topic of forgiveness can go in a thousand different directions. We taught from the perspective of complete openness and confidentiality that anyone could share or comment, thus creating a safe environment where all would be comfortable. We created a learning environment where participants would speak, ask questions, and learn from others' experiences.

John 8:31-32 (NIV)
To the Jews who had believed him, Jesus said, "If you hold to my teaching, you are really my disciples. Then you will know the truth, and the truth will set you free."

OUR BEST SPIRITUAL TRUTH IS OUR CHARACTER AND INTEGRITY, SO WHEN WE TEACH THIS TRUTH, OUR LIVES REFLECT THE FOCUS AND PURPOSE OF WHO JESUS IS IN OUR LIVES.

I began to share my story - the intimate details of my feelings, hurts, fears, and shame from my experience of being tied up, robbed, and held against my will. Nothing made up, nothing embellished, just sharing my story from my heart. I spoke from the perspective of pure, honest, and raw emotion. The room was quiet as everyone listened. We connected through the realities of life. Most everyone has been hurt; some hurts are easily visible, while others' hurts are buried deep into their subconscious minds, where their pain lies hidden behind their hearts' guarded walls.

That is the way it happened. I was open and vulnerable in a room of strangers as I described my trauma. The group looked on as I walked through my moments of sheer terror that still awaken me at times from a sound sleep over forty years later lapsing into nightmarish panic attacks. This was me being authentic in front of a room full of strangers. I would share this uncomfortable truth because that is who I am. Our best spiritual tool is our character and integrity, so when we teach this truth, our lives reflect the focus and purpose of who Jesus is in our lives. Our story changes from that of some religious element to the powerful, intimate personal relationship we have with Jesus Christ.

Robin and I are good at working off one another and know when we can respectfully add a comment or help clarify a point or topic. As we taught, the group was quiet but made a few comments here and there. For the most part, everyone was quiet. It was this way for the first few weeks, however, everything started to change in the fourth week. Faces were smiling, and everyone was beginning to open and share more.

Corinthians 13:1-3 (NIV)

"If I speak in the tongues of men or of angels, but do not have love, I am only a resounding gong or a clanging cymbal. If I have the gift of prophecy and can fathom all mysteries and all knowledge, and if I have a faith that can move mountains, but does not have love, I am nothing. If I give all I possess to the poor and give over my body to hardship that I may boast but do not have love, I gain nothing." - **Apostle Paul**

By the fifth week, one of the ladies in the class made us a homemade loaf of banana bread as a gift. Something was beginning to change, and where we were once outsiders, people were beginning to trust us with the hurt and abuses in their lives. Robin and I did not come to judge, but to bring hope and healing to those hurting, through biblical principles and the trauma of my robbery experience. Our culture has taught us to stuff down and suppress the hurts and feelings throughout our lives; that is what I had done for forty years following the trauma of my robbery experience.

In the following weeks, the hurts came out as the class began to share some of their childhood experiences where very extreme child abuse had occurred. Most of these abuses were caused by parents who were highly addicted to heavy drugs and/or had alcohol issues. Some stories were so horrific they would form tears in our eyes. I began to think my robbery story was minor in comparison!

As the weeks progressed, the closeness of the group came together. People began to support each other and pray for one another. When this happens, it is incredible; the hurts and burdens of the people in the class begin to heal! People have carried these hurts locked inside their hearts for years if not decades. As the group opened about their past hurts and experiences, we prayed, laughed, and cried together.

These suppressed feelings over time can quickly build into the hardest of hearts; anger and shame can set in, and when they do, there is a personality shift. The abuses run deep, and their hiddenness can stop personal growth. The innocence of normal childhood development has been hijacked. It is surrounded by a heavy cloud of shame where children were exposed to and have seen behaviors years or even decades ahead of their maturity level. They are most certainly things children should never see.

Part Three

As Carol Began to Share Her Life Story, The Bible Study Group Sat Up and Took Notice

Carol grew up with her parents and siblings; her home was full of love, and she felt loved and secure as a little girl. Carol's nature is to be trusting - to take someone's word and believe it's true. Being a trustworthy person is a fantastic attribute of her character. The difficulty of trusting is the vulnerability of being used and taken advantage of.

Carol's security was shaken at the age of thirteen when her parents separated and then divorced. Carol began hanging with the wrong crowd, first smoking some cigarettes, and then using other substances regularly. Carol would stay at her grandparents' house for a while to find some normalcy there. After establishing some trust, a relative entered her bedroom, and abuse began. Carol ran from her grandparent's home to hang with a close group of friends, who introduced her to other bad substance use. Then, she was introduced to harder substances, to which she was instantly addicted. The guys in the group were hustlers manipulating her into human trafficking.

Still a teenager, she began the human trafficking to support her drug addiction. The hustlers supplied her with the needed drugs; in turn, they would rape her and beat her to a bloody mess daily. Almost thirty years of substance abuse and escort service led her to being arrested, landing Carol in prison and jail for over thirty incarcerations. Carol wanted to be done with this life, but the strongholds that held her down were powerful. During her last time in prison, Carol cried out to God. Surrendering her life to the King of Kings and the Lord of Lords. The Holy Spirit comforted her as Carol sought a new life from the one, she had not known for most of her adult life on the streets.

Titus 2:14 (ASV)

"Who gave Himself for us to redeem us from every lawless deed, and to purify for Himself a people for His own possession, zealous for good deeds." - Apostle Paul

Carol's life is still a work in progress; however, today, she is a strong woman of God. Carol now owns a successful business and praises the One who freed her. After all the forgiveness, Carol still struggles with the shame of her past. Understand that those memories are a lie from the devil trying to keep her tied to her past. Jesus took the shame of her past mistakes and nailed them to the cross. I am thankful that Robin and I can walk alongside Carol and others and see the power of forgiveness and the story of her great redemption in Jesus Christ.

As the months passed, the success of the study began to grow. I made myself vulnerable, open, and honest. I openly shared the story of my armed robbery, being tied up and almost killed. Being authentic about my fears and feelings connected with our group. Most people we met in our class

30

had been hurt or abused by someone in their lives. We learned and healed together, and they began the journey of forgiveness. I spoke to Pastor Moses months after the class ended. "The class was beneficial", he said. "The church members still discuss it and want to do the class again". Moses smiled, saying, "lives were changed, strongholds were broken, and people were walking around being freed from decades of heaviness."

Ephesians 2:10 (NASB)
For we are His workmanship, created in Jesus Christ for good works, which God prepared beforehand so that we could walk in them. **- Apostle Paul**

I held my story inside for about forty years, and through Robin's encouragement, I began to draft my book, which was later published in 2017. The Holy Spirit knows when and how to 'knit the stories' of our lives together, and it is never by coincidence but by His perfect timing for each of our lives. The journey of forgiveness for each of us begins at the foot of the cross, giving our hearts and lives to Jesus Christ through the forgiveness of our sins.

Part Four

The Spiritual Gift of GIVING

The Holy Spirit imparts this gift to meet the needs of the church and to help those who do not have the means to provide fully for themselves. Those with the 'gift of giving' love to share with others the overflow of blessings God has given them. They are grateful when someone shares a need with them and are always joyful when they can meet it.

Philippians 4:10-18 (NIV)
"I rejoiced greatly in the Lord that at last, you renewed your concern for me. Indeed, you were concerned, but you had no opportunity to show it. I am not saying this because I am in need, for I have learned to be content whatever the circumstances. I know what it is to be in need, and I know what it is to have plenty. I

have learned the secret of being content in any and every situation, whether well-fed or hungry, whether living in plenty or in what I want. However, I can do all this through him who gives me strength. Yet it was good of you to share in my troubles. Moreover, as you Philippians know, in the early days of your acquaintance with the gospel, when I set out from Macedonia, not one church shared with me in the matter of giving and receiving, except you only; for even when I was in Thessalonica, you sent me aid more than once when I was in need. Not that I desire your gifts; what I desire is that more be credited to your account. I have received full payment and have more than enough. I am amply supplied, now that I have received from Epaphroditus the gifts you sent. They are a fragrant offering, an acceptable sacrifice, pleasing to God." - Apostle Paul

The Journey Begins with One

I prayed and processed how God could use me in the inner city. I made a list of core values not just for the inner-city ministry but also for how I would live my life. This was how I would approach each day, which would be my gift of service.

Proverbs 11:25 (NIV)
"A generous person will prosper; whoever refreshes others will be refreshed." - King Solomon

The journey to serving begins with one person at a time each day - and more if it happens! Making the relationship connection with others works best for me; however, I have been spontaneous when led.

We will never be able to reach the lost until we have deep, heart-felt compassion to see them saved.

The heart of inner-city ministry breaks down like this:

- Share Jesus with everyone, speak life, and hope for a better tomorrow.
- Share with them that their identity is in Christ, not in life's mistakes.

- Love unconditionally whomever I meet.
- Listen to their story with Holy Spirit-filled ears.
- Pray with them and offer encouragement.
- Serve everyone the same.
- Give of myself, share my testimony.
- Seek forgiveness, offer salvation in Jesus Christ.

My faith journey is an intentional walk every new day. I want to be used to grow, help, and serve others. In my heart, I care for others. I asked God to send me to where He would have me go. Sometimes, these divine appointments are big and powerful, and other times, they are simply casual moments sharing the love of Jesus. Throughout the years, the message has been clear - Bring hope and encouragement to the casualties in society. (The early years were the most difficult. I lacked the courage and self-confidence). When the Holy Spirit speaks to you, listen, pray, and let Him lead the conversations for you.

Moses and Diane began a meal program serving the homeless and the addicted in one of the inner-city parks. Robin and I were asked to take part. We recruited my friend Tom and others. The challenge was that we never knew how many people would show up. We began with hot dogs, chicken, and burgers. My friend John bought some grills to the park for the cookout.

I love smoking meat, so we shopped for briskets and chicken legs a few weeks before a planned event. The process of preparing the meat precisely and right is labor intensive. Seasoning the meat usually takes 24-48 hours (about two days) to let the marinades season into the meat. With five briskets and fifty pounds of chicken legs, the process begins.

I enjoy the low and slow smoke process, in which I fire up the smoker around six in the morning, and somewhere between twelve to eighteen hours later, everything is done. Great smoky taste, and the smoke ring looks exactly right! I refrigerate the brisket overnight, then slice the meat into serving sizes, reheat it, and bring it to the park to be served. Someone asked me once why I go through so much trouble and expense when hot dogs would be sufficient. I respond, "Nothing but the best for God's people!"

Preparing the food is excellent, but I love speaking and ministering to the people, praying for their needs, and encouraging those we serve. Every one of us has come from diverse backgrounds. I had the blessing of coming from a strong family structure, where my parents took us to church and taught us kids' strong values, so why not pass that along?

In The Face of Risk,
I Choose Courage

Life has been challenging for the many we meet on the street or in the park. At times their life was going along perfectly until a circumstance derailed them, spiraling downward into substance abuse and homelessness. We are the messengers of hope in a dark world. People in the park need hope and Jesus Christ in their lives. God has called us to serve, to love the unlovable in society, to be the source of encouragement, and to share the good news of Jesus Christ.

Deuteronomy 15:11 (NASB)
The poor will never cease to be in the land; therefore, I command you, saying, "You shall freely open your hand to your brother, to your needy and poor in your land." - **Moses**

While planning our most recent Labor Day lunch in the park, the Holy Spirit was moving in my heart, and I prayed to seek clarity. I shared with Robin what I was feeling. This prompting for me was taking a risk, to lay it all out on the line and follow the Holy Spirit's leading. In the days leading up to our lunch event, I smoked about twenty-five pounds of pulled pork, which I added to large batches of homemade mac and cheese, and then smoked the meal for another four to five hours.

Tom and I arrived at the park early; we contacted other event leaders. I pulled Pastor Moses aside for a word on what God had prepared for me. Pastor Moses told me some time back, "If God is laying something on your heart, do not hold back." Pastor Moses had given me complete approval to speak into the hearts of the park's residents. Pastor Moses and Chris, a church volunteer, and I addressed the crowd before they ate. I then shared what the Holy Spirit laid on my heart. I was to gather the people in the park in proximity while waiting in the food line. The time was now. I began to share what God has done for me, my salvation, and my relationship with Jesus Christ.

Ephesians 6:12-13 (NIV)
For our struggle is not against flesh and blood, but against the rulers, against the authorities, against the powers of this dark world and against the spiritual forces of evil in the heavenly realms. Therefore, put on the full armor of God, so that when the day of evil comes, you may be able to stand your ground, and after you have done everything, stand. **- Apostle Paul**

THERE IS NOTHING GREATER THAN HAVING A SECOND CHANCE.

When I am about to experience a significant move of God, I expect powerful opposition to my plans - and this day lived up to those expectations. On this day, Robin chose not to serve in the park, but instead, was going to walk around our property at home and pray and intercede for the rest of the volunteers and me. She prayed for strongholds to be broken and for the Holy Spirit to lead us into our day, into conversations and interactions with the people we met. Understand this is 'ground zero' where the most difficult homeless persons, prostitutes, heroin, and cocaine addicts live (and openly use) and will trade anything for their next fix.

With heads bowed and eyes closed, I asked those who wanted to receive forgiveness for their sins to raise their hands. Some of their hands went up to the sky while others raised their hands just a little. God knows the intention of each hand raised. We began to repeat aloud a prayer of salvation. As I spoke, hundreds repeated the prayer. Twenty-five to one hundred-plus people were saved at that moment. This was just as the Holy Spirit showed me it would be a week before.

The meal was nearing completion when I saw a young lady named Mary. I motioned her over to Pastor Moses and me. As we talked, she said she was twenty-one but looked about fifteen. She came from a horrible home environment and said, "life in the park and on the streets was better than her home." She said she hustled in the park, getting and selling illegal substances and other things to make money. We spoke of Jeremiah 29:11, explaining that God wants to give her hope and a future. I told her I saw a leader inside of her and a successful person and gave her the vision of leaving the streets. Before we parted ways, Moses and I led Mary into a prayer of salvation.

Part Five

Ephesians 2:8-9 (NIV)
"For it is by grace you have been saved, through faith—and this is not from yourselves, it is the gift of God—not by works, so that no one can boast." - **Apostle Paul**

PEOPLE CAN TELL WHETHER WE CARE
**No one is beyond the reach of God,
no one should be left out,
and no one should be written off.**

God uses everyday people like us and the wonderful volunteers at Acts Gospel Church to be a light in a dark place - to be honest with a woman named Mary or a man named Greg, as someone who brings the love of Jesus to the street.

As Tom and I were ministering to the people in the park, we met a man named Greg. Greg was fifty-five years old, and he wanted prayer for his addiction. Greg shared that when he was twenty-three, he was at a party and was introduced to drugs for the first time. The first time was followed by thousands of times. Greg was instantly addicted from the first time. Greg's marriage spiraled out of control, and he lost his job. The substance abuse destroyed his life, marriage, and relationship with his children.

1 Corinthians 10:13-14 NIV
"No temptation has overtaken you except what is common to mankind. And God is faithful; he will not let you be tempted beyond what you can bear. But when you are tempted, he will also provide a way out so that you can endure it. Therefore, my dear friends, flee from idolatry." -*Apostle Paul*

Greg told us he would be taking a Greyhound bus to the Seattle area the next day, entering a treatment program, and re-establishing relationships with his children. Tom and I prayed for Greg that Jesus was Lord of his life and then to release the demons of hell that kept him bound to decades of cocaine addiction. We prayed for healing in his body, that he would be healed from the top of his head to the soles of his feet, and for an immediate release of his addiction in Jesus' name. We said goodbye, believing God would provide the best for Greg.

As the days and months passed from our meeting with Greg, I wondered if he followed through with the prearranged treatment program set up by his children in Seattle. Greg's children had 'drawn a line in the sand' for Greg by entering him into the treatment plan. Pending his success, they would reestablish their relationship. Hard, tough love and difficult love were the boundaries. Nothing more, nothing less. When Greg comes to mind, I pray for him and wonder if he followed the plan. I pray that Greg's life is restored, his life that the enemy came to steal, kill, and destroy. Greg's story could become a testimony of God's healing, redemption, and that of an overcomer, understanding his identity in Jesus Christ.

The inner city is filled with every story imaginable. Every hardship in life is revealed through the faces of its residents. The pain in their eyes shows that lives once full of promise have now turned to heartache and despair. On this day, I helped man the grill for a few hours, and my friend Will led the charge in preparing 550 meals that we would serve. This was a typical day for our group of volunteers. Will led a simple message about overcoming addictions. The message was based on his decades of substance abuse. Will spoke of his life changed by the power of God and his relationship with Jesus Christ. He was a just another face in the crowd a few years before. Will's life was changed, washed clean from the shame and power of addictions.

We offered a prayer for salvation. About a dozen people confessed their sins, and these lives were changed for all eternity. I am always amazed when God moves in the hearts of his people, just regular, everyday people being used to share their faith to invest in others. As the meal was winding down, a woman approached me. She thanked me for the meal. It meant a lot to hear that. I asked her name, and she responded, "Kathy - "I'm from Texas. "After some small talk, I asked, "Why are you in the park? What brought you here?" Kathy stated, "I am a low-dollar escort who has lost her way." She was an escort, or someone caught up in trafficking.

Romans 2:1-2 NIV
"You, therefore, have no excuse, you who pass judgment on someone else, for at whatever point you judge another, you are condemning yourself, because you who pass judgment do the same things. Now we know that God's judgment against those who do such things is based on truth." - **Apostle Paul**

LOVE AS CHRIST LOVES

When in the city, judgment has been cast aside; these are children of God, His children. I represent myself as a beacon of light in a very dark place. This perspective levels out the playing field. We can share a meal and God's love with everyone we meet, not just a few; everyone's the same. Before the meal, Kathy responded to our simple message of salvation and surrendered her heart to Christ. Kathy looked down, feeling unworthy. I said, "You are a child of the King, and He loves you and knows you by name." Her eyes opened wide, and the smile hidden by years of shame came forth. As this happened, her whole demeanor changed in an instant! Kathy said, "He loves *me*?" I responded, "Yes, He loves *you*". I watched as tears ran down her face.

Kathy's life was filled with guilt and shame. She felt unworthy because of the choices that brought her to this point. Deep inside her is the likelihood of abuse from her childhood that turned her toward substance abuse, leading to escorting and homelessness. The power of God changed her life. She was no longer a woman held back by guilt and shame, but a new person born again, a child of God, washed clean from the sins and shame of her past!

GOD HOLDS US BLAMELESS FOR OUR FORGIVEN SINS - AND HE WILL NEVER ALLOW US TO BE HELD GUILTY FOR THEM.

And then, we spoke about a plan to help her with her future. My friend Steve and I prayed for Kathy that God would align the right people in her life so that good choices could be made, and that God would see her through to the destiny He created for her. We prayed that Kathy would become the woman that God created her to be, that she would develop her testimony and glorify God, who had changed her life. I cannot wait to hear her story and see what God has planned for her life!

Part Six

The News Story Felt Like a Punch to the Gut

A few weeks before I served at the July fifth event in the park, the Pastor asked me to share my heart and then pray for the meal. This was a regular event staffed with lots of volunteers and some excellent food for the folks gathered in the park. I walked over to a group of about fifteen park residents. I began to share my relationship with Jesus Christ, salvation, and a testimony of God's actions in my life. Whenever I am asked to give my testimony or to pray, I ask the Holy Spirit to use and anoint my words.

Jude 5:20 (NIV)
"But you, dear friends, by building yourselves up in your most holy faith and praying in the Holy Spirit, keep yourselves in God's love as you wait for the mercy of our Lord Jesus Christ to bring you to eternal life." - Jude

It is All About Eternity
Breaking The Cycle
And Moving Forward

Before I left for the park that morning, I asked friends and Pastors Doug and Don to lift our group in prayer, along with my wife Robin, that God would prepare the hearts of the listeners and that HIS words would speak out of me. The time had come, and I spoke to the group. I shared as they listened. We prayed, and twelve to fourteen people gave their hearts to Christ. God is tremendous! Our group had served 420 meals to the park residents.

When the event ended that day, I thought back to the faces in the crowd and to those who gave their hearts to Christ. I continued to pray for them as the days passed into weeks, hoping this was the change needed for a successful transition from the streets into everyday life.

Headline news broke with the story of a man killed in an area downtown park. This murder took place in the very spot where our group serves. My mind raced back to the faces in the crowd - of those who raised their hands and surrendered their lives to Christ a couple weeks previous. Maybe a drug deal had gone wrong, or a fight ensued over food or blankets. Sometimes, turf wars are started by residents' seniority or hierarchy within these groups. Some who heard the news that night might not think anything of the story. The Holy Spirit reminds me that therefore we do what we do. It hurts not knowing whether the deceased person's heart was made right with Jesus before he perished into eternity.

My friend Don reminds me that the places in which we minister are different yet the same. People are dying everywhere in every way. They may or may not know Jesus. We must press into the darkness and reach as many as possible before it is too late. I am thankful that God has paired me with like-minded believers. Brothers and sisters in Christ ministering the love and the cause of Christ in each of our communities, wherever the Spirit leads us.

Jeremiah 29:11(NIV)
*"For I know the plans I have for you", declares the LORD,
"plans to prosper you and not to harm you, plans to
give you hope and a future." - Prophet Jeremiah*

My faith-walk makes me believe that Greg will succeed in his treatment plan. Greg's life, like everyone's, is always in God's hands. I live my life with the hope that Greg has made better choices for himself and is a changed man by the power of the Holy Spirit. God knows the plan, for our hope and a future lies within His hands. When we accept Jesus as our Lord and Savior, we can remove the distractions that cloud our decisions and trust Him with the days ahead for a bright and prosperous future.

Several years earlier, we met Nancy - a middle-aged woman with a heart for God. Nancy walks through the park and the nearby streets, praying for people. She just asks the people she meets what she can pray for. The Holy Spirit leads her as she prays for their needs.

One day, as Tom and I left the park, we found a woman lying on the city sidewalk. We woke her, then helped her up and brought her back to the park for a warm meal and ministry. Nothing supernatural - just helping someone in need, loving the unloved in our community, leading her to a warm meal, and to a wonderful group that would help care for her needs.

Part Seven

Conclusion

Focusing On The Mission

The mission is to be the 'hands and feet' of Christ. To break it down even further is simply to love others in Christ. And that begins with the basics of feeding and clothing people. Our mission does not enable unruly behavior. Our efforts show people that they are loved unconditionally and that all of us are sinners saved by grace.

The journey of life brings people to this point. Our group happily loves, feeds, and clothes people where they are by surrounding them with prayer and sharing Jesus for the hope of a bright and better future. Some residents receive and embrace that hope, while others continue live as if nothing has changed. The mission is still to connect with someone, develop relationships, and be the vehicle of hope for a brighter tomorrow in a very dark place.

Encouragement

Through every meal event in the park, we feed and minister to an average of five to six hundred people. With so many faces in the crowd, the Holy Spirit identifies the one we are to talk with. He singled out one to me - Greg. I encouraged Greg by praying with him and then speaking about life in his family situation. We discussed reestablishing relationships with his children and making positive declarations and goals, like meeting his grandchildren for the first time. I encouraged Greg to stay the course and walk firmly in his new life in Christ, to turn from his past, and live it out one day at a time.

Speak Life

I was taking a break in the shade with Pastor Moses when I saw Mary for the first time. The Holy Spirit said to speak with her. I got up, walked to her, and asked her to sit in the shade with Pastor Moses and me. Mary spoke, and we listened to her story; she was such a vibrant young girl to be caught up in a life of homelessness and, as she said, hustling. Moses asked her about her relationship with God. Mary said she "believed in God"." Moses responded, "It is not enough to believe in God; the demons of hell believe that God exists." Moses and I offered to pray with her and explained what it means to be saved. Mary accepted Jesus as her Lord and Savior that day. I told Mary before she left us that I saw her as a leader and a successful businesswoman, and I encouraged her to go be the woman God has created her to be.

New Identity

The afternoon in the park was beginning to wind down when a lady approached me and said, "I want to thank you for praying for me and feeding me today." The woman I am talking about is Kathy from Texas. Her self-esteem was low when she described herself as a "low-dollar harlot". An hour before, Kathy accepted Jesus as her Lord and Savior. I told her that that was the 'old' Kathy. "You are a new creation in Christ. God loves you so very much! He does not see the mistakes you have made in your life." God sees Kathy forgiven for past mistakes. We spoke about the good things ahead of her in life. That afternoon was a new day for Kathy, now full of hope and promise!

Acts 20:35 (NIV)
"In everything I did, I showed you that by this kind of hard work, we must help the weak, remembering the words the Lord Jesus himself said: 'It is more blessed to give than to receive.'" - Luke

Rejecting The Feel-Good Moments.

Living out Acts 20:35, giving is more blessed than receiving. It feels good to serve others in the service of the Lord. After serving others, I feel good knowing I have made a difference in someone's life today. I have also learned that serving from the heart makes a difference. It helps me encourage the weak to help lift the ones who need it most.

Our group does not seek the attention of the media or any other publicity in doing good works; we just simply serve and care for God's people. This could sound like a feel-good story, but it is not. The people we serve alongside know that this is their mission- the mission to lift, love, and care for the hurting. Some of the people we serve with were rescued from the streets and alleyways where they overcame addictions, trafficking, and homelessness years or decades earlier. Seeing their lives changed and transformed and serving the people they used to be is nothing short of a miracle!

From my childhood memories riding through the inner-city, Mom's voice rings loud and clear: *"Lock your doors and roll up your windows"*. Today, I walk confidently, knowing the Holy Spirit goes before me. There is no shortage of needs; everywhere you look around, there are needs.

MINISTRY IS SIMPLY WHERE YOU ARE.
Do not fear but answer God's call in these awkward spaces.

I have changed from my past, as we are all sinners. Some sins in people's lives are played out on the street corner or under a bridge, while others are the moments played out in the mind behind closed doors, secretly hidden from view. Gone are the fears instilled by my mother as a child. I am wonderfully led by the Holy Spirit to go where HE leads me. The change in me is not just the desire to serve others but a matter of the heart.

My words today are a call to action: GO and SERVE! Go, and love, and care for people who are hurting - and show them that you care from the heart. Every one of us has a calling to be involved and to share the message of Jesus Christ with a lost and hurting world. Everyone has a voice to share the good news of Jesus Christ. Give them your best; give them your absolute best! This is a ministry and one of the many ways we can serve the body of Christ as Everyday Believers.

Thoughts and Footnotes....

In reflecting on my life, I can say with certainty I have, and am still enjoying it. For most people, along with myself, life has some significant 'bumps in the road'. My life could have taken a negative turn on several occasions. During the tough times, I had people close to me who cared enough to help me through the challenges. Life is difficult for most and harder for some.

Throughout my life, I have chosen to stay close and focus on my relationship with God. That relationship with God has made me realize and understand my life's mission. That mission is to love and care for those who are hurting. Then, God can use me as a lifeboat for someone who might be drowning and gasping for air. I want to be rock steady when someone is enduring life's storms.

Throughout my success in raising my family and in my business life, the one thing I can point to with assurance - is knowing and understanding my life's mission…loving on people, caring for people, and sharing Jesus with them.

MAIN TAKEAWAY

Feeding people in the park, the difference in life dynamics between the inner city and suburban areas, importance of walking in faith and serving from the heart.

The aspect of serving, the giving of ourselves for the benefit of spiritual nourishment and feeding people life-sustaining food.

We are the hands and feet of Jesus.

Chapter 2 Study Guide Questions

The mission field is all around us. I respect the calling on believers' hearts to go to a foreign country or even Africa. What special calling has God put on your heart to share the love of Jesus with those around you?

Serving in the inner city is not for everyone but caring for people is. Has God spoken to you about serving in a specific ministry?

Can you think back to a time in your spiritual journey when you had a priority shift to help or lead in ministry?

A word of caution about inner-city ministry:

Go with an experienced group. I ask for a prayer of 'covering' for the group before we minister in the inner city. Crime and unruly behavior can be dangerous even during daylight hours. Even with the risk of ministering here, the rewards are great in feeding people and ministering to their spiritual needs.

Does your town have an established inner-city ministry in place?

Can you think of a time when the Holy Spirit spoke to you about giving up some of your free time for ministry? For myself, I gave up an evening each week for six months' time to teach a class. At other times, we are busy serving on holidays like the Fourth of July, Memorial Day, Labor Day, etc. Note that the ministering opportunities were always met with personal growth.

How can you explain the value of reward that comes from serving others?

CHAPTER THREE

PRAYER WARRIOR

Part One

Ephesians 6:18 (NIV)
**"And pray in the spirit on all occasions with all kinds of requests.
Be alert and always pray for all the Lord's people." - Apostle Paul**

I remember the words I heard over thirty-eight years ago that I would be a dad. My then-wife had just returned from her doctor's visit, confirming she was pregnant with our first child. Becoming a father at that time was a fantastic dream that turned into a reality. Then, it never mattered whether it was a boy or a girl, but just to become a father. I prayed for the possibility of attending dance recitals and Little League ball games or sitting on the bank with fishing poles in hand, enjoying quiet, heartfelt conversations as I had done with my dad.

Throughout those times with my father, my life was shaped and molded by my time with him. These times with my dad were when we discussed the questions of life that helped me develop into the man I am today. I dreamed of those opportunities with my child - teaching how to bait a hook, properly field a ground ball as a shortstop, or just answer thousands of questions about life. Through childlike eyes, children trust their dads for everything.

My time with my dad was ending; my dad died of cancer when I was twenty. All too quickly, life changed, and my time with the man in my life was forever gone. He could never hold or see his grandson, see a new generation that started after his life ended, or witness his family name being carried on.

I reflected on praying for my father's healing and the birth of my first child. Throughout these times, I just prayed to believe and trust that the God of the universe is in control and has these matters and requests in His hands. There were thousands of prayers in developing my faith as I grew into a man. A time such as this was pivotal in each of life's challenges to grow into a deeper relationship with God the Father, Jesus the Son, and the Holy Spirit.

I prayed and asked God for a life-saving miracle for my dad. God answered that prayer mightily! My father gave his heart to Jesus while in his hospital bed, removing any questions I had about his salvation and where he would spend his eternity. God blessed our family with knowing Dad's heart was right with Jesus. A few days later, Dad was weakened, left us, and passed into Jesus' loving arms. Nothing is more satisfying than our loved ones' hearts being right with the Father.

The purpose of prayer is a spiritual discipline and our way of communicating with God. "Our day begins by thanking and praising God for the many blessings He has given us," says my friend Julie. Prayer deepens our relationship with God, which then strengthens us spiritually. The beauty of prayer is that nobody can stop us from praying, not even the devil. We can pray anywhere and at any time, whenever we are, - nobody can stop us.

God commands us to pray.

1 Thessalonians 5:16-18 NIV
**"Rejoice evermore, pray without ceasing. In
everything, give thanks, for this is the will of God in
Christ Jesus concerning you." - Apostle Paul**

**May we go forth with humility before God in prayer
and bring honor and glory to His name.**

My friend Dan Seaborn, founder of Winning at Home (a Christian marriage and counseling organization), recently said, "Approximately two percent of church-going Christian couples pray together daily." Prayer does a couple of things. First, the divorce rate in America is about thirty-three percent overall. (The divorce rate has dropped due to more couples living together rather than a marriage commitment).

47

When couples pray together, the odds of divorce change from the national average of one out of three or (thirty-three percent) to 1 in 1,255. These prayers are more engaging than mealtime prayers and are often more critical. But the prayers of couples take on a whole new meaning when they lovingly bring their needs together before the Father. These prayers are for complete covering, growing together, seeking God's will for their lives, and taking an offensive position against the adversary's attacks.

Those are interesting statistics. It also emphasizes the importance of not only prayer but couples and families praying together.

Acts 6:4 (KJV)
"But we will give ourselves continually in prayer, and to the ministry of the word." -Luke

There are a lot of people saying, "all we can do is pray." Last on the list, all hope is gone... Prayer is for the moment and FIRST on the list! When the thought or circumstance comes to mind, I pray until the Holy Spirit releases me from the burden.

Praying For the Spiritual Gift of KNOWLEDGE

Pray when the Holy Spirit moves you to pray. Pray without delay. Pray now. The Holy Spirit gives this spiritual gift to bring about understanding to Christ's followers. The person with this gift is usually well-versed in the Scriptures and often has much committed to memory. Therefore, they can retain the truth and communicate it effectively.

In a few examples below, the Holy Spirit told me to pray deeply and sincerely at night for the complete healing of employees and friends. God knows all and will reveal His plan in His timing through the sensitivity of the Holy Spirit and acts of obedience. God's love showed in protecting those in danger and for the complete healing of the body.

1 Corinthians 12:8 (NIV)
"To one there is given through the Spirit a message of wisdom, to another, a message of knowledge by means of the same Spirit..." - Apostle Paul

Part Two

PRAYERS FOR A FRIEND

The Holy Spirit speaks to me throughout the day and night. He has no specific times. It just happens in His time. I have awakened in the middle of the night with prayer needs, so real and timely; this is the Holy Spirit's prompting. On this night, we had been praying for a sick friend. His lungs were full of pneumonia and another cyst-type diagnosis. Sam did two hospital visits before he was transferred into intensive care.

We prayed with Sam and his wife for the complete healing of his lungs and entire body. During these moments, he was moved from prayers for a sick body to a worship experience. We finished praying then Sam spoke some words I would never forget. He stated, "Enough about me, and now I want to share what the Holy Spirit has given me in a vision." Finally, Sam described God's plan for him and his wife.

Sam was an extremely sick man with his eyes on Christ and His plan for their future. Sam believed in something greater than himself. Sam stood on the Word and the vision God put in his and his wife's heart. Sam's lungs worsened, and as a group, we prayed harder. After the transfer to intensive care, Sam stayed hospitalized for the next four weeks.

I woke again in the night and began to pray for Sam. I was pleading for his healing. All at once, I was released from the burden while praying for Sam! There was peace, complete peace. I felt at that time Sam had been healed, and I rested in knowing Sam was restored. I returned to bed and slept. The call came around 8:00 AM. I learned that Sam had passed away in the night. I shared with Robin my prayers for Sam and then the release of the burden.

Sam was healed in a separate way than I understood at that time. Sam was completely healed and in the arms of Jesus. Sam's passing was not due to any lack of faith or prayer from our prayer group. His healing was as complete as anyone could imagine; he was whole, healed, and with Jesus. The prayer release of the burden was amazing in that GOD was in the moment! Sam was running like a child on a baseball field. Sam was free of pain and sickness that had overtaken his body for many years in his earthly body. We prayed hard, extremely hard. However, Sam's healing was complete, just as God had planned.

Part Three

PRAYERS FOR OUR EMPLOYEES

When Robin and I were in business some years back, we made it a part of our nightly prayer time to pray for the safety of our construction crews. With teams working in several states, we prayed for their safety while driving and covered all other circumstances they would encounter. With as many as eighteen teams working nationwide, these prayers were necessary and needed.

I was awakened one night from my sleep. One of our construction crews was working in central Illinois. The groups are made up of day and night shift crews. At the time, we owned the largest big-box trucks available; the cab was the size of a semi-tractor with an enclosed box of around thirty-two feet. The box truck was a mobile shop for our employees for tools, supplies, and equipment.

The truck was parked that night behind the building we were working on. I was awake and praying for our employees around two in the morning. I was burdened to pray for my employee's safety. I was genuinely concerned for their safety and could not let it rest. After some time, I returned to bed. A few minutes later, my phone rang. The group at this location told me there had been a terrible accident! They reported that all our employees were safe, and they repeated, "Everyone was accounted for and safe!"

Our employees had entered the mobile shop truck to retrieve a specific tool, closed the rear doors, and locked it. Then, they walked away a safe distance, returning to their job site. Suddenly, out of nowhere, a car raced through the rear parking lot hitting our truck head-on! The force of the impact had ripped the car almost in two! Yet somehow, the car was able to be driven a short distance! Once stopped, the police arrested the driver for drunk driving.

Being awakened in the night to pray for the safety of these specific employees is a complete miracle of God's goodness. A moment earlier, the workers would have been inside the truck or walking around it and could have been killed or very seriously injured. We thanked God for covering our employees' lives (and for the drunk driver) - who was not hurt. Trucks and tools can be replaced, but lives are eternal! The police investigation showed the drunk driver was going at least 100 miles an hour when he impacted our truck.

My prayer life changed when I decided to be "all in" on my faith, holding nothing back, and being available for anything the Holy Spirit brought my way. In my life, Christ is first, without wavering, indecision, or question. When I hear and understand the voice of the Holy Spirit, I can say with reasonable certainty that I will stop and pray immediately for the situation without hesitation or delay.

PRAYER CHANGED ME AND BROUGHT ME INTO AN INTIMATE RELATIONSHIP WITH THE FATHER.

I can't remember when the change began to take place. The time when I went from being a Sunday and Wednesday church attender to where God is taking me now. I understand I may never arrive at my appointed ministry position or destination; a ministry is fluid, and that is where I am now. I am hungry for God's word. I want to learn, grow, and develop to where He will take me and use me next. I can say my prayer life accelerated with my spiritual maturity is taking place.

My friend Gregg states a prayer like this:

"We fight with spiritual weapons to release God's power and provision into life's circumstances."

When I pray, I know God sends the power of the Holy Spirit and ministering angels into the situation. The blood of Jesus Christ provides overcoming power; in God, we have authority over the enemy's work. I like the imagery in Revelation 5:8 "...the four living creatures and the twenty-four elders holding golden bowls full of incense, which are the prayers of God's people". It encourages me to join my prayers with others and rise to God as incense before him. Our prayers are precious to God. God intervenes in our lives, and His kingdom advances in response to the prayers of the saints. The intimacy of prayer unleashes the power of the Holy Spirit.

The Holy Spirit is the great equalizer, the tremendous force of mighty hurricane winds dressed in velvet-covered steel.

The power in prayer is based on the foundation of the blood of Jesus Christ and His ministering angels. The Holy Spirit and my relationship with Him inspire my prayers. I am asking for the day's opportunities for His presence in business meetings and other daily encounters. I pray that I am sensitive to the Holy Spirit to hear His voice and to go boldly, taking risks, and speaking the truth in love to whomever needs it, and most of all, being obedient and submitting my will to Him.

Part Four

Colossians 4:4-5 NIV
"Pray that I may proclaim it clearly, as I should.
Be wise in how you act toward outsiders; make the
most of every opportunity." - Apostle Paul

PRAYER OPENS THE DOOR TO SHARING CHRIST'S LOVE WITH THOSE WHO ARE HURTING.

A few years back, Robin and I were on a trip to Florida for a much-needed relaxation from our business. Being from Michigan, early March is still very much winter, and after many months of winter, you are ready for a break from the cold and snow. The Florida sunshine feels indescribably wonderful after leaving the frosty winter weather in Michigan! We needed some old-fashioned relaxation, a time to reconnect and talk as a couple, as husband and wife, not as business partners.

Marriages can get left behind when couples own a business together, and everyday conversations can sound like corporate meetings instead of the intimacy of caring for one another. The timing of this trip was perfect in many ways. First, our day started with prayer. Then, we had unexpected opportunities to pray for the needs of others.

The temperature was in the mid-eighties with not a cloud in the sky as we headed toward the hotel pool. We gathered some podcasts and books and chose our lounge chairs. The warm sun was a great feeling. We settled into our pool chairs, enjoying the moment, reading without distractions, and listening to soft music. Watching families around the pool area enjoy themselves on vacation is pleasant and interesting. This "rest" feels so incredible!

My previous week's work had been exceedingly difficult. In addition, my schedule was leading up to this anticipated vacation. My schedule went as follows:

Monday

I flew early to Arkansas to attend some corporate meetings on Monday night and returned home late.

Tuesday

I flew early to Minneapolis on Tuesday morning, drove to several areas in the state, and arrived home late on Tuesday night.

Wednesday

I made an unexpected trip to Baltimore to access some emergency work on Wednesday.

Thursday

I caught an early flight to Minneapolis, then on to Duluth, and returned to Grand Rapids around 11 p.m.

Friday

Robin and I were back at the airport early in the morning by 5:30 a.m. to fly to Orlando for vacation.

What made this more difficult was each day trip required multiple connecting flights and rental cars. Most days between rental cars consisted of four flights each day. In addition, during this period in our business, we were averaging 2,300 jobs annually in 18 states. So, as you can imagine, I was worn out and tired entering this vacation time of rest!

The pool waitress staff dropped off their menu for the meal and drink options; this was great!! We ordered, and a tray of food was delivered to our chairs. As the afternoon progressed, I noticed an older woman having difficulty getting her husband into the pool. I got up from my chair, walked around the pool, and asked if they needed some help. The wife assured me it was okay, so I returned to my chair. Unfortunately, it appeared that the husband had some form of severe illness. I wondered if he had (ALS) Lou Gehrig's disease or had suffered a stroke.

2 Peter 3:8-9 (NIV)
"But do not forget this one thing, dear friends: With the Lord, a day is like a thousand years, and a thousand years are like a day. The Lord is not slow in keeping his promise, as some understand slowness. Instead, he is patient with you, not wanting anyone to perish, but everyone to come to repentance." - Peter

Their struggle was difficult as the wife managed to get him into the pool. The Holy Spirit began to work in my heart; I felt a connectedness toward them as they started enjoying their time. First, I would go back to reading – when again, my attention would be drawn to the older couple. Finally, I began to feel the Holy Spirit speak into my heart to go pray with them. I confess I pushed it off. Was it my exhaustion - or thinking, "these are 'strangers'?" What would I say? How would they react to a stranger walking up to them and asking to pray for them?

The minutes passed, and the conviction was absolute; go pray with the older couple. I told Robin I felt that the Holy Spirit would have me go over and pray with them, but somehow, I continued to resist the Holy Spirit. Then, as the Holy Spirit does, He spoke deep into my heart, then asked me to pray with this older couple. This was the Holy Spirit's third time urging me to go to them. So, I told Robin I was going over to pray with that couple. I prayed that God would give me the words that needed to be spoken. Robin agreed as I committed to getting out of my lounge chair.

I confess to you that I pushed it off. Was it fatigue, or being jet lagged - or just simply being overly tired? These are strangers; what would I say? How would they react to a stranger walking up and asking to pray for them?

I AM A VERY SELF-MOTIVATED GUY, I'M CERTAINLY NOT LAZY. I WAS, HOWEVER, VERY FATIGUED IN MY HESITATION.

Often, the physical aspect is just getting up and starting to walk (in this case, to the couple across the pool). Then, the supernatural energy of the Holy Spirit comes over me. I then began the walk toward the pool steps putting one foot into the water and then the next, asking God to give me His words. This is now going to happen. "Lord, soften their hearts and give me Your direction" I prayed as I moved forward in waist deep water.

Robin prayed as I continued toward the couple. I am now a "messenger of hope" on a mission, totally trusting the Holy Spirit with not a clue of what I might say! They were at the pool's far end as I neared the halfway point; again, I was still unsure how to do this.

WHEN A BELIEVING PERSON PRAYS, GREAT THINGS HAPPEN.

"Lord, let me give Your message and share with them softly and clearly what You want them to hear." I continued toward them, and they began to look at me. I felt awkward at first as I introduced myself. They were from the Boston area; her name was Mary; her husband was Bob. We began to have some light conversation, but eventually I learned that Bob was suffering from a severe health crisis. Finally, I 'broke the ice' and said, "I feel the conviction of the Holy Spirit to come over and pray with you." I said, "I am unsure what is happening in your life, but I want to pray with you." The wife's answer to me will live on in me FOREVER; I was floored and shocked at what she said next!

Mary then turned and looked into my eyes, her eyes showing the strain of a wife carrying the heavy burden for her husband and family. Her response was loud and clear - and full of emotion! With tears streaming down her face, she cried,

"WHERE HAVE YOU BEEN?"

"WE'VE BEEN WAITING FOR YOU!"

"WE HAVE BEEN STRUGGLING FOR SO LONG."

"AND WE HAVE BEEN ALL ALONE…. UNTIL NOW".

Wow…I thought back to my resistance and lack of obedience to the Holy Spirit's call to pray with them. O Lord, I am sorry, so, so sorry to have been selfish and to have resisted your calling! Then the three of us joined hands in a resort swimming pool and prayed for God's healing and that God would supply their every need as they walked through their crisis. The barriers broke, and a new fresh anointing was upon them. Then simply, I prayed a prayer of blessing and healing over their lives. Whatever God put on my heart came out of me as an expression of His love that poured into their hurting hearts that afternoon.

This simple act of obedience blessed this couple beyond words. With tears running down their faces, they were spiritually loved and cared for in the body of Christ. I was the vehicle the Holy Spirit chose to give them this message. Even in complete exhaustion, God used me at that moment, which was one of the most profound experiences I have ever had.

Our most fulfilling purpose is found when we align ourselves with God's divine plan and use our talents and abilities to bring glory to Him. It is then we feel most alive, living out our purpose for what He has created us for.

PRAY AND SEEK GOD'S LEADING IN YOUR LIFE.

My goal in sharing these testimonies is to inspire you. Seek out your gifts. With sensitivity and boldness, live out your mission. The simple act of obedience blessed this couple beyond words. They knew God had not forgotten them; they were loved and cared for by a stranger in the body of Christ. The simple act of a stranger who stepped out of his comfort zone and shared his faith made all the difference to them. They had tears running down their faces and were smiling with joy. Did their church or their small group of church friends simply walk away from them at a time when they were in their greatest need? As a result, had they never developed close relationships with other couples?

I cannot answer that; however, going back to the early words written in this chapter, I emphasized the need to stay in the community of like-minded believers. He is God, sovereign- and He is never late! He sends a 'messenger of hope' at just the right time.

Couples need to grow together, and teams need other like-minded, believing couples to grow and go through life with. Life is full of twists and turns. There have been times when we needed others to stand with us as prayer partners and warriors. And other times, we have been rock solid for others in their most significant times of need and crisis.

As I write this, I am still bothered by my hesitation; why did the Holy Spirit need to prompt me three times before I committed myself to get up and go over to pray with them? I am very self-motivated by nature; if I see something that needs to be done, I just get up and do it. I did not feel fear of rejection. I honestly did not. I have confidence in the Lord for the task at hand. I am glad I have a faithful wife and prayer partner who prays for me in these unique situations. I need to just believe it was God's perfect timing.

God, the Father, loves and adores His children no matter their circumstances. His love is not based on anyone's performance or good work. He loves the most excellent servant and the person on skid row the same. There is no favoritism in His eyes, just pure unconditional love. He desires a relationship with each of His children so that none should perish, and all have everlasting life.

Part Five

PRAYER CHANGED THE MAN INSIDE OF ME. I NEED ALL OF HIM.

My life began a shift and changed from my ways to His ways, from laying down my agenda to what is next. I now understood that change could come in a couple of ways - voluntary or involuntary. Throughout my life experience, I voluntarily work best when I push myself into the unknown and the most uncomfortable situations. I feel alive in the perspective of a new challenge that God and only God will know the outcome of as I nervously ease into a unique opportunity to serve Him. Many times, I could have said, "how hard is it, how long will it take?" Or, "I am not qualified. Use someone else," and He said, "I pick you for the task."

Involuntary change comes as a rough and tumble ride. Usually, a passage is made up of unpreparedness and needs more choices. My thoughts go toward being pushed into a role that I am most uncomfortable with and, certainly in my human flesh, I do not want to do. People are resistant to change. People become comfortable with their routines and dig their heels to protect themselves.

When your heart connects with the Holy Spirit's heart, this is where transformation takes place. From the Holy Spirit's heart to my heart is where the relationship began, to yield myself to the Creator where I can feel an inner movement of my spirit and connection, sometimes numerous times a day.

Those early morning prayers started a change in me years ago, and I continue to feel the changes today, many years later. Yet, those prayers began with no plan or structure for two or three-hour segments of praying in the Spirit while driving across America. I paid complete attention to my driving. However, those hours and hundreds of miles passed like a few moments.

Philippians 4:6 (NASB)
"Be anxious for nothing, but in everything by prayer and supplication with thanksgiving let your requests be made known to God." - Apostle Paul

As you read this, I hope you know - and are confident that God hears your prayers and cares for you. You are His chosen one, and He desires this relationship with you. His love for you is consistent, unconditional, and more profound than the deepest sea. His love never changes, even when you may not feel His presence.

My adult life is being shaped into becoming an encourager and prayer warrior. I pray for the underdogs in society, I pray for our government leaders, and I pray for the sick. I have a network of believers who send prayer requests for sick friends and relatives or those needing God's favor regarding a particular issue or circumstance. We stand as believers in agreement that these needs are to be met nationwide.

Conclusion

Warriors Get Ready for Battle!

For as long as I can remember, I have received prayer requests from others and have sent back others' prayer requests. It is my honor to pray for healing for someone who is sick. I have seen miracles where someone's health has been restored, and others pass away and meet Jesus - face to face. I do not judge or question the love of the Father for I have come to understand. His love is more powerful than the most potent sicknesses and diseases in our human bodies. When the most grueling cancer diagnosis is not cured here on earth, or when doctors have exhausted all possibilities – It is then that Jesus steps in and welcomes those individuals into all eternity with His great love that we here on earth cannot even begin to imagine or understand.

We are the 'light' of the world, the light that gives and shares hope with the hurting. Pray without ceasing until the Holy Spirit releases the burden or the prayer has been answered. The prayers of believers standing in unity pray to the God of the universe for a revival starting in our homes and spreading like wildfire across towns and state lines to the far ends of our country's borders and worldwide. In these last days, many millions or even billions will call out to the mighty name of Jesus for the forgiveness of their sins so that the multitudes are saved and come into a lasting, eternal relationship with God the Father, Jesus the Son, and the Holy Spirit.

I pray that the power of God will change people's hearts for the unified body of Christ that all come together just as God has aligned these matters for His glory. I pray against the sinful nature of men and women and the evil forces of darkness that feed these unquenchable thirsts for sin. Make no mistake about it. This is a spiritual battle and spiritual warfare needs prayers to the highest degree! God calls all believers to prayer, from the casual church attender to those called to pray on the front lines.

These are prayers full of purpose and expectation that GOD WILL MOVE 'MOUNTAINS' and everything between them! These are the prayers of His people - prayer warriors that are "all in" and holding nothing back, understanding and believing that this is war. These are prayers against the forces of evil and sinful nature everywhere. Prayer warriors know and understand that they were born and created for this time.

I will pray for elected officials from any political party. I pray for county commissioners and small-town mayors right up the chain to state representatives, governors, members of Congress, Senators, Supreme Court Justices, and Presidents. My prayer is simply that the Holy Spirit touches their hearts and transform them into the believers God has called them to be, and that they govern and legislate according to the word of God. I pray for the forgiveness of our nation for the sins and mistakes we as a nation have made.

There is a never-ending list of elections and legislation to pray for. I pray that Godly men and women be elected and appointed in all positions of authority. I pray that these men and women govern according to the word of God, and If they refuse - they are swiftly removed from their appointed or elected positions. These are sometimes difficult prayers because some leaders are offensive and ungodly. I pray because He is the God of possibilities and can change their hearts.

My friend Sandy says, "I know my God hears my prayers. My heart aches when someone is hurting and needs prayer, whether for themselves or someone else. But most of the time, this is the best way I can help lift the needs of others before God in prayer." What a magnificent way to stand in the gap for others to 'raise them up' for their healing or other life circumstances.

Robin's and my relationship with Sandy is unique. Wherever Sandy is, her prayer life is in the here and now, not later, not tonight, but right now. I love surrounding myself with people who will stop immediately and pray to the Lord. Sandy's life is not a 'back burner' kind of faith. It is now, full throttle, as she goes to battle until the Holy Spirit releases her from the burden. Robin and I have lots of "Sandy's" in our lives. Prayer IS powerful, and we believe it has the power to move mountains.

When I received Jesus as my Lord and Savior, my heart changed from simply offering the standard 'meal and bedtime' prayers. God created us - you and me, for His pleasure and, most notably, for relationship with Himself. My prayer life has taken on a new meaning as I have grown. It is personal, and there is a closeness between Him and me that it is new and refreshing every time and every day.

I stay in contact with others in my day-to-day human relationships with open and transparent communication. This keeps me and others growing and enriching our lives and friendships. The same is true for our prayer time with God - this continual conversation throughout the day or the night, always on my mind, always present, and always relevant to the issues and the world around me.

Our relationship with God the Father, Jesus the Son, and the Holy Spirit, is different, yet the same. Christ is always on my mind. The Holy Spirit is always close and leading and guiding me throughout the day. This intimacy is so personal, rich, and fulfilling - knowing that the God of the universe loves me in a close and unique way! When I worship Him, it is not in a mechanical way with well-rehearsed songs, and prayers, but it is new, and from my heart and soul that everything is His and belongs to Him.

In my life, He created all things and can immediately change His course or course of action. All things are possible through Him, who made all creation and knows everything. His ways are not man's; they are infinite and without end. And He still does miracles every day, from the healing of sick bodies to the power of forgiveness where a sinner's heart is now made right in Him. There is no end to the possibilities of prayer. Jesus has been given all authority and all the power over the adversary. Prayer has more power than most believers know and understand. I am moved to pray by the leading of the Holy Spirit.

I am called to pray because God has called me to do this. To further explain - this is difficult to put into words - but my human spirit aligns with what the Holy Spirit is asking me to do. That can mean praying for someone on a moment's notice or a long-term proposition like Fred's back in Chapter One, where I prayed earnestly for Fred every day for six years, and sometimes praying multiple times each day.

Then after a mighty move of the Holy Spirit, Fred submitted his heart to Christ, breaking the spirit of atheism and the strongholds on that family for generations. When the Holy Spirit speaks to me, His voice isn't mistaken. His voice speaks right into my spirit. The best way I can explain this: My consciousness moves inside me with a word of instruction that completely overtakes my thought process. I am then moved to pray and confidently take a risk when sharing Christ with a stranger.

Morning Prayers Set the Tone and Pace for The Day

Our days start with this prayer: "Holy Spirit give me the sensitivity to hear your voice, speak clearly, and remove distractions from my busy mind. Today, as I seek You out, give me the boldness to speak and enable me to provide a word of encouragement to someone, to feed and love them in Christ, then possibly walk up to a stranger and pray with them." There is a tremendous risk of being rejected, or I may be the answer to somebody's prayer.

As you read this book, know, and understand there is no time for "sideline" Christians. The call is now. The media promotes and describes sin as normalcy, then laughs in the face of believers. But we are not left to fight this alone. Seek the face of God and find your part in this battle. The most vital thing that every one of us can do is to pray.

Thoughts and footnotes.

Prayer is the most important way to connect with the Father. Nobody can take that away from you. We can pray anywhere and anytime, silently, or aloud, day or night, in every circumstance. Prayer is the single most powerful tool that believers have. Nothing can stop you from praying.

I am called to prayer because prayer creates intimacy with the Father. I am not a huge fan of traditional rehearsed reading of prayers. Instead, prayer is spontaneous out of my heart to Him. Traditions are important, and I have respect for that. However, my relationship with God is in the moment throughout the day or night. I pray for what is on my heart when it is on my heart.

As a Christian, I am called to pray, encourage, and give hope to others. Yet, these prayers are often done to be anonymous to the world around us. I am happy that we have such a loving God and Father that I can be chosen to pray, speak the truth, and care for others in their most incredible time of need.

Prayer changes things. Through prayer, there are a lot of things that can happen. For example, during my business life, I prayed before meetings that His will would be done and that we completely understood the tasks at hand. One perspective on this is listening and taking notes. The other is being prayerful during these conversations.

I am moved to pray because God has called me to pray for others. We are instructed and encouraged to pray for our own needs, and we are also commanded to pray for the needs of others.

I have changed from saying to someone "I will be praying for you" to "let us pray right now" and believe this will happen wherever we are.

God loves His children and wants to have close relationships with everyone. The easiest way to have this relationship is through prayer and worship. Prayer is as simple as a conversation with God. Do not complicate it but be authentic from the heart!

MAIN TAKEAWAY:

Pool Story: The impact of aligning with God's will and the notable reaction of a stranger saying, "Where have you been? We have been waiting for you."

Step out in faith, even when exhausted!

Focus on Gifts: I was encouraged to match my wife's strong and consistent prayer life, recognizing her as his Proverbs 31 wife. Always be in prayer for your spouse.

Chapter 3 Study Guide Questions

How do you pray for your family?

I learned from my friend Brent that he often prayed throughout the day. Before meetings, seeing someone walking down the road, and so on. Brent had a closeness with the Lord that I had never witnessed before. I have written that my prayer life communicates with God the Father, Jesus the Son, and the Holy Spirit. Can you describe your prayer life?

I am a believer in non-rehearsed prayers. I feel prayers should be prayed from the heart, often spontaneous expressions of our love for God. Prayers could be mixed with praise and worship, and thankfulness. There is no more excellent way to give God our day than submitting our will to His.

How do you start your day in prayer?

Does your prayer life continue throughout the day?

As a Christian, I am called to pray for others' needs. I am connected to others like prayer warriors. We are always available to pray that these needs are brought before the Father.

Have you considered joining a prayer group or starting one of your own?

My relationship with the Holy Spirit is unique. When a need arises, I pray for whoever I am with. The Holy Spirit quickens my heart in real-time. Consequently, I moved past the ideology of telling someone I would pray for them "later."

Do you or can you pray for someone in their time of need?

Often these times are in a public setting. Can you or do you do this? Why or why not?

Prayer is something that can be private and quiet. Yet, nobody can stop you from praying. You can pray virtually anywhere and at any time. This is because God loves to hear our prayers.

Prayer changes relationships from casual to intimate. Prayer can change things NOW. Describe how your prayer life can be more effective.

My prayer life is never a wish list of my wants and desires. It is petitioning the Father for His will to be done and for opportunities to share the gospel with others and serve and care for those in need. I seek His divine appointments as the "messenger of hope and good news."

The world calls "divine appointments" coincidences. Reflecting upon this statement, can you describe any "divine appointments" that God has placed in your life?

CHAPTER FOUR

ENCOURAGER

Part One

Romans 15:5 (NIV)
"May the God who gives endurance and encouragement
give you the same attitude toward each other
that Jesus Christ had." - Apostle Paul

FOLLOW THE HOLY SPIRIT.
GO BOLDLY,
AND SHARE JESUS
SIMPLY BY
LOVING
ONE ANOTHER.

As much as I try to describe this, I will never find the right words to match the feeling of the Holy Spirit speaking to me. I am reminded each day to dedicate my day to the Lord through prayer. But, can I do it? Never has there been a time in history with so much noise and information; humanity is under full assault and bombarded with information and misinformation. The world is screaming for your attention, your money, and your soul. And they will do anything to get it! There is no lie nor deception that the media will not use to bend a shred of truth to get you to believe their way.

Spiritual Discipline

Peace and calm are rare commodities, so how can I surrender myself to Him long enough to rest in His presence? Simply to pray, submit my heart to Him, and just say, "Jesus use me to help and love someone today." Discipline is prioritizing my time and thought process to be available for this relationship to flourish. Relationships will become stale and boring without the attention and effort needed to make them grow.

This book does not reveal my life as a life of perfection. It does, however, reflect a humble human heart, made right in my relationship with Jesus Christ.

As we journey through life, we can draw people closer to Christ or push them away - making us all missionaries in our own right. Understanding this principle is vital in sharing our faith.

We are missionaries wherever we go - what a thought! Those are wise words to live by. The road before us is the mission field whether that be the neighbor across the street or the person next to us on the assembly line. There are no training or special assignments. Just be the missionaries God has called us to be!

I love that we are so full of the Holy Spirit that the atmosphere changes, and people want what we have. Our lives radiate the goodness of the Lord in whatever we do, so that people see Christ in us and want what we have.

Part Two

The Spiritual Gift of Exhortation,

The spiritual gift of exhortation is often called the "gift of encouragement." The Spirit of God gives this gift to people in the church to strengthen, encourage, uplift, and motivate others.

Romans 12:8 (NIV)
"If it is to encourage, then give encouragement; if it is giving, then give generously; if it is to lead, do it diligently; if it is to show mercy, do it cheerfully. "
-Apostle Paul

Acts 11:23-24 (NIV)
When he arrived and saw what the grace of God had done, he was glad and encouraged them all to remain true to the Lord with

all their hearts. He was a good man, full of the Holy Spirit and faith, and a great number of people were brought to the Lord.

The value of a friend is immeasurable, for they accept us as we are and can leave us better than they found us. They lift our spirits, offer words of encouragement, and provide support. As true friends, we make ourselves readily available to those who require our assistance without hesitation or delay.

I am a blessed man. I have some wonderful close friendships that go back to my early childhood. These are some guys from our neighborhood, where we walked to elementary school and middle school and graduated high school together. We played minor league baseball, fished with our dads, and invested in each other's lives. Although now we are retired and talking about our kids and grandkids, our lives are still close because we took the time for each other. Like our relationship with God, we invest time in prayer or quietly sitting in His presence. Just listening is connecting your heart to Him. Time spent in a relationship is invested in Him. Discipline throughout the day, in prayer or mini prayers, establishes intimacy and connection with the Father.

The day had come for my friends Dan, Rick, and I to leave for our trip. We arranged and rearranged our gear as we packed my truck. Finally, we had completed our task and were ready to go as we stood in the driveway. Robin, my wife, gathered around us. She laid hands on us individually and prayed a blessing over us. Her prayers were for God to reveal Himself in fresh new ways. She prayed for our safety, that God would use us, and that we would hear and seek the presence of the Holy Spirit.

This trip would be an outdoor adventure we had planned for the last year. The three of us had meetings and emails covering every detail. There was joy in the planning process, and now it was *'game on'!* After a seven-hour road trip, we pulled into a small farming town. After unpacking, we had time to go to a local taxidermy shop. We asked some questions to the counter salesperson when an older gentleman walked in and made some small talk, introducing himself as David. I thought he was a nice guy, a local to this area, who was a wealth of knowledge. The Holy Spirit caught my attention. Dave and I shared some conversation, and we were on our way.

The following morning found us at the local restaurant eating breakfast as we chatted about the upcoming week. Then, David, the older gentleman we had seen at the taxidermy shop the evening before came up to our table. He jokingly said, "You will never get a big buck sitting in a restaurant." The Holy Spirit moved inside me when he said, "Good morning," then left for another room. It was hard for me to define; I waited, then after a minute or two, prayed, then went into the room to find David. I went to his table and said a few words and introduced myself. We spoke for a while, and he then agreed to meet me after he left the restaurant.

1 John 4:21 KJV
"And this commandment we have from him, that he who loveth God loves his brother also." -John

Thirty minutes later, he drove up in his truck, so I went over to meet him. I boldly asked him if his heart was 'right' with Jesus. He looked at me and said, "Yes, it is. I love the Lord with my whole heart." I then said, "The Holy Spirit wants me to pray with you. I am not sure what it is about, but I feel the need to pray for you." I asked what I could pray for. He looked down, then looked away as I patiently waited. Finally, he said "It is my son. Scott is living a wayward life along with his children." David mentioned that others in his family were also wayward.

1 Thessalonians 5:11 NIV
"Therefore encourage one another and build one another up, just as you are doing." - Apostle Paul

My friend Rick walked over, and then Dan met us, as well. We prayed the Holy Spirit would surround Scott and Scott's children and shower them with His compassion. To bring them unto Himself, in love - not in condemnation but in love that surpasses understanding. We prayed that Scott would be released from his addictions.

This act of obedience did not end with miraculous salvation or instantaneous healing. It was, however, more important than my words can describe. David knew the love of the Lord was upon his shoulders; this was the work of the Lord and nothing else. So, when the Holy Spirit spoke into my heart, all I could understand was that I needed to pray for this gentleman and, from then on, let the Holy Spirit lead me. He knows the need and restlessness in a father's heart for his son and grandchildren. I rejoice that God chose my friends and I to minister to someone experiencing hurt and rejection, to share His love, and pray for David's lost family members. The need was deep and personal to David, and the ache in his heart was immeasurable. David carries a burden for his family, as he fears they will be lost for all eternity and separated from God.

Hebrews 10:24-25 (ESV)
"And let us consider how to stir up one another to love and good works, not neglecting to meet together, as is the habit of some, but encouraging one another, and all the more as you see the Day drawing near." - Apostle Paul

When we finished praying with David, there was a look of relief on his face. Indeed, David's prayers may have been prayed a thousand times for his family. And maybe David kept these prayers between himself and God alone.

But today was a new day when a stranger showed up and simply said "How can I pray for you?" God revealed to David that he was not forgotten and was loved and faithful under all circumstances and in all situations. This encounter was nothing short of a miracle. Our prayers were for the softening of Scott's heart, and then letting the Holy Spirit do His work. We continue to pray and trust; Scott will hear the Holy Spirit's voice and respond obediently. God desires repentance and restoration for anyone who has gone astray. We are all created to be in a relationship with the Father.

It's amazing to see how God used the three friends who had taken a year to plan this trip to love on a stranger in a hotel in a parking lot. The timing of God's divine appointments to unite everyone and everything was more than amazing. No embarrassment, no awkwardness, just the love of Jesus reaching out to a father and grandfather in his time need.

How do we continue to pray for our loved ones day after day, then for months, and year after year? Is there ever a sense where one might feel that

God has forgotten me? Does He even care anymore? The adversary would lead you to believe that you are alone, and that God does not care. But NOTHING could be further from the truth! God says He will never leave you or forsake you. NOTHING CAN SEPARATE US FROM GOD. Our prayers are being heard, and God's timing is God's timing. The will of our friends and loved ones must submit to God for any actual, lasting change to happen. However, we can be the faith-filled encouragers to those like David praying for his son and his family. Having someone alongside us can help carry the burden and lessen the load.

Part Two:

Our week-long adventure ended as the three of us began to pack our truck for the ride home. We stayed the last night in camp with plans to leave at about four-thirty the following day. I set my alarm only to awaken an hour late. The alarm did not go off; we hurriedly made coffee, said our goodbyes, and headed home. The three of us traveled back in the early morning darkness, conversing. It had been a terrific week to meet with some old friends and make some new ones. God is always at work, and iron sharpens iron when Christian brothers come together! I have been to this lodge many times and always leave refreshed and fulfilled that God has moved in my life throughout the week.

The darkness turned into early morning daylight when I asked the others if they would like to stop for breakfast. Within a few miles, we passed a sign for a national restaurant that sounded good to the three of us. We exited and parked the truck. We were seated when our waitress came over. Her apron spelled out her name, "Debbie", and she had four stars embroidered below her name - with 5 stars being given for the most experienced waitstaff. Debbie's four stars meant she was a veteran waitress for many years.

An individual who can spread grace and blessings and uplift others with words of encouragement possesses one of the world's most appealing and refreshing personalities. God's people are responsible for building people up through realistic expectations, leaving them hopeful for a better future in Christ Jesus.

We ordered coffee and breakfast. A few minutes passed when Debbie returned with our food. She said, "I am sorry guys, I am a little 'off my game' this morning." Debbie went on to explain that today marked the fourteenth-month anniversary of her husband's death. As she talked about walking through her pain in the last fourteen months, her eyes revealed a woman in grief. When people tell you something, there is always a deeper reason. The Holy Spirit is always at work in these moments. Debbie then apologized for her candidness. Rick and I asked Debbie if we could pray with her and she agreed to that, so, in the middle of a busy dining room restaurant, we prayed for God's peace, comfort, and love to surround our server Debbie - to heal her and help her with her grief process and that He reveal Himself close to her.

God was in this moment. When we ended our prayer, Debbie's eyes had tears running down her face. We told her that God loves her and will see her through the pain and loneliness of missing her husband. The grieving process is different for everyone. There is no right or wrong way to grieve. Everyone will eventually go through these valleys in their lifetime, then level off, then continue climbing through each step to the top. One thing for sure is having close family and friends to support you through these times! It is essential in navigating through this process. So, the Holy Spirit does what He does best to send a friend - or, in Debbie's case - some strangers to love on and minister to her without hesitation. Right now, even in the busyness of a restaurant dining room.

Minister In The Moment

When the Holy Spirit speaks, I do my best to listen, give Him my full attention, and then let Him lead me in whatever He chooses. I have moved away from ideology, saying, "I will pray for you", then walk away. I pray right here, right now, wherever I am. I will continue to pray for these needs in David's and Debbie's case until the Holy Spirit releases me from those needs.

No one can relate to the loss of a spouse unless you have walked through this journey yourself. Debbie was coming home to a quiet, empty house with no one to say "good morning" to or enjoy a peaceful cup of coffee together. The thought of loneliness seems unbearable to me as a bystander in these people's lives. This must be so hard and difficult to walk through alone. The comfort of the Holy Spirit will draw us closer to God and as we draw upon His strength, as He carries us through these most needed and challenging times.

Debbie's moment was filled with God's presence. There is no way to calculate God's timing for her and three friends returning from our outdoor adventure. To oversleep by over an hour, to finish packing our personal belongings, then drive down the highway, get hungry, and make a choice to stop at a restaurant, only to be seated in Debbie's section - is a divine moment only created by God and expressly for Debbie's needs. Like every other day for me, this was about being available to the voice of the Holy Spirit, being sensitive to His voice, and going boldly to where He led. Then, simply get out of the way and allow Him to use me (or us) in these situations!

Blessed To Be A Blessing ...

Every one of us has heard this statement, and we ARE blessed to be a blessing! In the couple of examples, I have shared, they cost me nothing financially. While other times we have invested time and money into feeding, clothing, buying cars, and so on in ministries.

The point is, that we look for the little signs around us and ask God to make us sensitive to His Spirit. He can use us to bless someone, through prayer and encouragement. In the above testimonies, the God of the universe chose Dan, Rick, and me to pour into the lives of those who were hurting. In David's case, his hurt was deep down inside of him. David carried a burden inside his heart for his son Scott and Scott's children. Scott is wayward, and so are his children. From a dad who wants the best for his son and his grandchildren, our God is amid his late-night prayers for deliverance from his addictions. Where Scott goes, his children will follow; in this case, their lives are far from God. When I met David in the taxidermy shop, I knew I could feel that the Holy Spirit was working.

I was "heart checked," meaning there was something different about David as he shared the story about a big buck, he had taken years ago while hunting with a young youth pastor. As the story goes; the deer ran by David, he shot, then the deer ran by the youth pastor and he shot - but not knowing, missed - and the deer fell dead. David said the youth pastor could not have taken the buck. Still, the youth pastor was SO excited - David extended himself to the youth pastor and congratulated him on a massive 200-pound whitetail. That is a world-class whitetail deer anywhere in the world! David shared that he had taken many large bucks in his life; he simply stepped back and shared in the youth pastor's excitement as he tagged a once-in-a-lifetime trophy buck. That is a giving spirit that wanted to see another man succeed as he stood in the background and understood he was 'blessed to be a blessing' to a younger, less experienced hunter. David's character showed he was a man who would rather see someone else succeed, then stand in the background, and enjoy someone else's success. The Holy Spirit brings people together for His glory and for the ability to share one another's other burdens. Months later, I still pray for David and his son Scott and grandchildren that they would be delivered from addictions and caught up in the Holy Spirit's plan for their lives so that their life plan is fulfilled.

Part Three

Pam's Story

Many years ago, Robin and I understood one of our missions was to give away gospel-related books. One of the books we had chosen to give away was Sarah Young's best-selling book, *Jesus Calling*. Over the years, we have given away about a thousand copies randomly and purposely. Books can be an easy evangelism tool. The *Jesus Calling* book is a daily devotional supported by Bible scriptures. Each day is exciting and reflective to read as it ministers to its readers.

My work travels took me from West Michigan toward upper Wisconsin through Minnesota and beyond. After I crossed the Mackinac Bridge, I headed west on US 2, a beautiful scenic drive along Lake Michigan's northern shoreline. Several hours west of the bridge, there is a little market where I would stop to stretch my legs to buy a few road snacks. This market sold everything from sporting goods to fresh food. In addition, the market sold homemade fish decoys that ice fishermen used to spear pike through the ice-covered lakes. I like hand-carved decoys as folk art and have collected twenty-five or so throughout the years.

The owner of the market is Pam - and Pam is a true 'Northern Michigan' woman. Pam and I would talk about deer hunting that she enjoyed doing with her granddaughter. I would pay for my purchases and then return on the road again. After about one hundred miles down the road, the Holy Spirit began speaking to me about Pam. I was on a tight schedule with over a thousand miles to go and could not turn around and return to her store. I prayed about it and then sent Pam a copy of the book, *Jesus Calling*. I wrote out a note saying, "I was in your store a few days ago and wanted to give you this book. I just remembered after I was hours down the road."

My travels would take me through Pam's store several times a year. A year later, I stopped to see her and made some purchases. I asked her, did you receive a book in the mail called *Jesus Calling*? She said, "Yes, are you the one who sent it?" I said, "Yes", then she pulled it out from under the counter. The book was well-worn from lots of everyday use. Pam held the book up and said, "This book is a daily inspiration for myself and others."

Pam mentioned that this part of Michigan's Upper Peninsula is sparsely populated. She continued that, "I have people walk into my store from great distances to read the daily devotions." Then she said, "This book is read by six to eight others on a daily basis."

The Upper Peninsula of Michigan is amazingly incredible in its natural beauty, with bountiful lakes, streams, and vast woodlands. Unfortunately, weather in this area can be brutal, with some areas of the Upper Peninsula receiving three hundred inches of snow or more. Pam told me that people walk through very harsh conditions to come into her store to read the day's devotions every day, no matter the weather. To those unfamiliar with Michigan's Upper Peninsula, it ranks in the top three coldest and snowy places in the continental United States.

Ministry is all around us; we just need to stop and listen to what people tell us, then ask the Holy Spirit for discernment and direction. The need is great; we live in a lost and dying world. The body of Christ needs to show love and embrace those who are hurting, letting them know that there is hope in Jesus. Despite our differences, the body of Christ must come together and be united to share the love of Christ.

Part Four

WE NEED TO BE THE MESSENGERS OF HOPE. AS BELIEVERS, WE ARE THE MESSENGERS OF HOPE! We are moved by the Power of the Holy Spirit.

One recurring theme or idea throughout this reading is my love for the Holy Spirit. Our pastor spoke of the 'Holy Ghost' in our services as a child. As a small boy, I could not understand the connection of the Godhead. The name "Holy Ghost" sounded scary at the time because I did not understand what that meant. As I matured both in my physical age and spiritual development, I began exploring and studying the Holy Spirit. Looking back at my life, I can say with certainty - the hand of God has guided me throughout EVERY STAGE of my life and still does today. I have previously written about early morning prayers while traveling for my job in the country's Midwest. At the time, my focused prayers were to 'hear the voice' of the Holy Spirit and to feel His presence.

IF CHRIST IS THE LORD OF YOUR LIFE, THE PRESENCE AND THE POWER OF THE HOLY SPIRIT ARE YOURS. THEREFORE, WALKING IN THE SPIRIT MEANS WALKING WITH CHRIST.

I wanted a close and unique relationship with the Holy Spirit, asking in my prayers to grow into the man He created me to be. First, to have sensitivity to hear His voice with clarity, and secondly to go forth with boldness, go and do whatever He asks me to do. My prayer is to go wherever needed whether that be to speak to strangers across the street or go into a foreign land. I studied and prayed, and little by little, my eyes were opened to the gifts of the Holy Spirit. To grow in this area of my spiritual walk was more than exciting because situations change quickly. Sometimes, just a thought or an idea for something to work on or to pray for occurs immediately in these moments of ministry.

One such time happened like this: My sons and I were camping near Traverse City, Michigan. My sons were three and four years old at the time. We were running some errands when two cars collided in the intersection right before us. The vehicle's impact was significant; both occupants had severe injuries and were trapped inside their vehicles as the first responders arrived. I began to pray for the injured people, and we prayed for the first responders to help give first aid to the hurting. Next, I prayed for the doctors, nurses, and hospital staff - that God would provide them with wisdom and knowledge on how to help them and save lives. I then prayed that there would be no loss of life without the injured knowing Jesus as their Lord and Savior. Prayers now and in moments of crisis for God to intervene quickly! In times like these, prayers are not the last resort, as I have heard some people say they are the "first line of defense" or, instead, an "offensive move" to petition the Father. God's timing is God's timing, and His love is His love; there are no surprises to Him. With all due respect, we understand that He holds time in His hands and that when someone passes away, I trust He loves that individual more than my human mind can understand. He loves us so much that He brings us to Himself in His time.

Part Five

One of the benefits of social media is the connection between far and distant relatives. My wife, Robin, connected with distant cousins from the Texas Gulf Coast. We were contacting her cousins to share family memories with other cousins she had never met. These introductions have led to some beautiful relationships. Robin was sharing with her cousin Rick and his wife, Mary, about one of our corporate fishing trips coming up in the fall. Rick is an avid outdoorsman and fisherman. We had a late cancellation, so Rick gladly accepted our invitation to fly in from the Texas Gulf Coast and visit us for a few days. Rick and Mary would stay in our home a few days later, and we would travel north for our fishing event. Robin and I attended church on Saturday evenings. We extended the invitation to our guests, and they accepted. Our church is large and might be intimidating for some. Nevertheless, we arrived and were seated with the praise and worship service starting. Our senior pastor spoke the message, and Rick raised his hand that night and gave his life to Christ.

Like most new converts, Rick had many questions about his newfound faith.

We fished and bonded as a family and as brothers in Christ throughout the next few days. Finally, Rick and Mary's trip ended, and they were on their way back to Southwest Texas. A brief time later, Mary was diagnosed with cancer. Throughout her treatments, we stood closely with her in prayer, but after many months, she passed away from the disease. Some years have passed since Mary's death, and I have stayed connected with Rick daily through a daily devotional that I forward on from my friend Doug.

Rick recently stated that he was overseas with one of his sons. Rick said he was leaving and traveling to Costa Rica to visit one of his sisters. When Rick arrived in Costa Rica, he mentioned that one of the sisters was in poor health and not expected to live much longer. His visit was planned in part to say their proper and heartfelt goodbyes. Hearing this news, I began praying for his sick sister. The Holy Spirit's voice was clear to me as I began to pray for the sisters' salvation, not knowing where her heart was or if she was 'right' with the Lord. I urgently pursued the Holy Spirit as Rick felt his sister was within a few days of her passing. The Holy Spirit spoke in unbelievable clarity on what to do next. I went to my first book, *The Power of Forgiveness*, and looked up page 146. This page lists the prayer of salvation. I took my phone, took a picture of this page, and texted it to Rick in Costa Rica with this statement - "Rick, this picture is from my book. It is the prayer of salvation. Your sister is about to enter eternity. Can you speak with her and pray with her as soon as possible?" Rick had yet to respond or confirm if he even received my text. So, we prayed and waited to trust that he could follow through.

Often, the most challenging, complex thing is to pray with or share our faith with our family. This can be a real struggle! We prayed that Rick would have the sensitivity to the Holy Spirit and the boldness to say what was necessary, being able to share his faith and pray with his sister. A few days passed, and Rick shared that his sister had died. Without knowing the outcome - or if Rick had prayed with his sister, I rested because I did what the Holy Spirit had wanted me to do. I obeyed His call, and now I must simply trust that God is God, and He is in control. My thoughts played out over the last few days, and I needed to trust the process, knowing that

I did everything the Holy Spirit asked me to do. But, as always, this is the Lord's business, and everyone will stand before Him on judgment day.

I asked Rick, "Did she ask for forgiveness and accept Jesus as her Lord and Savior?" Rick had arrived to say goodbye, which he did. However, Rick was the messenger of hope and where she would spend eternity.

Rick brought the love of Jesus that was missing from his sister's life. A week or so had passed, and Rick sent word that he could and would pray with her a prayer of salvation, and as he said, "she was ready, ready to meet the Lord of her life." The Holy Spirit released me from this burden, and I thanked Him for using me as a vehicle in this unique and unusual set of circumstances to share Jesus with Rick's sister. I always ask the question, "why" or "why me?" I live in Michigan, and Rick and his sister were in Costa Rica, thousands of miles away. God could have used anyone to send this message of salvation in this circumstance, but He chose me. I am delighted that He chose me to supply the necessary information to help Rick in this challenging situation. The distance from Michigan to Costa Rica, for God, is an inch. His love transcends physical distance and time for His will and His purposes to be complete.

The testimony words you have read are nothing short of a modern-day miracle. The Holy Spirit speaks, and the message is heard. The receiver is sensitive to the voice. The receiver soaks the news in and then responds with love, kindness, and respect. The Holy Spirit's words speak softly and right into the heart. It is precisely in God's timing, in God's perfect way. His love is not trickery, just His wondrous love with arms opens wide to be in a relationship with His children. It does not matter where I am in ministry; I never want to see a life lost for eternity. I will always try to minister and follow the leading of the Holy Spirit. Every life is one of God's chosen people; He loves them deeply and beyond my imagination. So, if I am determined to help or minister to someone, I will go.

Conclusion

The relationship with the Holy Spirit is one of the greatest of them all. We will never know the scope or the depth of our acts of obedience until one day God reveals them to us in Heaven.

We were created by God to be in relationship with Him. We are designed to hear the voice of God. Look for and experience the closeness of His presence. Because I am looking for Him, I am seeking to see Him in all situations. In the uniqueness of life's circumstances, ask God what He is saying, what is He revealing to you. Ask and seek Him for these answers in how you can be used.

Not everything is prophetic. There are many distractions along the way. Learn to discern the difference. Ask God "what are You trying to tell me?" Look deeper into the word and pray to seek clarity.

As we stood in the driveway, Robin prayed over us asking the Lord that He would use us. These are a few examples of how God has used me. Nothing on earth can compare to living out these moments as He leads us.

It is always worth the risk to love someone through God's word or through a simple act of kindness. My morning prayers are to be used for His glory and my testimony. We will never understand how sharing our faith or praying for someone makes them feel. All this costs us absolutely nothing but our time and a little effort. Like the "David and Debbie" experiences I shared - encouragement was effortless on my part but meant the world to them. I shared and they received. When led by the Holy Spirit, know that His timing is impeccable and perfect for those who need to hear an encouraging word to help them make it through the hour, the day, the week, or the year!

GOD IS GOOD! I proclaim and shout that from the mountain tops! JESUS IS ENOUGH!

Thoughts and footnotes.

I cannot think of anything more valuable or rewarding than the spiritual gift of exhortation, more commonly, known as 'encouragement'. For the giver of encouragement - it is free to give away and one of life's most valuable gifts. In this chapter, I have shared some examples with the utmost sensitivity regarding hearing the Holy Spirit's voice and moving naturally as the Holy Spirit leads.

Everywhere you look, people are hurting. Each of us has been wounded at some point in our life. Take the example of Debbie when she was serving our breakfast. She hurt so bad she could not contain herself any longer. It was visible by looking at her and then as she spoke. But, most importantly, WE LISTENED before speaking as she shared her grief. When she finished, we looked into her eyes with compassion and then shared that Jesus is enough, in her hurt, pain, and loneliness. We prayed in public as tears streamed down her face. Debbie was surrounded by strangers ministering to her needs.

Then we met David in a taxidermy shop. While exchanging small talk conversation, the Holy Spirit began checking my heart to see something more. I did not understand then, but while eating breakfast the following day, it became evident that David needed prayer. Imagine the awkwardness of asking him if he could meet me in our hotel parking lot after breakfast! God knows the hurts inside of a man's heart. David arrived, and we prayed for his son and grandchildren. The pain in his heart was deep into his soul as we bound the enemy and claimed his family for the kingdom of God. This was a divine appointment that only the Holy Spirit could have orchestrated. When we finished, David knew and understood that God was at work and that he was not forgotten in his prayers. I do not know the rest of David's story, but God does. As for David and me, our faith grew deeper that day.

Every one of us must recognize the evil forces of the adversary. The most incredible tool for combating these attacks is to pray for a covering over yourself and your family.

None of these testimonies would be possible without surrendering our hearts to God, the Father. You and I are far from perfect but made 'right' in Christ's image. Amazingly, all God wants from us is our availability, no qualifications, or requirements. Simply go when you see a need, serve others in their time, and be available to the Holy Spirit's call on your life. Go boldly stepping out in faith; these costs you absolutely nothing but might be the greatest gift you can give to others. As previously stated in this book, we are the vehicles to deliver the Holy Spirit's message. All the honor, glory, and praise go to God; none of this would be possible without Him.

MAIN TAKEAWAY:

Missionary Life

Main Point: We are missionaries wherever we find ourselves.

Personal Gifting: Recognizing the gift of encouragement (Romans 12:8).

Debbie's Story: Highlighting the impact of being open to the Holy Spirit.

Being sensitive to the Holy Spirit, both David and Debbie were ministered to through the act of obedience, ministering in the moment.

Chapter 4 Study Guide Questions

Exhortation can also be described as "encouragement."

Everyone we meet has been hurt or wounded at some point.

For some, these wounds are open and accessible to see; the scars are a little deeper for others. One of the keys to encouraging others is to LISTEN TO THEIR STORY.

Can you describe a time when you were able to encourage someone?

I wrote about meeting David in a taxidermy shop and restaurant. This was an extraordinary meeting. I felt the Holy Spirit's attention because I wanted a further conversation with him. So, I prayed and asked for clarity. Initially, it was for his salvation, but I discovered it was for his son Scott and grandsons. I spoke to David when he was with a group of men and asked him to meet me at the small town's hotel. Very awkward! The Holy Spirit guided our meeting and our conversation.

Have you ever had difficulty speaking to a stranger about their relationship with God?

Rick, Dan, and I met Debbie in a restaurant. This meeting was utterly random or the exact divine appointment that Debbie needed in her life. I believe in praying NOW - if the moment presents itself. There can be some nervousness around strangers. If the Holy Spirit is speaking to you, I encourage you to step out and try. The Lord is using you. In Debbie's example, it was exactly what she needed.

If the opportunity presented itself, could you pray with someone like Debbie in a public place or restaurant?

When we encourage someone, it always starts with a heart full of prayer.

For myself, personal study of the word, several devotionals, and devoted prayer time are the keys to listening to the Holy Spirit and asking Him to use me and point out the world around me and in front of me.

What does your study life and prayer life look like?

Describe a time when you stepped out in prayer, successful or unsuccessful.

Everyone's prayer lives are different. Life as a single mother raising children differs from that of middle-aged retired adults. Study habits in the Bible can be 'caught' between business and self-discipline.

Describe how your prayer life has changed through the years. Or has it stayed the same?

CHAPTER FIVE

COMPASSION AND FORGIVENESS

Part One

Deuteronomy 31:6. NIV
"Be strong and courageous. Do not fear or be in dread
of them, for it is the LORD your God who goes with
you. He will not leave you or forsake you." - Moses

THE IDEA OF TRUSTING THE PLAN
TO AN UNKNOWN OUTCOME TAKES FAITH.

God is in control. That has been my perspective regarding my faith for a very long time. Even in the hard times and disappointments, I have trusted God and His process. God is always at work. He is working on His plan. Therefore, as the Holy Spirit leads, we follow.

Sometimes, His plans come moment by moment, and other times, it has taken years to understand the plan. The idea of trusting the plan to an unknown outcome takes faith.

Frequently, the 'detour in the road' was for my greater good. It was saving me from an unforeseen pitfall or accident. I rest today knowing God is good. God is in control and knows the plan for my life and the days ahead.

He is working ALL things together for my good. We use our experiences, talents, and creativity for His glory and our testimony. Life can be challenging at times, however, if we can learn and grow from these good and challenging times - we mature in our faith, which becomes our life story of His goodness.

I have had times where I have asked God, "Why, why me, why now, and why not now?" It is fair to ask. However, we may get more than the answers we hope to receive. I could write a mile-long list of examples when someone has been hurt, taken advantage of, or abused. At times, life simply is not fair. People sometimes hurt people at the very lowest times of their lives.

At the end of chapter one, I wrote that Fred had developed a rare blood disease. I shared in section one I had also had the same (ITP) blood disease - a rare form of Hemophilia. ITP is very close to a leukemia diagnosis, but not any form of cancer. I was almost thirty-three years old and a single father of two young boys when I received my diagnosis. I was treated with many blood transfusions, heavy steroids, and experimental drugs. My energy levels would increase with new doses of medicines. Then, soon afterward, my energy levels would quickly drop.

These drugs kept me alive. The side effects were complex. I gained forty-five pounds in thirty days and sixty pounds in forty-five days. I looked and felt horrible.

After I had received a blood transfusion, my energy levels would spike, and I would feel alive and full of energy. Then, after a few days, my internal system would kill off all the good cells and platelets. Within hours, fatigue would set in, along with uncontrollable bleeding from every place imaginable.

BE STRONG AND COURAGEOUS EVEN WHEN THE NEWS GOES FROM BAD TO WORSE.

Months had passed without gaining ground on this disease which was slowly taking my life. My only hope was that a miracle from the Lord would happen soon! But the clock was ticking with no possible cure in sight. Finally, my doctor called me in for a consultation. After four months, my doctor elected to end my treatments without more blood transfusions or medicines. The doctor's statement shook me like an earthquake to my core.

"There is nothing more we can do for you." The doctor advised me, "This is the time to get your affairs in order, Mike. You have about thirty days to live." He continued, "Every day from this point forward will be more complex and more complicated. Without the proper number of platelets in your bloodstream, you will bleed to death. I'm sorry, but we can do nothing else."

My doctor was kind and compassionate as he shared the news with me. But my God promises to walk beside me even in and through my darkest valleys!

Time stopped in its tracks with his conversation. This sickness had just taken an abrupt turn - like hitting a wall at one hundred miles an hour. There is no cure, no more medications, and no more treatments. The air was just sucked out of my lungs. Unable to speak, I held my head in my hands as the world began to spin around me as I looked down. My hands filled with tears as I tried to make sense of his words.

2 Corinthians 1:3-5 (NIV)
"Praise be to the God and Father of our Lord Jesus Christ, the Father of compassion and the God of all comfort, ⁴ who comforts us in all our troubles, so that we can comfort those in any trouble with the comfort we ourselves receive from God. ⁵ For just as we share abundantly in the sufferings of Christ, so also our comfort abounds through Christ." - Apostle Paul

I recognized that God had given my doctor an extraordinary gift of compassion.

My doctor treated me kindly and with respect. His bedside manner and doctor-patient relationship were more than I could ask for. As I reflect, I believe God worked within me to develop compassion for hurting people during this process. In my case, I was hurting, dying, and scared. Yet, I was confident I would be with my Lord and Savior. I thought about this much sooner than I could have ever imagined. I feared my two young sons would grow up without their father.

As a dad, I would sacrifice everything and anything for my children. I would give up my life so they could live. This, however, was not in the realm of possibilities. I was a very sick dad, and in this process, I surrendered my children to the Lord, knowing He would care for them. Nothing can prepare you for this; nobody is prepared to die this young.

I could never willingly walk away from my young children; this would be impossible. This could only happen through the Lord's closeness and presence. This was a full-on surrender of my life to Him. In my humanness, this is not possible. As the days counted down, weakness was overtaking my body. The Holy Spirit eased my anxiety and worry for my children's future. Trust the Father, trust His plan, and trust His process.

There is nothing more I can do; I am all His. That's a beautiful sentiment about faith in God. Trusting in His timing and methods, and being willing to follow His direction, brings peace and guidance in life's journey.

GOD IS BIGGER THAN THE STORM

Praise God that He lives within us and has promised, "Never will I leave you; never will I forsake you." These were some very dark days. I cried out, prayed, and negotiated with God to heal me. But, in the end, His time is His time. I reconciled my heart to Him and submitted myself to the fact that He knows best.

Giving up control and yielding to God's will was made slightly more manageable in my humanness because there were no other options. Looking back at this moment, I handed myself over to Him totally and completely without holding anything back. I was all His, not my will - my selfish, self-centered will - but His will be done. I surrendered myself fully to Him.

Even in my death, my sons would be cared for. That is the most challenging reconciliation any human can make. This was a complete and total surrender to Him. As hard as that is, I trusted His plan and His purpose. I am a strong man. Honestly, I didn't understand this, but there comes a moment when you can no longer 'fight the fight'. I surrendered this to my Lord and Savior. I can honestly say, "To God be the glory!"

This will be HIS outcome.

(Hebrews 13:5). NIV
And He, (Jesus) has assured us, "Surely I am with
you always, to the very end of the age." (Matthew
28:20 NIV) - Apostle Paul & Matthew

CHOOSE NOW

There is no easy way to tell an almost thirty-three old man he will die very soon. I cried as I drove home from the doctor's office. He didn't give six to eighteen months. I will die before the END of the month! There is nothing that prepares you for this kind of news—even though I was surrounded by family and friends who loved me through this process. Everyone was praying for me. The prognosis didn't look good as the doctor had said, "Each day would become more and more difficult." The doctor gave me some good advice on deciding. Choose NOW where you want to pass away. You will most likely choose a hospital or at home under nursing care.

Psalm 142:3 NLT
"When I am overwhelmed, you alone know how I should turn." - King David

God is good and faithful. Often, He uses our times of hardship to open doors for us to glorify Himself and share the gospel with others through our testimony.

HURTING PEOPLE NEED SOMEONE TO COME ALONGSIDE THEM AND HELP CARRY THE BURDEN.

When your blood counts are so low, when you rub or scratch your arm - blood simply comes through your skin. Blood comes out of everywhere, with no clotting factors that can stop it. I will not go into any more details, which is unnecessary. The fact is, death was close - closer than I could ever have imagined! I didn't understand why or how this could be happening to me. I made peace with God, and to die is 'gain'. Nobody knows the exact times or days we are given. But God does.

Being critical is not what hurting people need, rather, we need to be encouraging. Hurting people need someone to come alongside them to help carry the burden - in every facet of life and in every aspect of caring.

While walking through the church one day, a friend approached me and said some words. First, let me explain. I have forgiven him, but I will never forget how much he hurt me when he said these words. He pointed his finger at my face and spoke, loud enough for everyone to hear, not just loud enough for me. Everyone listened to his religious public shaming of a man who now had less than twenty-one days to live.

"Get the SIN out of your life, and God will heal you!"

He threw his head back and proudly walked away as if he had the last word. I had no rebuttal because I was just too sick to even respond. My mind raced. Is this how you treat a friend? What he said couldn't be true. It was the coldest, cruelest thing you could say to anybody. It was utterly heartless.

If someone has an obvious sin issue, a private "one-on-one" or a church leadership conversation is a more appropriate way to speak to a friend. I cannot say I knew any reason for his judgment about me. However, he seemed satisfied with himself as he felt the need for this public display of his self-righteousness.

Let me say, if you have a sick family member or friend – THEY NEED LOVE! They need a hug and a listening ear, and THEY NEED PRAYER. They need encouragement from a brother or sister in Christ. My healing was paid for on the cross at Calvary. Jesus died for me and paid the price for every one of my sins.

I DID NOT HAVE THE ABILITY TO UNDERSTAND MY CIRCUMSTANCES. I CONTINUE TO PRAISE HIM IN THE MIDST OF THE STORM.

The cross is where my healing comes from, nothing more or nothing less.

I stood there, as he walked away, with a steady stream of blood pouring out of my nose and down my face with hundreds of people watching. I knew right then that I would never treat anyone like that. Instead, I would be compassionate to others' circumstances, no matter where I was or whatever someone's story might be.

I was disappointed that no one came to my aid within the large group surrounding me. That morning, I walked out of the church with my head down, completely discouraged, and defeated. Truthfully, forgiveness was not necessarily immediately on my mind, but I soon forgave him. I swallowed deep, sucked it up, and went on to get my affairs in order.

In my spiritual walk, I learned to bring honor and glory to God. This should be a single purpose and guide in every human conversation. I'll pray that my friend will one day understand this meaning. Honestly, you wouldn't treat a dog like that man treated me in this case, in public or in private! I am not telling you I was perfect; I am human, and we all make mistakes. But God doesn't expect perfection. He does, however, expect obedience. I strive to live a closer and deeper relationship with Jesus Christ daily.

Joshua 1:9 NIV
"Have I not commanded you? Be strong and of good courage; do not be afraid or dismayed. The Lord, your God, is with you wherever you go." - Joshua

Today is my birthday. I turned thirty-three, sat with my sons, ages five and six, in my attorney's office, and drew up my will. I watched the boys play with Matchbox cars on the carpet. They had no idea what lay ahead. Although I got through it, this simple act of drafting a formal will was tough on me. This was yet another stark reminder of life and my impending death.

GOD HEARS THE PRAYERS OF HIS PEOPLE.

Ephesians 4:2 ESV
"Be completely humble and gentle; be patient, bearing with one another in love." - Apostle Paul

My brothers and sisters in a small group Bible study ministry are my most incredible friends - although I am reminded of where one person let me down. The Lord provided a group of people to help me in every way. I will always be grateful for each person who 'stood in the gap' in prayer, providing meals and childcare.

My small group leader's wife, Jo, said, "Let's pray for Mike's doctor. Let's pray that the doctor is an extension of God's hands." Praying for the doctor sounded like a great idea. So, I surrounded myself with a small group that loved and cared for me deeply as I walked out of these challenging days.

THERE IS NO GREATER PLACE TO BE THAN OUT ON A LIMB WITH THE LORD!

My pastor, M. Wayne Benson, and Evangelist, Dave Roever, prayed with me on Sunday morning at the end of our church service. After the prayer, Dave and Pastor Benson said, "There is no greater place to be than out on a limb with God." That statement has reminded me that there are no more distractions in my life.

My total dependence is now on God - and God alone. There is nothing else that matters - only me, and the Lord. All the worries of life, jobs, and money mean nothing anymore—just the closeness with my Lord. If a miracle does not happen, I will meet Jesus soon. No more cares about this world and the responsibilities of life—just Jesus. My divine Lord and Savior.

Studying God's word taught me that genuine trust may not eradicate fear. Yet, faith sometimes requires one to move forward despite trembling hands and butterflies fluttering in their stomach amidst a raging storm.

A few days passed, and the phone rang. My doctor, a Hematologist (blood specialist), devised an idea. He called me into his office for a consultation. He said to me, "We have nothing to lose". I want to open you up and look at your internal organs surgically."

The doctor thought deeply throughout the night and then said he "woke up and could not rest without at least trying" this. He continued, "Maybe we can find something wrong inside of you that can save your life." I am reminded of the prayers that were offered up for my doctor...

GOD HEARS THE PRAYERS OF HIS PEOPLE.

I woke from my surgery in the recovery room. My doctor leaned over me and said, "I have great news, Mike! You are going to live." The surgery revealed I was born with two spleen organs, and the surgeons removed both. Both were removed due to the uncertainty of one or both spleens being sick. This was a surgical decision done in the moment. (The medical reasoning for this was I was almost a set of twins!) Thirty days to live is now thirty-five years ago—GLORY BE TO GOD!

Isaiah 40:31 (NKJV)
"But those who wait on the Lord shall renew their strength; they shall mount up with wings like eagles, they shall run and not be weary, they shall walk and not faint." - Prophet Isaiah

Going through this journey made me evaluate how I treat others. This became a matter of heart and my Christian witness. My character and integrity demand that I be authentic, kind, and compassionate.

Choose the kind of friend that you will be today. Consider how you would have reacted to my actual life story. I have gone out of my way to extend grace to the friend who shamed me in the church that Sunday morning.

I learned long ago that living up to someone else's standards is impossible. I lived then and today with my identity in Jesus Christ. He is my Lord and Savior.

When I began writing the paragraph regarding my 'friend', I stated I had forgiven him. I will explain this because most people have difficulties with forgiveness. In my prayer years ago, I told the Lord I forgave the man who said this to me. I didn't go into any great details. The Lord knew what was said and what had transpired. I left this hurt at the cross, and that's where it will stay. I have no desire to continue any kind of friendship or relationship with him. I have no desire to meet with him and talk it out. I have just moved on and left this issue at the foot of the cross.

My message goes beyond my words. Those victimized worldwide might think they need further conversations to bring closure. Hopefully, victims seek professional counseling from those who can help navigate difficult times.

I'm speaking from the heart when I tell you I didn't need any closure or further conversation. To connect and relive this conversation would have no gain. Instead, it would force me to walk back down a 'dark road'. So, if you're struggling with difficulties from your past, forgive the offenders. When you do, you set the captive free that is holding you down and connecting you to your history.

Before I write, I ask the Holy Spirit what he wants me to say. My healing from a severe blood disease is a remarkable story. But the real story is compassion and forgiveness. If God had healed me from the blood disease - and I hadn't matured into a compassionate person - this would have been only part of my story.

Part Two

GROWING FROM DIFFICULTIES

God has a way of strengthening us. Strength comes from the trials in our lives. The critical point here is how we navigate these moments. As you have read, I choose life and live it abundantly. Every day is a gift to be lived to its fullest. I am grateful for life. I will not sabotage the promise of today by looking and living back at my past. The exception is whether my past can bring glory to God through my testimony, by showing God's goodness in my healing and inspiring hope in others.

As God imparts insightful wisdom about the grand scheme of our lives, He equips us with the essential qualities of faith, perseverance, and patience, which enable us to fulfill His purpose and persist in times of hardship and adversity.

The Bible is filled with stories of great men and women of faith; almost all had one or more defining "wilderness experiences" that God used to prepare them for even greater use. So, God used my story and sickness to witness to Fred thirty years after my illness. It's amazing how HE works!

"Every day brings us opportunities to serve God, to love others, and to live obediently. Those living with an evident appreciation that each day could be the day He comes will act accordingly."

I am confident God used these moments to give me a heart for the hurting, along with compassion. Had I not gone through the spiritual abuse from the guy at church, I would not have learned forgiveness. Through my doctor, I learned compassion. My doctor didn't 'sugarcoat' the details of my medical condition. He gave the news as a professional with much more care, which, in turn, opened my eyes to a very caring individual, and for that, I am eternally thankful. God brought a man into my life who helped heal me physically and opened my eyes to help care for others. Without this experience, I may have never developed the sensitivity to minister to the homeless community in the inner city.

Forgiveness would have never occurred if I didn't forgive the man who hurt me - when I needed him the most. Here is an image inspired by the phrase: "He wants to free you from your past and lead you into a new future. Forgiveness can never be purchased; it is always a free gift given." Forgiveness is better done as soon as possible! Sometimes, it's a process through professional counseling, but always best left at the foot of the cross!

As I mature in my faith, I choose to forgive others quickly. Give it to the Lord. Leave it there and move on. Rehashing old wounds does nothing for my Christian witness. My identity is in Christ, not in the injustices done to me by others. It is a sign of strength to surrender everything unto the Father, and then move on to the life God has set before me. Sharing this testimonial story is by my example. During the most challenging time in my life, FORGIVENESS BROUGHT FORTH HEALING.

Forgiveness plays a more significant role in our lives than most people understand. I do not think I have publicly or privately shared this spiritual abuse story. But, had I not forgiven the man who needed to prove himself self-righteous to a dying man, I may have become bitter and angry. Instead, forgiveness opened the doors to my healing.

Forgiveness is a process. The sooner you forgive others for their infractions against you, the quicker you move on. The healing in both the physical body, and forgiveness, glorifies God and now becomes part of your testimony. Your testimony is one of the most potent evangelizing tools you have in sharing the gospel with others.

There's a saying, "Whatever doesn't kill you will make you stronger." It has strengthened me and made me more compassionate about our hurting and lost world. Another way to think about this is everyone has a choice to be a "bridge builder." I am bringing forth healing and calmness amidst calamities. The other option is to live in the chaos and destruction of the past. God is glorified when we forgive as He has forgiven us. Overcoming the wounds gives God the glory and sets the tone of our testimony's foundation.

Part Three

Difficulty Brings Forth Compassion

True happiness lies within living out our purpose. Some of the happiest people I know understand their purpose in life. Quite simply, they look for the good in life and find ways to serve to make it better for others. They find significance in everyday living, have a relationship with the Father, and know the world doesn't revolve around them. We are placed here by God to make an impact, big or small, for the kingdom of God.

I remember my purpose every time I reach into my back left pocket when I open my wallet. My wife, Robin, had a custom wallet made for me. Inscribed in the leather is - "You are created for such a time as this," Love Robin. What an essential daily reminder to step out and share Jesus with the world. This gift reminds me of who I am and that I am created uniquely for God's plan and purpose for my life.

I have shared throughout this book about my ministry in our inner city. During one such event, I met Edna, an older woman whom I had helped with her meal. When I spoke to Edna, she was as sweet as any grandma you would ever meet. Before her dinner, I asked her if we could pray together. I asked her what her needs were. She wasn't specific, so I asked her if Jesus was the Lord of her life. Edna responded, "I believe, but I'm not good at it." I then asked her, "Would you like to make Jesus your Lord and Savior?" She said "yes," and we walked through the sinner's prayer together. Her life changed, and the trajectory of her eternity did, as well.

Being truthful but needing to be respectful - these are moments of coaching. This made me think of others' backstories and the issues deep inside their hearts—secrets of self-made mistakes and regrets and the possibilities of abuses suffered earlier in life.

I then started walking away when another older woman approached me. She introduced herself and said, "I am Debra." Debra started to speak. She said, "I want you to pray for me too!" I like what she had referred to, same as Edna. "I want to be counted." Debra and I shared some light conversation. I walked her through the salvation prayer and prayed for healing in her failing knees. I gave Edna and Debra communication cards, so follow-up care and ministry would be available for them. These are just a few times and examples that I am "living out my purpose" as the Holy Spirit leads my days.

I didn't ask these ladies what had brought them to this 'place' in their lives. Sometimes, it is a mental illness. Other times it's bad choices and substance abuse. But God has revealed to me to see the hurt in someone's eyes. God has given me compassion for the inner-city community.

Conclusion

SOME OF OUR BEST 'PREACHING' IS DONE THROUGH OUR ACTIONS AND HOW WE TAKE CARE OF OTHERS.

Christians need to look at the world through the eyes of Christ - beginning with simply caring for one another. My doctor truly cared for me in my sickness and throughout his care for me I saw a man with a big compassionate heart. I never asked him if he was a believer however, it was evident in every part of his mannerisms. Some of our best preaching is done through our actions and how we live and take care of others.

The bridge for this community is forgiveness. To be a "bridge builder" means to meet each person exactly where they are in life. But, unfortunately, listening to their story often is filled with a long list of hurts and abuses (like in my example of the man who pointed his finger in my face telling me I needed to "get the sin out of my life" in order for God to heal me.) I hope no one would ever have to go through this unfortunate situation. There is no superiority in Christianity - just believers willing to serve, and not condemn others.

This world needs to be introduced to Jesus. This is done by laying our own interests aside then listening to what others are saying and helping them find a solution. Caring for others is not complicated, we just need to take the focus off ourselves.

Don't overcomplicate the message.

Just share Jesus.

The message is clear and straightforward.

No fancy sermons. Only grassroots faith, and unconditional love.

It is not enabling people, it's just simply loving them, just as Jesus did (and still does!)

Lastly, let God be God.

At times, the most impactful action we can take as believers is surrendering to God's sovereignty. By entrusting Him to fight our battles and patiently await His response, we acknowledge His presence amid chaos and His advocacy on our behalf. Although we may feel compelled to retaliate verbally against those who wrong us, it is wiser to release our grip and rely on God as our defense.

Thoughts and Footnotes

Deuteronomy 31:6. NIV
"Be strong and courageous. Do not fear or be in dread of them, for it is the LORD your God who goes with you. He will not leave you or forsake you." - Moses

When facing challenges and battles in life, what matters most is not whether we measure up to someone's idea but whether we seek and trust God from the heart.

We will never live up to another person's expectations.

My journey through this health crisis changed me in so many ways. I have had times in my life where I have been far too intense on things or overly concerned with issues that didn't matter. But, after being sick, I slowed down enough to see the 'little' things and to "stop and smell the roses." The 'little' things in life became big things to notice and enjoy.

I am thankful for my doctor. I hope you can see how God used the prayers of His people, in this case, my small group. When Jo said, "Let's pray for the doctor," this was a divine word from God to pray and intercede for my doctor, so he could not rest without rethinking my case. My illness was a year-long journey to wellness.

Always pray for your doctors and medical care professionals. Always surround yourselves with solid, mature Bible-based believers. All I wanted was extreme prayer warriors in the battle, no pity parties, just solid Christians that believed their prayers could move mountains. In my case, prayers that God would bring forth healing in my body.

I hope that everyone can understand how to minister and be friends. As believers, we are the 'light' of the world. I encourage everyone first to love others, then listen and minister to those others in their time of need. Cast your judgments aside and be the loving brother or sister in Christ He has called you to be in times of someone's most significant time of need.

Always learn to forgive quickly. As I explained - Unforgiveness leads to negativity, and negativity will likely never lead anyone to Christ. Unforgiveness lives in the past and hinders our testimony. Our testimonies are some of the most powerful words we can speak to others in leading them to Christ.

I came out of my sickness with a heart of compassion, to help and love others. The Holy Spirit has a way of redirecting our steps. My life today is one hundred percent different from what I ever dreamed it would be. I am happy and fulfilled to be ministering in the inner city - or wherever He has called me to love and pray with others. I am thankful for this day, another day of life to use my time wisely for the kingdom of God.

MAIN TAKEAWAYS:

Facing Mortality

Initial Hopelessness: The ITP - initially hopeless from man's perspective.

Psalm 142:3: Biblical reflection during overwhelming times.

Mike's Birthday: Preparing a will, facing death with his children, reassessing life's priorities.

SEEING FORGIVENESS AND LEARNING COMPASSION

Learning to forgive at the lowest moments in life opened the door to compassion and ministry.

Always pray for your doctors' to be an extension of God's hands.

Chapter 5 Study Guide Questions

In the severity of my sickness, my life changed quickly. My condition caused me to reevaluate the relationships closest to me. Some people ministered such incredible Christ-like love to me - while others did not. This was a challenging season.

Choose the kind of friend that you will be today. Consider how you would have reacted to my actual life story. I have gone out of my way to extend grace to the 'friend' that shamed me in the church that Sunday morning.

How would you react?

Either in sickness or a loss, how have your experiences brought you closer to the Lord?

My doctor was a fantastic man. He 'walked' through my sickness with me, doing everything he could. In difficult conversations, he was truthful and kind. As I have written, I am so grateful for his compassion. At one point, he gave me no hope. How difficult that must have been for him to share that information with me! The other perspective is to be brutally honest and heartless in approach.

Being truthful, compassionate, and authentic must be a part of every believer's life.

Have you ever needed to share difficult news with someone?

Were you able to do it with honesty, kindness, and compassion, or must you learn to be more compassionate?

Forgiveness plays a more significant role in our lives than most people understand. But had I not forgiven the man who needed to "prove himself righteous" to a dying man, I may have become bitter and angry. Instead, forgiveness opened the doors to my healing and later, my ministry.

Forgiveness is a process. The sooner you forgive others for their infractions against you, the quicker you move on. The healing in both the physical body and through forgiveness glorifies God and now becomes part of your testimony. Your testimony is one of the most potent evangelizing tools you have in sharing the gospel with others.

Have you ever felt the need to stop and reevaluate your life in terms of forgiveness?

In quiet reflection...

Do you need to forgive others who may have hurt you?

Have you discovered ministry opportunities after going through challenging times?

How do character and integrity add value to your testimony?

CHAPTER SIX

COMFORTER

Part One

Matthew 6:33 (NIV)
"But seek first the kingdom of God and his righteousness, and all these things will be given to you as well." - Jesus Christ

I often pray that God will lead me into conversations where I can be used to share my Christian witness and testimony. By setting my agenda aside, my thoughts and ideas can align with God's so that my experiences and testimonies can be used to help others and offer comfort.

By submitting our lives to Christ, we recognize God is in authority. As we put our faith in Jesus Christ, we submit ourselves to His watchful care. Understand that God is fully aware of every occurrence in our lives. NOTHING ESCAPES HIS NOTICE. He has complete authority over all our lives.

You can be a tremendous influence in other people's lives. It does not a require a Biblical degree or influential positions in life. It has everything to do with yielding to God's call on your life, then, living it out through obedience.

Our routine was to leave work early on Fridays to load up and get to the cottage before the Friday afternoon rush began. Our two dogs, Sig, and Lacey, each took their respective positions in the back seat. As a result, the driving time and arrival at the cottage were usually a couple of hours from the time we left our suburban country home. Finally, walking into the cabin, I secured the dogs, my wife unloaded and unpacked, and began to start dinner.

After all this, I was met with physical exhaustion. After some food and light socializing with our neighbors, I built a campfire and kicked back, enjoying the solitude of the moments before bedtime. Getting away is refreshing to my soul, as I sit on the deck watching the brown trout rise to the sound of their slurp as they feed on the evening hatch of insects rising to the top of the water. Occasionally, I would grab a fly rod and swing a few dry flies into the current that worked around the rock eddies out in front of our place. Traveling from Michigan to Minnesota each week, I enjoyed this time of reflection and types of moments that would help the miles pass.

There is little that compares to swinging a fly into the river and being in conversation with the Lord! More specifically, when the Holy Spirit is present, the praises come out of me naturally as I am not singing but praying and conversing in the Spirit. My mind would think back to a successful week, safe travels for me, and up to eighteen crews working throughout the Midwest United States. After the work conversations, I moved into the personal stuff about how I could grow closer to God. He knows I'm a work in progress, but He uses me in a unique way in this chaotic world. I asked Him to "speak into my soul" so that I would hear Him without questioning. I would 'hear' His voice as I moved throughout my days.

When I pray, I ask God to use me, send me, and clear my mind of the noise of the day. I pray believing He is creating divine appointments ahead of my steps. The thought of my prayer is that not my will, Lord, but Your will be done. Scary prayers when you think of where and how God will take you and use you throughout this day, this week, and this life!

I pray for the 'gifts' of the Holy Spirit to grow me into the person He wants me to be. As I stated in previous chapters, - I don't want to be in the same place spiritually for even two days in a row. I want to be where the action is! I like being on the edge of my comfort zone, trusting that God is leading me throughout my conversations or situations with strangers, supplying me with words of knowledge. Using both 'gifts', the Holy Spirit will speak into my life regarding an issue, which usually means praying for a hurting person. I trust Him, and I don't question the Holy Spirit.

AN ORDINARY PERSON DOING EXTRAORDINARY THINGS IS ALWAYS POSSIBLE WITH GOD.

To put this another way - the right word at the wrong time is the wrong word. So, waiting on the 'right time' is imperative to the Holy Spirit's leading. A good thing to remember is that I'm a man here on earth. I am not the Holy Spirit, so I want to avoid getting ahead of His plan.

God's timing is perfect and He's always on time, so there is no need to hurry or rush according to my schedule. If I'm uncertain about 'timing', I just go into prayer, asking God to clarify the moment for me. At times, I have driven away from a location to have the Holy Spirit give me a 'heart check' on something - sometimes when I'm a couple of hours away after leaving someone. I ask God to preserve their lives until I can return to present the Gospel to them, and sometimes, I have led them to Christ. I have also had moments where I turned around because that's what He wanted me to do.

AN ORDINARY PERSON DOING EXTRAORDINARY THINGS IS ALWAYS POSSIBLE WITH GOD; that's the perspective of *The Everyday Believer.* No unique talents or doctorate degrees, just the power of the Holy Spirit and the obedience to His call. That's my prayer - to be used and available for divine appointments orchestrated by the Holy Spirit.

Part Two

We usually would leave to come home on weekends because we attended Saturday night services at church. I consider Sundays a day of rest, mostly without schedules or deadlines, just relaxing Sundays... So, leaving our cottage this Saturday afternoon was an ordinary occurrence for us as we packed the truck and headed south on the highway.

We were nearing home when the Holy Spirit spoke into my heart. While driving on the highway, we noticed a low-flying helicopter flying quickly by. My wife thought that a local business family was heading home. The Holy Spirit "spoke" into my heart SO clearly that there was a thirteen-year-old boy from White Cloud, Michigan that had been in a severe ATV accident. I heard Him saying, "his leg is severed, and he has had significant blood loss. He is going into shock and could die." I said to Robin, "Let's pray; this is what God just said to me." She looked at me with a surprised look on her face. So, we prayed for the helicopter pilots, the onboard nurses, the doctors, and the young boy.

As we neared the town, the hospital was in view, and we watched as the helicopter touched down on the hospital helipad on the rooftop. We continued to pray for the receiving doctors - to give them wisdom and knowledge on treating this young man. We prayed that this young man would not pass away without knowing Jesus as his Lord and Savior. We prayed for the anesthesiologist, operating doctors, nurses, and even for the technology God created to be used for this young man at this moment in time. We prayed that God would use their wisdom and knowledge to save this boy's life as an extension of God himself.

Several times throughout the evening, I continued to pray for the boy's well-being. I never knew the exact specifics - only what the Holy Spirit shared with me, the wisdom and word of knowledge as we drove down the highway. I felt happy that God chose me during this family crisis. Almost unbelievably, the next day, the news reported that "a thirteen-year-old boy was severely hurt, had injured his leg from an ATV accident, and underwent emergency surgery to save his life." The boy had been airlifted from the small town of White Cloud to a Grand Rapids hospital and was expected to survive. Praise and glory be to God that He met the young boy in his greatest need! A young life was preserved but could have been met with greater disaster.

My salvation began the process where I was becoming more connected to Jesus and more specifically to the Holy Spirit. The Holy Spirit lives inside me through my salvation, as He does with all 'born-again' believers. The presence of the Holy Spirit allows me to live 'less of myself' and 'more of Him'. Little by little, my life began to produce the 'fruit' that He has created for me in my relationships here on earth - but more importantly, with my relationships with the Father, Son, and Holy Spirit.

You might ask, did I do a follow-up visit with the boy who had been injured? I didn't feel led to do so; I did precisely what the Holy Spirit asked me to do at that moment. I would have been there if He had led me to visit the boy - without hesitation.

The Spiritual Gift of KNOWLEDGE

The Holy Spirit gives this spiritual gift to bring about understanding to Christ's followers. The person with this gift is usually well-versed in the Scriptures and often has much of God's word committed to memory. This person can retain the truth and communicate it effectively. Here is another spiritual gift that involves understanding truth with an insight that only comes by revelation from God. Those with the gift of knowledge understand the deep things of God and the mysteries of His Word.

1 Corinthians 12:8 (NIV)
"To one there is given through the Spirit a message of wisdom, to another a message of knowledge by means of the same Spirit..." - Apostle Paul

To receive a word of knowledge with such clarity for this young man is truly a gift from God. I am glad for the sensitivity and the discernment to have made a difference for that young man, which could have been the difference between life and death. Although, as a Christian, I am called to pray, encourage, and give hope to others, these prayers are being prayed so that they are anonymous to the world around us. I am happy that we have such a loving God and Father - and that I am chosen to pray, speak the truth, and care for others in their most significant times of need!

Part Three

THE HEART OF A MAN IS DEFINED BY WHO HE IS IN CHRIST.

I have traveled extensively with employees and other contractors throughout my years in the construction business. The heart of the man is easily understood when he is away from home, either for business or pleasure.

Man can sometimes be described in two ways—committed or non-committed men in Christ. I have seen behavior in both types of men that would be downright shameful. Some consider being away from home a return to "locker room" talks somewhere between ninth-grade behavior and college fraternity life. I love to laugh and have fun, but my language and behavior do not change when I drive out of my driveway. First and foremost, I represent Christ. My values and behavior must be held to my Christian witness.

It takes faith to stand up for the truth. But unfortunately, the truth is not popular in today's culture or society. Those who believe in God the Father, Jesus the Son, and the Holy Spirit understand they are looked upon as old-fashioned and have a traditional conservative mindset.

The Spiritual Gift of EXHORTATION

The spiritual gift of exhortation is often called the "gift of encouragement." The Spirit of God gives this gift to people in the church to strengthen, encourage, uplift, and motivate others.

Romans 12:8 (NIV) "...if it is to encourage, then give encouragement; if it is giving, then give generously; if it is to lead, do it diligently; if it is to show mercy, do it cheerfully." - Apostle Paul

I was in a hunting camp in the western Wyoming mountain country some years ago. The ranch totaled about fifty-five thousand acres. Where I'm from in the Midwest, fifty-five thousand acres is a big piece of ground!

I was a guest at this ranch, and when I walked in - I was amazed at this beautifully decorated "Western-style" lodge. There was a table of various foods and snacks and a table with a fully stocked bar. All alcohol goods were self-serve; drink as much as you like. The outfit had strict rules regarding alcohol and the use of guns.

Standing Up for the Truth -
It Isn't a Choice - It's The Lifestyle in Which I Choose to Live.

Our first evening at the lodge was a meal of salads and ribeye steaks. I went through the food line and gathered everything for this feast. I sat down, bowed my head, and prayed for the meal I was about to eat. I looked up, and a man was standing there, looking me in the eyes. He had had a few drinks and, with a beet-red face and loud voice, gathered everyone's attention and spoke. "Hey, I see this guy praying for his meal; maybe he would like to pray for all of us!"

Mind you, this man was making great fun of me and my beliefs and trying to get the others to join in by laughing at me. So, I stood up and said, "I would LOVE to pray a blessing over this meal and for every hunter here." I asked God to bless the food to our bodies for strength and nourishment. I then prayed for the hunters' safety, that God would reveal Himself to them during their time on this ranch, and that each hunter would shoot the buck of their dreams!

I sat down only to have the other guests thanking me for the prayer. The prayer wasn't condescending to others or some big drummed-up pre-planned prayer, but rather the words of my heart. And looking back, the prayer spoken was much more than thanking God for our meal. It was the Holy Spirit opening the door to much bigger things. That prayer began relationships with other 'strong-believing' guys growing to where "iron sharpens iron" now more than a decade later!

My morning prayers include asking God to have His way. I pray, "Lord, use me to do your will. In obedience, I submit this day to you. Give me the boldness to speak your truth into others' lives in Christ's love."

OUR CHRISTIAN WITNESS IS ALWAYS ON DISPLAY - NOT AS A FLASHING BILLBOARD, BUT IN THE HEARTFELT CONVERSATIONS LED BY THE HOLY SPIRIT.

The dinner-time prayer started many conversations within our group of hunters in this camp. One of the most interesting conversations was with the gentleman who was a little tipsy and then asked me to pray for our meal. He began by asking about my church and where I was from. I simply shared a brief testimony of my life, family, work life, and faith in God. So naturally, I asked him what town he was from. He replied, "I'm from Amarillo, Texas." I told him, after some small talk about work, family, etc., "My church has a pastor that visits occasionally from the Amarillo area." I said, "He's one of my favorites. His name is Jimmy Evans. Jimmy's ministry is geared toward marriage. Have you ever heard of him?" He looked away, stared at the floor for a moment, looked up into

my eyes, and said, "Yes, I have heard of him," and after a long pause…
"He's, my pastor."

CHOOSING GRACE

I remarked that "Jimmy is an incredible teacher, and you have an outstanding pastor. I love it when he comes to my church and teaches about marriage and family!"

I responded out of love for him. I didn't need to call him out on trying to make fun of me while praying or for his immature behavior. I just loved him and allowed the Holy Spirit to work through me to infiltrate his heart. I encouraged him to follow Jesus and to be the man he was created to be. We shook hands and hugged as we parted ways.

I hope he is vital in the Lord, continues growing as a husband and father, and as a leader in his family, fulfilling his calling and God's purpose. From our conversations, I could tell he is a good man. He just let the situations of life take over his better judgment. Our Christian witness is always on display, not as a flashing billboard, but in the heartfelt conversations led by the Holy Spirit. The atmosphere changes when we enter a room, a business meeting, or anywhere. God opens the doors to conversations we might never have thought of.

THIS WAS NO 'BOOT ON HIS THROAT' MOMENT!

How do we respond to someone who is seemingly out of line? My experience is that I don't have to point out someone's sins or mistakes. They know what they are doing. I disagree with taking the stance of public shaming or gang-piling on the guilt, then shooting off Bible verses pointing out someone's sinfulness and condemnation to make them feel bad.

I can't think that this type of behavior would ever lead anyone to Christ! Instead, our lives should represent the best of LISTENING, UNDERSTANDING, and SHARING our faith as the Holy Spirit leads. In someone's failure, let them speak - carefully listening to what they have to say - without rattling back with rapid-fire answers and responses.

THE HOLY SPIRIT WAS ALREADY AT WORK IN THIS MAN'S HEART

As believers, we are called to be 'bridge builders' to help someone in their time of need. By responding in love, we can close the gap between bad behavior and Christ-like behavior or witness. I can't think of anything worse than Christians 'looking down their noses' with a "better-than-you attitude."

I certainly am not advocating being someone's doormat or tolerating abuse by someone. Let your 'light' shine in a way that God has called you to be His witness. Often, people don't want Bible verses thrown at them, but they simply want to be loved and heard.

These are often teachable moments best done with Christ-like love and encouragement. There is no value in 'rubbing someone's nose' in their mistakes, even when their intent and actions are meant to make fun of or embarrass someone else.

No preaching, no condescending attitude from me to him, just love him as Christ would love him, wishing him the best for himself and his family. The time away spent on a remote Wyoming hunting ranch might be a "good old boys' club" for some, but as believers, we are called to always represent Christ - even while staying in a remote hunting camp in the mountains, far from home.

Part Four

How To Love A Hurting Man

With great anticipation, I was off to a west Texas hill-country hunting camp. The flight from Michigan to Dallas is just a few hours long. Before the trip, my pastor friend encouraged me to write a small-group study guide from my first book, *The Power of Forgiveness*, so I used my book as a reference tool while writing the study guide. A gentleman named Greg, who was seated next to me on the flight to Dallas, saw the book's title and asked me how it was possible to forgive someone who hurt you so deeply as a child that you believed you could never forgive them. So, I shared my experience with forgiveness. Most people have been hurt by someone or some circumstance in life. Forgiveness is more than saying you're sorry. Forgiveness begins at the cross, and our hearts are made right before God for our sins to be forgiven.

I told him that most of us have been hurt deeply by someone, down to their soul; these examples are too many and far too numerous to list. I shared my story on how deeply the pain went down inside me and how the Holy Spirit allowed me to forgive the men who almost killed me during the robbery attempt. I explained that by finding forgiveness, I could move forward without living in the identity of my robbery event.

Traumatic events leave scars deep into the layers of someone's soul which are almost impossible to get over on their own. Only God can heal the brokenhearted and the abused, while often, with others who have experienced traumatic events - it becomes their identity. My identity is in Jesus Christ and not in the events of a grocery store robbery when I was victimized as a sixteen-year-old young man. Greg said, "I would never tell you or anyone else about my childhood." I said, "that was fine." I encouraged him to "bring it to the cross" and leave it there and let God work through the circumstances of what happened to him. He had been very deeply hurt for decades. Greg was a man in his forties, longing for the wholeness and healing that only God can provide. I gave Greg a copy of my book, and I pray that he can surrender the circumstances of hurt, abuse, or abandonment to the cross. I hope that Greg's life is restored. He is growing into the man God has called him to be. Finally, a man is free from childhood pain, shame, and unspeakable hurt. That is a miracle that only God can do!

Conclusion

For believers in Christ, there are always ministry opportunities all around us. These are divine appointments brought before us by the Holy Spirit. I am reminded to be a good listener and ready for a word that can encourage someone in a difficult time. Our conversations can lead to 'bridge-building' without compromising our faith.

I have a little sign on my mantel saying, "The best sermons are lived, not preached." I have heard some outstanding teachings and sermons, but our life stories, testimonies, and character will ultimately draw others to

Christ. Our lives will either attract people to Christ or repel them from Him. So, I want to live so that my life models Christlikeness in all aspects.

Whether we are leaving home for a business trip or for pleasure, our Christian witness is always on display. Certainly not in an 'act' or for the benefit of others to see, and for our own glory - but in the character of our hearts. God has used me to listen, pray, and encourage others in my travels.

Thoughts and Footnotes

I pray God leads me into conversations with others and that He creates divine appointments where I can be used to share my Christian witness and testimony. To set my agenda aside, my thoughts and ideas must align with God's. My experiences and testimonies throughout my life can be used to help others and bring them comfort.

We believe we do not have control over our lives; God is in charge. By putting our faith in Jesus Christ, we submit ourselves to His watchful care. As a result, God is fully aware of every occurrence in our lives. Nothing escapes His notice, and He has complete authority over all our lives.

You can have a tremendous influence on other people's lives.

It is not a matter of Biblical degrees or influential positions in life.

It has everything to do with obedience to God's call on your life.

Then, through obedience, living it out.

As we journey through life, it is meaningful to 'sacrifice' ourselves for others. Every one of us will meet people who will cause us offense. Our ministry takes place in how we react or simply don't react.

The world teaches us to hit back with a rude comment - or we could choose God's way by listening with maturity to the Holy Spirit. A quick response to a rude comment completely blows our Christian witness. This is much easier said than done, but the rewards of sowing back into the person with love are priceless. Nothing can be gained by pointing your finger at someone, 'getting the last word', thus creating more resentment and shame.

These words were written as examples of the ways that life has changed. For some, it was the healing needed in their physical bodies, while others were hurt decades ago when torment entered their lives as young, innocent victims. While some may need to evaluate their lives more closely to live and understand that others and Christian witnesses are always being viewed - our lives are always on display, not in the form of a show but rather a matter of character and heart.

MAIN TAKEAWAYS:

Lodge Prayer:

Being identified as a Christian (to embarrass me) yet placing myself to lead a transformative prayer to the entire lodge. The prayer opened the door to deeper conversations with many men.

Chapter 6 STUDY GUIDE QUESTIONS

The gifts of the Holy Spirit are truly unique. When we accept Jesus Christ as our Lord and Savior, the Holy Spirit now lives inside of us. After giving my heart to Christ, I began to experience the Holy Spirit and His voice directing my steps. One of the most extraordinary things I have ever done was to forgive others. That forgiveness opened the door to His blessings.

Have you held back forgiveness towards others who have hurt you in the past?

I pursued the Holy Spirit through study, prayers, and reading the Word. I would pray to be sensitive to the Holy Spirit's voice and to submit my will to His. Then, God opened the door to a new realm of faith for me.

Explain how you are pursuing the Holy Spirit.

It has taken years to understand and hear the Holy Spirit's voice. Yet, the Holy Spirit spoke to me clearly regarding the young boy injured in an ATV accident.

Has the Holy Spirit ever told you with such clarity that you needed to pray immediately to save someone's life?

If so, share your testimonial experience.

I shared that the Holy Spirit goes before us through prayer and prepares His meetings and encounters. Therefore, our Christian witness is always on display for others to observe.

Sometimes in life, we encounter a person who is rude or trying to embarrass or shame us publicly. Often, these times are awkward and full of challenging moments.

How can we step back without reacting or overreacting?

How can you do better at being a 'bridge builder'?

Can you ask a family member, friend, or stranger the 'hard' questions like these about their faith?

Where is their heart with Jesus Christ?

Where will they spend eternity?

Why do you think this is this so difficult and how can we do better?

CHAPTER SEVEN

MEANINGFUL RISK

Part One

1 Corinthians 16:1 (NKJV)
"Watch, stand fast in faith. Be brave and strong" - Apostle Paul.

It's easy to think that our lives are insignificant, or that we have nothing special to offer. But the truth is, God has uniquely gifted and equipped each of us for His purposes. We just need to be open and willing to follow His lead.

Esther 4:14 (NIV)
"For if you remain silent at this time, relief and deliverance for the Jews will arise from another place, but you and your father's family will perish. And who knows but that you have come to your royal position for such a time as this?" -Mordecai

Esther was a young Jewish girl who became the queen of Persia. She could have easily kept her head down and enjoyed the privileges of her position, but instead, she was willing to risk everything to save her people from destruction. God had placed her in that position for a reason, and she was ready to use her influence to make a difference.

In the same way, God has placed us in our specific circumstances for a reason. Whether we're stay-at-home parents, teachers, business owners, or anything in between - we can make a difference in the lives of those around us.

LIVING A LIFE OF GREATER SIGNIFICANCE

We may not always know God's plan for us, but we can trust He will guide us and use us for His purposes. We just need to be willing to take the small steps of obedience that He asks of us and trust that He will use them to bring about something more significant than we could ever imagine.

So, let's embrace the ordinary moments of our lives, knowing that God is at work in them. Let's be open to His leading and willing to step out in faith when He calls us to something greater than ourselves. And let's trust that He will use us to make an extraordinary difference in the world around us.

There are only rewards with significant risks. Throughout this writing, I share some of my life stories and testimonies where I stood at the doorway and consciously chose to step forward, freeze in place, or simply turn away. Through the Holy Spirit's leading, we are vehicles carrying the message of hope and love of Jesus Christ. Through obedience, we are the messengers of light in a dark world. As we journey through these testimonial stories, God is the hero, and to Him be all the glory; without Him, none of this could have happened for His timing, purpose, and destiny for whom God uses and chooses in these times.

I have never woken up in the morning and told myself, "Today, I will run into a burning house and carry an older woman in my arms to safety." I have no aspirations to be a hero, only to be the man God has created me to be. Sometimes, that man must be courageous in the face of danger. As a Christ follower or someone who's experienced the redeeming love of Jesus, He has shown me what love looks like. Love looks like doing anything I can to help another person in crisis, sometimes disregarding my safety to help another. I cannot stand by and watch another person suffer without trying to help.

The Holy Spirit designs our appointments for us, often during personal inconvenience. Doing the Lord's work must be a joyful opportunity to surrender my will to His. When He opens doors, I must recognize the opportunity and walk through it to do ministry. The church body is built up because somebody cared enough and took the time to share, do the work, and minister - no matter the size of the task.

One recurring theme or idea throughout this book – you may have noticed - is my love for the Holy Spirit. Years ago, the pastor spoke of the "Holy Ghost" during our Methodist Church services when I was a small boy. At that time, I couldn't understand or 'get' the connection of the Godhead. The "Holy Ghost" sounded scary then because I did not understand what that meant or who He was.

As I matured both in my physical age and spiritual development, I began exploring and studying the Holy Spirit. Looking back at my life, I can say with certainty the hand of God has guided me throughout every stage of my life and still does today. I have previously written about early morning prayers while traveling for my job in the country's Midwest. I remember thinking - my focused prayers were to hear the Holy Spirit's voice, seek His presence, and be used by Him.

IF JESUS CHRIST IS THE LORD OF YOUR LIFE, THE PRESENCE AND THE POWER OF THE HOLY SPIRIT ARE YOURS. WALKING IN THE SPIRIT MEANS WALKING WITH CHRIST.

I wanted a close and unique relationship with the Holy Spirit, asking in my prayers to grow into the man He has created me to be. With sensitivity, to hear His voice with clarity, and then with boldness, go forth and do whatever He asks me to do. To pray these prayers without limitations means going wherever led or needed to speak to strangers whether that is across the street or across the continent.

I studied and prayed, then gradually opened my eyes to the gifts of the Holy Spirit. To grow in this area of my spiritual walk was very exciting because situations can change quickly! Sometimes, with just a thought or idea for something to work on or to pray about are in these moments of immediate ministry.

Reflecting on my life, it's clear that God uniquely 'wired' me. Like every one of us, we are made in His image. When my talents and abilities align with His will, my ministry is as natural as anything I have ever done, and much can be accomplished with seemingly little effort on my part. Indeed, sacrificing ourselves for the sake of another is a powerful act of love and selflessness. It is the essence of being a guide, of leading others towards a better path or outcome. It is also a vital element of the 'hero's journey', where the hero must often make sacrifices or face significant challenges to achieve the goal.

When we sacrifice ourselves for others, we demonstrate compassion and empathy for their struggles and needs. We are putting their well-being above our own and showing that we value them. This sacrifice can take many forms, from giving up our time and resources to help someone in need, to risking our safety or comfort to protect or care for others.

But regardless of its form, sacrificing ourselves for others is a significant and transformative act. It changes us, and it changes the people around us. It can inspire others to follow our example and create a ripple effect of kindness and generosity. So, let us embrace the power of sacrifice and be willing to give of ourselves for the sake of others. In doing so, we will not only make a meaningful difference in their lives, but we will also discover our true purpose and meaning in this world.

In previous chapters, I have written that I am a relationship guy. This is a crucial factor in the spiritual gift of mercy. As I have matured in my faith, the gift of mercy continues to come forth and develop in my life.

Relationships, caring, and compassion are attributes of my personality and how I live my life. Mix these with surrendering myself to Him daily and being available, and you can easily see the needs of others right before your eyes.

Developing my confidence as a Christian took some time to reach maturity. I was born with a naturally shy personality, so walking boldly in this area took some real effort. I remember the defining moment when I pushed myself for the breakthrough.

Part Two

The Spiritual Gift of FAITH

Those with the gift of faith trust that God is sovereign, and He is good. They take Him at His Word and put the full weight of their lives in His hands. They pray for God to move and are not surprised when He answers a prayer or performs a miracle. I expect that in my prayers.

I Corinthians 12:9 (NIV)
"...to another faith by the same Spirit, to another gifts
of healing by that one Spirit." - Apostle Paul

Hebrews 11:1-3 (NIV)
"Now, faith is confidence in what we hope for and assurance
about what we do not see. This is what the ancients were
commended for. By faith we understand that the universe
was formed at God's command, so that what is seen
was not made of what was visible." - Apostle Paul

Confidence

Enrich your life by surrounding yourself with high-quality individuals - those who possess intelligence, kindness, ambition, and admirable qualities that inspire and uplift you. Being in their company will raise your expectations, encourage you, and help you become a better version of yourself. This is true in the business world, ministry partners, and your personal friends and relationships.

Your confidence influences your success in accomplishing the task and your faith in God's capacity to address your shortcomings and rectify any mistakes. Confidence in my life, and maybe for most people, was one 'growth step' after another. Building my business through the years started small and grew into a nationally recognized company – one step at a time.

The same can be said about my spiritual life. I started by attending fellowship groups, small in-home Bible studies, and classes in my church on Wednesday evenings. We made friends with vital people in the faith with many years of evangelism experience. I was determined to grow in my faith, and my friends and mentors led by example. I took in what they shared and eventually began to step out and never looked back.

CRITICAL STEPPING-STONES FORM
A VALUABLE FOUNDATION!

I took several connecting flights on this day to ensure my on-time arrival. I was attending corporate meetings at one of the largest home improvement retailers in the country's home office the following day.

At about 8:30 in the evening, before our scheduled meeting, one of the corporate managers called me at my hotel room. He said, "We heard your company has an excellent safety program. We would like you to present it at our meeting in the morning. We have a thirty-minute time slot for your presentation."

My office sent many faxes and emails to my hotel. I worked well into the night to compile the information into presentation form. The following day, the meeting was in the executive board room, attended by several divisional Vice Presidents and other nationwide peer contracting companies. The attendees stood to their feet when I finished, and I received a standing ovation. God used that moment to help me become the confident man I am today. The lifetime of shyness slowly began to fade away.

> **There is no growth in your life without change.**
> **There is no change without loss.**
> **And there is no loss without pain.**
> **You've got to let go of the past,**
> **To become a newer version of yourself.**

At that time, I was not comfortable speaking in front of large groups of attendees. God uses moments like these to grow and develop His children - rarely comfortable, but necessary in maturing each of us into the individuals He will use in the future! These moments are critical steppingstones that form a valuable foundation for how God will use us when the Holy Spirit leads us into His divine appointments.

Part Three

When I was in my twenties, I attended a large church. The church choir presented an Easter program that was truly amazing. The rehearsals for this program started many months before. The church had a heavy emphasis on prayer, especially for attendees before the rehearsals. We prayed for the power of the Holy Spirit to touch people's hearts and that many would be saved. We performed eight or nine presentations each Easter season, attended by approximately twenty-five hundred people each night.

I was one of the Roman soldiers who would whip and beat Jesus and then hang him on the cross. I was chosen because of being tall and intimidating - and it worked well in these productions! Wigs, makeup, and the Roman soldiers' dress and helmet completed the look.

There were many thousands who had given their hearts to Christ through the years through these Easter productions. I was genuinely amazed to be a part of these presentations. It was difficult being one of the Roman soldiers killing Jesus and then hanging Him on a cross night after night. It was so real you could see and hear people crying in the crowded church sanctuary, whose set was nothing short of a Broadway production.

The practices for these productions went on for months as we pursued perfecting every song note and all other aspects of a fine arts production. This group had hundreds of volunteers, from set designers, costume and makeup artists, and sound and lighting to custodial staff and ushers. The discipline in praying for our guests, with the understanding this might be the only time someone might ever be in a church and possibly their only opportunity to hear and see the gospel - played out before their eyes. This might be when someone's heart is changed for all eternity. Our pastor had a message that spoke to every person from every walk of life. At the appropriate time, he offered a prayer of salvation, and many gave their hearts to Christ after every presentation.

Everything was done to perfection, and nothing was left to chance. When doing anything for the Lord, we learn to do our best. After all, we represent Christ as His ambassadors in this production in everyday life.

The lessons learned from these Easter performances have stayed with me for many years and still to this day. Always strive for excellence with the integrity and character that represents Him in every aspect of our lives. This was an amazing ministry season that I was a part of for seven or eight years, eventually handing my position over to younger who were guys eager to minister in this role in Easter productions.

God's Timing Is Everything

I believe in our lives, God is always at work, either preparing us for something new or using something we have done in the past for His glory. Nothing could have prepared me for what happened next!

Even as a small boy, I have loved the outdoors and the outdoor lifestyle. As kids, you could find us fishing in Buck Creek for trout most days in the summer. Every year, there was a sports and RV show that came to town. Like most years, I attended this show with my young sons. They were five and six years old at the time. The show was sold out this Saturday afternoon, with thousands of people attending. We walked through the hundreds of booths, from Canadian fishing outfitters to boat and camper sales. Next, we walked into a large corridor filled with hundreds of people. The corridor connected the large showrooms, linking the show halls together. We patiently waited as we shuffled with small steps. The boys must have felt they were in the land of the giants! Suddenly, a man yelled loudly across the corridor, and everyone stopped and looked in his direction. The guy yelled again, "Hey," pointing in my direction. Not recognizing the man, we continued through the crowd. Once again, the man yelled, pointing right at me. I looked at him now, pointing at my chest. He looked and nodded back at me.

I motioned back and began working through the crowd toward him. I had no idea what was about to happen. He was a stranger to me. I reached him and said, "Hello." He asked me, "Are you the Roman soldier who killed Jesus in that large church's Easter presentation?" I was shocked by what he was asking me! Through the costume, wigs, beard, and spotlights in a massive church auditorium some five or six years after I had last played the role of a Roman soldier, he still recognized me! I replied, "Yes, I was a Roman soldier for seven or eight years at the Assembly of God Church in Wyoming during the Easter program 'The Last Supper'." He then looked into my eyes and spoke, "I gave my heart to Jesus at one of those Easter shows and remembered you." I said out loud, "You remembered me?" He assuredly said, "Yes, like it was yesterday." I then asked him the only thing I could think of. I asked him, "Are you still serving the Lord today?" He replied, "Absolutely, I love Him with all my heart."

We continued with some light conversation, then parted ways to the next room at the outdoor show. This 'chance' meeting was not a 'chance' at all. I pondered what happened when the man who attended the "Last Supper" Easter Presentation recognized me after several years. What sense did this make? Of course, I was delighted that he gave his heart to Christ and is still serving Him many years later. But why, Lord, why did this happen, and what is the purpose of my knowing? Was there a more meaningful message in meeting the man after so many years and in a crowded public place?

I prayed and sought an answer from the Lord. This is what He said to me, "Sometimes, it's the small parts of what we do either in life or in an Easter play crucifying Jesus. Or in bringing the Easter story to life, even perhaps a small word of encouragement, sharing our faith, or leading someone to Christ." It all matters to the God of the universe. One day, when we are in Heaven, all the small stories may be revealed to us in how God knitted everything together, everything in perfect symmetry and in perfect timing.

How marvelous might it be, when we shared our faith with someone who showed outright rejection towards us at that moment, that we were being used to plant seeds of faith into someone's heart? The next person comes along and 'waters' and shares some more faith and Christian witness, on and on. Will these stories be revealed in Heaven? I'm not sure, but it is a delight to be used by the Holy Spirit! God places every one of us in His appointed time for His purpose.

Will we ever know what happened through an 'act of obedience' or just simply an 'act of kindness'? Nothing can replace a heart that cares for others and serves from the heart. It's serving in the purest form. No arm twisting, no begging - just seeing a 'need', and naturally responding as a part of who they are in Christ. To everyone who 'hears' the voice of the Holy Spirit and takes risks to share their faith, these are the everyday heroes of the faith. This represents an amazing closeness with the God of the universe.

The maturing in our faith-walk must be a deliberate 'act of discipline'. God will reward everyone who seeks to grow and develop their faith. As I pursued my walk with the Holy Spirit, I developed an unquenchable thirst for the Word of God. The more I seek Him, the more I want and need Him. With this learning of who I am in Christ, I will never sit on the sidelines and let others do what the Holy Spirit has called me to do.

Part Four

Unwavering Faith

We have a close-knit group of like-minded couples and friends. This night was like many other Bible study group evenings. Our group arrived around five-thirty PM and sat down for my wife's prepared meal. Other attendees brought a dish to pass. We gathered for our meal and fellowship. It's fun and enjoyable for the group to catch up on God's actions in each other's lives. My wife has the amazing gift of teaching and hospitality, making each guest feel welcome in our home – which brings me to my next story!

The journey to this home, our home, was quite a process. It was an incredible move by the Lord to align our hopes and dreams to make this happen. There was no discontentment with our previous home. We just desired more of a country setting and more wide-open spaces. So, Robin began looking at different realty sights and began forwarding them to me.

We had some friends in the real estate business who also kept a casual eye out for something we might be interested in. My wife closed in on one home. We looked through the pictures repeatedly. Then, out of the blue, our realtor friend called and said,

"I found a home you might be interested in." It was the same house that we had been looking at. We agreed to a scheduled showing and did the walk-through. We stood in the kitchen when done, looked at each other, and said, "This house has everything we want,"- except a high price tag, besides needing fresh paint and decorating!

We prayed for God's will to be done. He would need to make this happen if He wanted us to move. Robin and I are true visionaries. From our work lives we see the opportunities before us. We see the possibilities in everything. We prayed and prayed and prayed some more. We attended church on Saturday nights, and after church, we would drive by this house week after week, then stop on the country road and pray for the possibility that it could be ours.

We both felt the Holy Spirit leading us to this home. However, this was not the typical emotional pull to a property. We acted on amazing faith where the weeks turned into months, sometimes standing in the middle of the icy road praying about this home in Michigan's winter weather!

Eventually, we settled into an 'offering' price that we felt comfortable with. We submitted our offer and patiently waited. There was no counteroffer, just simply a firm "no" from the sellers. Months passed, and we continued to pray. We had concluded that the deal was not going to happen. We rested in knowing that whatever God's will was, we were "okay" with whatever it was.

The listing realtor called us and wondered if we were still interested in the home. We noted a few things and resubmitted an even lower offer. Again, the sellers flat-out rejected our offer.

A few weeks passed, my wife had left work and was pulling into our garage. She felt contentment, and not moving was fine with her. On my way home from work, the realtor called me just a few minutes after Robin said she was okay with not moving. He asked if I could please stop by his office immediately. The realtor, his assistant, and I sat in his conference room. They looked at each other and then said, "In my twenty-five years in the real estate business, we have never seen anything like I have seen today!"

I listened as he spoke. "Your offer was low, and by most accounts, utterly offensive to the sellers." He then gave a slight pause before saying, "Today, they accepted your offer! Today, you bought a new home!" We were overwhelmed with excitement and gratitude as we shared the news with family and friends! God foreknew the people attending our Bible studies and how the relationships would grow in this new home. God knew the books written in the office study would change lives, heal lives, and help people worldwide find forgiveness and salvation!

The world will tell you repeatedly about their 'deals' or possibly taking advantage of someone for their financial gain. The point here is this: My purpose for sharing this story was not to tell you we got the 'deal' of the century but rather how we sought out God's will and trusted Him with the outcome. We prayed, believing we heard and understood the Holy Spirit's voice, and moved forward on His word. We moved by stepping forth in faith and boldness and taking risks well beyond our comfort zone. So, the question might be, why did God bless us with this home? He blessed us with this home simply because we asked for it. We patiently prayed and asked for this home and for the ministry it would provide to our community.

We stood in the middle of the country road in the brutal cold of the Michigan winter week after week on Saturday nights and prayed and claimed this house for the glory of God. Because we asked to receive His favor, our perspective is - God owns all of this. We are just the caretakers. What we have, we share with others, and ministries have used our home for fundraising events. Through that, without question, God blesses us beyond my wildest imagination, and we give all glory, honor, and praise to Him. God's answers are not always "yes" and "right now." God answers prayer in HIS appointed time.

Part Five

1 Timothy 6:7-8 (NIV)
"For we brought nothing into the world, and we can take nothing out." - Timothy

We will never find contentment in this world. There will never be enough 'things' to make you happy. True peace and joy are found only in the relationship with the Prince of Peace, the peace that only He can provide. The peace and contentment with a heart made right in Jesus Christ are worth all the money in the world. It is a peace only found through the submission of our hearts to Jesus Christ.

God's timing is everything. As I reflect on circumstances in my life, I stand in awe of His mighty presence. God has placed me in moments of crisis to be at peace 'within the storm'. In times of emergency, He has enabled me to be the person who not only helps another miraculously, but in some situations, save someone's life.

It always goes back to being available in my morning prayers - "Father, we come to You expectantly." Not just prayers are spoken, but prayers with great expectations. Radical prayers are life-changing prayers that inspire others. The world may talk about 'coincidences' - that you were "there by accident." I believe these moments are God's 'divine' appointments. These times were created for you and me to rise courageously to the occasion! God will use His 'divine appointments' for His glory and for you and me to give testimony where God meets us in a crisis. Sometimes, we are just to help in a time of need. Other times, we plant seeds of faith that lead to 'divine' appointments.

THE RIGHT TIME AT THE RIGHT PLACE

When you give your heart to God, your thoughts are, "God, what can you do FOR me?", but the more you understand who you are and who He created you to be, your thoughts become, "God, what can you do THROUGH me?" .... that's perspective, my friends. (Scott Smith)

I have had many times in my life where I have been at the 'right time' and the 'right place'. There is no question in my mind that God aligned the circumstances not just to help someone in need, but these were moments of divine appointments precisely in His time. Sometimes, I sit back and ask the Holy Spirit to verify what to do next within my heart. Other times, I quickly acted the way in which He was instructing me in that moment.

Thinking back on a particular crisis, I have always been a quick thinker. When I was twenty, I applied to be a police officer at our local police department. Being six foot five and having a large frame, I had the physical size for the job. The department wanted me, but I was twenty, and the state requirements stated you needed to be twenty-one years old. They asked me to come back on my twenty-first birthday. Time passed, and I was promoted where I worked and never fulfilled the dream of being a police officer.

Part Six

**Our love for another cannot be held back in times of crisis.
Love is an action, and love is something you do.**

As my life moved on, I went on to become successful in my job position, then marriage and family responsibilities, Years ago, Robin and I had a home on a small lake in Byron Center. The lake has beautiful higher-end homes built all around it. The view from our house to the houses across the lake was around half a mile. Our location was ideal; it was near restaurants, shopping, and hospitals.

On one evening, the weather for early December was unseasonably warm, with very high winds gusting forty-five to fifty miles an hour throughout the night. Robin's view from her chair perfectly aligned with one home across the lake. Robin commented it looked like someone across the lake was having a campfire. She couldn't believe someone would light a fire in such high wind conditions. A moment later, she said, "You come look at this!" We both agreed that the fire was getting 'out of hand' at a very rapid pace! I quickly grabbed my phone and drove my truck to the house's location. As I went up in front of the house, massive amounts of smoke were everywhere! I ran into the backyard and saw the flames under the deck, covering most of the back of the home's vinyl siding. This house was entirely on fire, so I called 911 to report the fire. I ran around the front of the house and saw the family watching television. I knocked on the door and frantically rang the doorbell, but obviously, they didn't hear me, as no one answered!

I had no other option but to lower my shoulder and forcibly push through the door. The family was shocked as they looked at a stranger standing in their living room! I quickly identified the situation as smoke began to fill up their house. The homeowners and I used buckets and hoses to slow the fire down. The fire department showed up with several vehicles and quickly controlled the fire. It was discovered that one of the adult sons living in the house had gone outside to smoke a cigarette and threw the smoldering cigarette butt into the fire pit filled with dry leaves and grasses.

The sparks ignited into flames quickly with such high winds, as you could imagine they would! This could have been a complete disaster. Sometimes, God gives perfect alignment for us to see someone else's tragedies in the making. Robin was aware of the world around her. Robin's chair was in exact alignment with their fire pit across the lake. The Holy Spirit quickens our senses and awareness of Him.

This is much like our human spirit connecting to the Holy Spirit. When we are sensitive to His Spirit, it opens a whole new world of opportunity to glimpse the world through God's eyes.

We find ourselves disconnected from Him only to be consumed by what's happening. I don't know if that's what happened to the family's home engulfed in flames. They were watching television, wearing earbuds, and disconnected from the world around them. Know that I'm not being negative. The family was unaware their house was on fire, and many lives were put at risk.

I am thankful Robin had a perfect nighttime view of their home. This house would have burned to the ground within three or four minutes, possibly with the family still inside their home. Robin's alertness saved a very expensive home from burning to the ground and potentially several other homes in alignment with the high-gusting winds. The most crucial possession here was the human lives that might have been lost for eternity.

These lives have a destiny created by God and for God's design and plan. Saving these lives turned from a tragedy of a burned home to the opportunity for lives to be lived - the lives of family members, marriages, grandchildren, and future generations are yet to come.

Part Seven

Thessalonians 5:17 (NIV)
"Pray continually, pray without ceasing." - Apostle Paul

The scripture tells you and me that we must always live a life with mindfulness and God's presence. We do this by acknowledging Him throughout the day and having continual conversations as we have new experiences daily.

My brother and I were leaving our farm on a Christmas Eve morning. We decided to take the backroads home on this typical winter morning. It was cold, with maybe a foot of new snow on the ground. Our conversations revolved around Christmas dinners, family gatherings, etc.

GOD ORDERS OUR STEPS. DO WE TURN TO THE RIGHT OR TO THE LEFT? IN WHICH WAY SHOULD I GO?

I have often wondered when I drive home this way (or another way) - if the Holy Spirit and angels are guarding me against a terrible accident or danger? We decided to enjoy a leisurely ride home on the country roads when we left the farm, taking a different route than we normally would take. As we proceeded down the road, we noticed heavy smoke pouring from a two-story home. The smoke was black and thick, and someone was most likely in trouble. We quickly pulled into the driveway. We knocked loudly on the door with no response. We decided to push through the door to see if anyone was inside. By now, the whole top of the house was engulfed in flames! Large flames were coming out through the eves! We saw an older woman standing on the steps going upstairs. She was walking into right into the fire!

Joshua 1:9 (NIV)
"Have I not commanded you?
Be strong and courageous.
Do not be afraid: do not be discouraged.
For the Lord your God
will be with you wherever you go." - Joshua

There is nothing in life that can prepare you to run into a burning building. This is not natural; this goes against everything I have been taught. The only reason to do this was to save someone's life. That morning, we did just that. To God be the glory, everyone was kept safe!

The elderly woman was paralyzed in fear and panic. She just stood there and couldn't move. I ran across the main floor and grabbed her to try to help carry her outside to safety. This was the first time I had ever been inside a burning house with a fire of this magnitude! You could hear the fire 'breathing' for air. It sounded like a big gasp followed by a roar that raced across the ceiling of the second floor!

The sounds of the fire were nothing like I had ever heard before, almost like the crackling of a campfire but louder and magnified hundreds of times! The living room ceiling above our heads became less visible as the smoke hung down about a foot. I won't ever forget feeling the heat across my face and throughout the main level of her home! Incredulously, this lady was refusing to leave her home and the Christmas gifts she had wrapped for her grandchildren. She turned and ran back into the burning house! We told her we would try to save the gifts, but she again refused to leave the house as she would try to run back inside yet again! I knew that she must leave the house right then, so I forcibly picked her up and carried her out the front door!

We finally got her outside, but she continued to try to get back into the house. A couple of others who were passing by stopped to help. Against my better judgment, I re-entered the home and threw gifts to others, who then put them safely in the bed of a pick-up truck. This was a fast 'production line' operation, as the fire trucks pulled up and the firefighters rushed in with their hoses and equipment as we exited the home. The firefighters were extremely upset with us for being inside a fully engulfed house!

I am thankful the Holy Spirit led us to take the backroads home that Christmas Eve morning. I'm not exactly sure, but we believe we saved her life that morning. I am very thankful for the Lord's hand of protection in our lives!

That day, a woman stood on the stairway frozen in fear. She couldn't move and had difficulty speaking. Indeed, she was in shock! She might have been walking directly into the fire while standing on the stairway when we walked in. God's timing is always right on time. It was at the right moment to help save her life. She was very distraught and in much distress.

Earlier that morning, we had driven to our farm, hunted in separate locations, and then agreed to meet at a prearranged time. Walking out of the farm in the twelve inches of new snow, wearing heavy boots and clothing, could have added valuable minutes to our time during our half-mile walk out. There could have been several reasons to slow down or speed up our timing. God knows the needs of his people. God aligns the right people at the right time to help someone in their greatest need.

The Holy Spirit put in our hearts to "drive the backroads" home. "Let's enjoy the slower ride home rather than the highway," we thought. It was Christmas, after all. However, God knew the needs of that elderly woman that day. My brother and I would always do our best to help anyone in an emergency. That's how God made us.

A minute or two earlier, the smoke may have looked like a fireplace chimney where we would have passed by without noticing. Two minutes later, the fire may have been so involved, she may have walked into the fire or been overcome with smoke and died of smoke inhalation.

John 15:13 NIV
"Greater love has no one than this: to lay down one's life for one's friends." - Jesus

To God be the glory that her life was spared that day. This is another example of God's 'divine appointments' using two ordinary guys and aligning everything at His appointed time to help to do whatever we could. That morning, surely, we saved her life. I know who God has created me to be. It would be impossible to fully describe the feeling of running into a house that was entirely on fire. I also know I would have died trying to save her.

As you read the verse - John 15:13 (NIV) "Greater love has no one than this: to lay down one's life for one's friends", I will add this to the verse or for a stranger in distress:

Our love for another cannot be held back in times of crisis.

Love is an action; love is something you just do.

Conclusion

Life is a series of small steps; these steps are easier for some and harder for others. For most of my early childhood, I was a quiet and shy personality. Elementary school book reports were a challenge for me, and I disliked every minute of them!

God has a way of developing each one of us into the person He is creating us to be. As for myself and maybe, like many of you, I can look back at key moments throughout my life that were 'growth-steps' into the person I have become. This development comes with going well beyond our comfort level. Every moment helps us gain the needed confidence in our journey.

I am thankful God has positioned me to notice situations from a distance. Followed by an obedience perspective, He then positions me for action. Being thankful to Him, for this positioning is truly a gift!

A few weeks after speaking on our Safety Program, I was asked to fly to one of the world's largest retailers and once again do the presentation in their corporate offices. These moments become stepping-stones in our personal growth.

Thought and Footnotes

GOD IS THE HERO - THIS TIME and EVERY TIME.

There are only rewards with significant risks. I share some life stories and testimonies of standing at the doorway and consciously choosing to step forward, freeze in place, or simply turn away. Through the Holy Spirit's leading, we are vehicles carrying the message of hope and love of Jesus Christ. Through obedience, we are the 'messengers of light' in a dark world. As we journey through these testimonial stories, God is the Hero, and to Him be all the glory; without Him, none of this could have happened for His timing, purpose, and destiny for whom God uses and chooses in these 'divine appointments'. The pain of regret is something most of us can relate to, whether it is things we have done or things we should not have done. The only way to avoid tomorrow's regrets is to walk in obedience and do what we should do today.

The feeling of running into a fully engulfed home and pulling an older woman frozen in fear is terrifying. I am thankful for the 'prayers of protection on that day and that everyone was kept safe. For that, I will always be truly grateful! All the examples in this chapter involved taking a risk, stepping well beyond my comfort zone, and then realizing God rewards us with confidence to go where others would not. God uses these opportunities to grow every one of us in our faith. So, with significant risk comes reward, sometimes in finding a new home, other times helping a family or saving a life.

Personal growth develops differently for each of us at different times. But the continual growth throughout our lives gives us knowledge and confidence to represent Him according to our specific gifts and talents. Our lives are unique because we are all different. Sharing your faith can have unexpected rewards – whether in "Mega-church" Easter productions or in everyday life when the Holy Spirit is aligning His people for His purpose.

MAIN TAKEAWAYS:

Divine Alignment:

Family Rescue: Seeing the fire due to DIVINE (God's) alignment.

Frozen in Fear: Lesson from a woman too afraid to leave her burning house. Step forth in courage and faith.

Chapter 7 Study Guide Questions

There are only rewards with significant risks. I have shared real-life stories and testimonies of standing at the doorway and consciously choosing to step forward, freeze in place, or turn away. Through the Holy Spirit's leading, we are 'messengers of light' in a dark world.

Each of us is created very differently. One person's assessment of risk is different from someone else's. No one should do anything uncomfortable with or jeopardize theirs or another's safety. Running into a burning house and saving a woman's life was most likely the riskiest thing I have ever done. I am glad it worked out safely for everyone involved.

Enrich your life by surrounding yourself with high-quality individuals - those who possess intelligence, kindness, ambition, and admirable qualities that inspire and uplift you. Being in their company will raise your expectations, encourage you, and help you become a better version of yourself. This is true in business, ministry partners, personal friends, and relationships. Most likely, you will be like the people you are closest to.

Are you learning and growing in your relationships?

The same can be said about my spiritual life. I started by attending fellowship groups, small in-home Bible studies, and classes in my church on Wednesday evenings. We made friends with vital people in the faith with many years of evangelism experience. I was determined to grow in my faith, and my friends and mentors led by example. I took in what they shared and eventually began to step out and never looked back.

Do you have faith-based mentors in your life with whom you meet regularly to study with a 'growth' plan?

Risk-taking can mean many things; from speaking to a group of business associates to risking injury in a problematic situation. Some may find praying with friends for a dinner-time meal beyond their comfort zone.

Could you walk up to a stranger and share your faith?

Would you be able to pray in public?

How would you describe taking a risk?

Some risks involve financial decisions, like buying a new home. Some might laugh at standing in the middle of a country road on a cold Michigan winter day. We claimed our house for the glory of God and watched Him make it our reality!

Do you and your spouse pray together for these types of buying decisions?

I have never woken up in the morning and told myself, "Today, I will run into a burning house and carry an older woman in my arms to safety." I have no aspirations to be a hero, only to be the man God has created me to be. Sometimes, that man must be courageous in the face of danger. As a Christ follower or someone who's experienced the redeeming love of Jesus, He has shown me what love looks like. Love looks like doing anything I can to help another person in crisis, sometimes disregarding my safety to help another. I cannot stand by and watch another person suffer.

Entering the elderly woman's burning home was the perfect scenario to step forward, freeze in place, or turn away. This was a split-second decision made from being a confident man. I did what I felt was best at the time. I was to create a five-second observation to help if I could - then quickly get out!

What does "be courageous" mean to you?

Do you have an example where you were courageous?

CHAPTER EIGHT

RELENTLESS ATTACK

Part One

John 10:10 (NIV)
"The thief comes only to steal, kill, and destroy; I have come that they may have life and have it to the full." - Jesus

STAY ALERT.
THERE WILL BE OPPOSITION FOR THOSE
WHO STAND FOR RIGHTEOUSNESS.

This winter morning was mainly dark. The ten inches of snow illuminated our backyard and surrounding farm fields. The thermometer read four degrees. The lone doe used her front hoof to scratch around the bottom of our bird feeders, looking for excess food. Some birds kick the seed out of the feeders, looking for the exact grain, while spilled seeds fall to the ground. No grain will go to waste.

The deer typically show up in groups in the late winter. Sometimes, we have had close to thirty deer some evenings searching for morsels before heading out to the neighboring crop fields for their nightly feeding.

I held my coffee and enjoyed the sight of her. Again, it was still dark when I saw two other darker objects against the pre-dawn snowy background. I first thought they were her fawns born last spring catching up to her. I grabbed my binoculars and then quickly realized they were two coyotes. They were angled low to the ground and most definitely on a hunt. Coyotes can take down adult deer and kill them.

The deer's head jolted up and locked in on the impending danger. The coyotes froze in their low stance. The doe instantly bolted off in a high-speed exit. The coyotes didn't run after her. They lowered their heads and snuck through the thick underbrush in the direction she ran off, perhaps waiting for another opportunity.

The Holy Spirit instantly quickened my heart. This is precisely what Satan does! He circles, tracks, and memorizes people's patterns and behaviors. The devil's schemes and plans quickly go into action, setting traps and pitfalls for the unsuspecting. I give him no credit for anything, but this must be known - He is out for evil and will stop at nothing to ruin your reputation, destroy you, and then take your soul and your life!

Satan is depicted in the Bible as a "lion seeking to devour and destroy." The hunting method of coyotes, as with many other predators, does not typically focus on a large herd of prey but instead looks for stragglers or loners and those who have become weak and separated from the group. It is far easier for a predator to take down a lone target than one that is part of a group. Therefore, we need to ensure we stay connected with other believers. It is a huge help and encouragement to have others standing with us as we face life's challenges and temptations. When we feel lonely or isolated, we are easier targets for the devil to attack.

The devil knows that you will become weak and vulnerable if he can separate you from God. Then, he can pick you off, like a lion going after the herd's most helpless and vulnerable animal.

Often, he seeks a solitary person who is alone. The devil will try to enter your life in the most innocent way. The easiest is allowing him to enter through the compromise of your values; you leave the door open a crack, and he's there. Though unintentional, you've invited him in. This is easy to see and understand through the slightest change in what you see in biblical truth. The parallels are clearly there.

So much influence from our culture and social media pulls people away from God's word. Yet, the 'word' doesn't change with cultural influence. It is truth, unchanged, and rock steady to build our lives upon.

Like the coyote, we can become fixated on something that appears suitable for us but will lead to our spiritual compromise and eventual death. Yes, we can list a myriad of temptations and sins that draw us away from Jesus, but in the end, it will take your life.

This also can happen with couples or groups of couples where someone gets offended. Then, they steer the others off course. I'm sure most of us have seen this with friends or families.

Part Two

Psalm 97:10 (NIV)
"Let those who love the Lord hate evil,
for he guards the lives of his faithful ones
and delivers them from the hand of the wicked." - King David

THE DEVIL HATES GOD.
HE HATES GOD-FEARING FOLLOWERS OF JESUS CHRIST.

The devil will try to draw away those faithfully working for God. First, he tempts them to become proud and lose their focus. Then, he lures them to sin, thus damaging their character's spiritual influence.

The attacks will come in a thousand different ways. If you're actively seeking the Lord, volunteering, or working in ministry, the likelihood of these attacks becomes much higher. Whether in church or not, a church-attending follower of Jesus, or even a non-believer - you are in the crosshairs of the evil one. Satan is hell-bent on destroying your life and will go to any means to see it through.

FEARS, WORRIES, AND DOUBTS

2 Timothy 1:7 (NIV)
"God has not given us a spirit of fear but power,
love, and a sound mind." - Apostle Paul

Psalm 23:1-6 (Easy)
"The Lord takes care of me like a shepherd with his sheep. I have
everything that I need. He takes me to green fields where I can
rest. He leads me to streams of water where I can drink. He gives
me new strength in my life. He is my guide to the right path. He
does this to show that he is good. I may walk through a valley that
is as dark as death. But I will not be afraid of any danger. This is

because you are with me, Lord. Your stick and your shepherd's pole make me feel brave. You prepare a big meal for me while my enemies watch. You put olive oil on my head. You bless me so much that my cup is full. I am sure that you will always be good to me. You will love me all the days of my life. That will never change. I will live in the Lord's house for as long as I live" - King David.

THE POWER OF GOD DISPLACES THE POWERS OF DARKNESS.

The ambush is planned to look for their weaknesses where, little by little, the adversary can bend the truth within his prey. Then, over time, the truth becomes a 'maybe', and then what was 'the fact' is now going in the opposite direction.

The weak or unsuspecting are then caught into not knowing what to believe. The answer to the traps, snares, and pitfalls is in studying the word of God, memorizing God's word in your heart, and then using it to ward off impure thoughts or other temptations of the adversary that come your way.

The coyote is not an evil animal. It was just the example I used. The coyote is a necessary part of the food chain. I don't like coyotes. The coyote slinks behind its prey, looking to kill its next meal. It must eat to survive. Coyotes know no boundaries, and neither does the evil one as he looks for his next opportunity to rob, kill, and destroy.

We need to be on guard while letting our pets outside. When my dog is out in our yard, our dog is in danger, as is every other animal or neighbor's pets. So, likewise, my focus is not on the evil one but on Jesus Christ, the Lord of my life. I am covered and loved by Him. It is in Him I take refuge.

THERE'S A WAY THAT SEEMS RIGHT TO MAN BUT LEADS TO DEATH. DISCERNING THE DIFFERENCE LEADS TO SUCCESS OR FAILURE.

You can discern the fears about your life by observing how the enemy attacks you. The enemy tends to target aspects in you that he can relate to, prompting his attacks. Additionally, when the enemy makes you question something, he will guide you toward deception and disbelief. It's important to note that the enemy doesn't always begin with an outright lie; he often distorts the truth as a starting point.

The devil is no different. The devil seeks unsuspecting people to destroy their marriages, families, and lives. The devil is a master of digging up the sins and mistakes of your past. He is the accuser of the brethren and will always point out your failures. You hear things like "You're not forgiven, and who do you think you are?" Yet, over, and over, the mistakes of your past keep resurfacing. Know who you are. Know the word in your heart. Immediately stop any thoughts and behavior that are not from the Lord.

We must follow God's instructions to be sober, watchful, and careful, keeping our mind set on Christ. The enemy is not visible - But understand that he is always around you! Listen to the inner warnings from the Holy Spirit and be sensitive to the dangers of being close to evil.

Part Three

DON'T GIVE THE ENEMY A SEAT AT YOUR TABLE.

Don't welcome the enemy into your house! Guard your heart, eyes, and ears on what you see, hear, and listen to. Sometimes, it's impossible to walk through life without the negative influence of others. In your spirit, quickly discern Godly vs. ungodly behaviors. Determine them, and promptly walk away from ANY negative impact or interaction.

LIVING INTENTIONALLY FOR CHRIST KEEPS OUR PRIORITIES IN LINE WITH THE WORD OF GOD.

With today's technology, we are bombarded with images, temptations, and information that will steer us away from our walk with Christ. Living intentionally for Christ keeps our priorities in line with the Word of God. Above all else, guard your heart and never compromise your values!

2 Corinthians 2:11(NIV)
"In order that Satan might not outwit us. For
we are not unaware of his schemes."
Apostle Paul

We place ourselves in great danger when we do not heed the warnings. God has given us guidelines and instructions that mark the difference between good and evil or another way between God and the devil. It should not be surprising how Satan tries to hurt or tempt us. God has pointed them out. Paul reminds us that we are supposed to understand how the devil works. In other words, "Do not open your door a crack and then allow a locomotive to come in and run you over."

This is where being in a community with other like-minded believers and memorizing Bible verses can quickly calm a restless heart. Satan will tell you, "It's impossible! You can't rebuild your life. It's impossible to rebuild your marriage. You will always have a broken heart!" Or, you may think, "this season of grief is more than I can bear." We must always believe that God has a more excellent plan, and that the growth in our faith comes from the times we 'put our shoulders to the plow' and push on and persevere. Personal growth never comes from being comfortable. Difficult seasons will reveal our true character and total dependence on God, but we also grow through the process.

God promises to define your future and mine. Stay firm in the promises of God. My confidence has been written in God's promises to me. Trust, trust, and trust some more when your problems become so overwhelming - and know that He sees you as His loving child. Remember, you are loved IN your circumstances. Hold on; He will see you through this, and this will pass.

I must look at my life and take inventory of my decisions, then accept responsibility for them. In the wake of bad things, did my choices play a part in negative consequences? Did I move on my own accord without God's leading, or did I simply want things my way and push God out of the way for my agenda? Or, did I even consult Him at all?

The importance of prayer cannot be expressed enough! Talk to God, stay on guard, always be on guard! The covering of blessing over your family is your first line of defense, or rather, - offense.

1 Corinthians 16:13-14 (NIV)
"Be on your guard; stand firm in the faith; be courageous;
be strong. Do everything in love." - Apostle Paul

Looking back through the years, the previous Bible verse above couldn't be more accurate. The attack was full on for this 'everyday man' of God, this Everyday Believer. I can recount the challenges I have faced as the 'flame' was turned up on my life by the adversary. The closer my walk with the Lord, the more things would happen out of the ordinary, and I would pause and try to comprehend it all.

When my wife, Robin, and I would support a mission, invest in a ministry, or head up a fundraising event, it almost certainly would be followed by some problematic circumstance or unforeseen accident or tragedy in the days or weeks ahead.

Deuteronomy 20:4 (NIV)
"For the LORD your God is the one who goes with you to fight
for you against your enemies to give you victory." - Moses

THERE ARE NO GREAT VICTORIES
WITHOUT GREAT BATTLES.

The closer we walked with God, (and I began to understand my relationship with Him), the more complex the outside circumstances of life would become. So, in the 'valleys', I trusted that God 'had' me, and everything would be okay. Stay the course. The times when things are good or even easy, my human nature can steer me sufficiently where reliance on my decisions or my abilities can begin to take over.

My prayer life quickly reminds me that my sufficiency comes from God. Once again, I am reminded of who I am in Christ and who He is. The compass needle quickly returns to the truth, and the truth points to the word of God every time. Emptying myself daily and giving Him my strengths and weaknesses remind me that my life is entirely in His hands.

Psalm 121:7 (KJV):
"The LORD shall preserve thee from all evil:
he shall preserve thy soul." - King David

Robin and I have prayed together for decades, seeking God's will in our lives, and praying for complete coverage for safety and health. For years we have prayed for the protection of our families, our children, grandchildren, and that generations yet to come will grow up to be Godly men and women who make a difference for the Kingdom of God. We continue to pray that their lives are lived according to the destiny only God has planned for them.

RESIST THE DEVIL

Our prayers continue, and we have a hedge of protection and a fortress around us. We understand that the adversary prowls around like a roaring lion, looking for whom he may destroy. The adversary will stop at nothing to destroy marriages and families through accidents, sickness and disease, relentless temptations, and financial woes. He will try to keep our hearts from focusing on God. Yet, because of these prayers throughout the days and nights, we are 'covered by the blood' of Christ.

TRIALS AND TEMPTATIONS

James 1:2-3 (NIV)
"Consider it pure joy, my brothers and sisters, whenever you face trials of many kinds because you know that the testing of your faith produces perseverance." - James

The forces of evil are ever-present in the world around us. When believers take a stand for the cause of Christ and begin to impact the world around them, the adversary is and will always be hard at work. More than ever, Christian families must be faithful in their prayer lives. I cannot think of a time in history, more than right now when Christians need to be on their knees. Husbands and wives should be developing their prayer lives deeply and more intimately with the Father than ever before. This is war, all-out war. Remember – the enemy will stop at nothing to destroy everything in his way.

Part Four

THE ATTACKS WILL COME - WAVE AFTER
WAVE OF RELENTLESS ATTACKS.

Joshua 1:9 (NIV) "Have I not commanded you? Be strong and courageous. Do not be afraid; do not be discouraged, for the Lord your God will be with you wherever you go." - The LORD GOD

Before I left my house early one morning, my wife and I prayed for a hedge of protection. Considering the time, our prayers were abbreviated but effective.

My business was off and running at a rapid pace, and my group of contractors left the shop at three AM. Trucks loaded some 'pulling job' trailers as we left Michigan for our project in central Indiana. Although the weather was unusually warm at this time of night, the Midwest was scorching hot for the third week of July.

Much of our business success was driven by multiple crews working in several states simultaneously. So, when we arrived this Monday morning, I would walk the project through, then leave to move on to other areas of the state to look at future projects.

While enroute in the early morning darkness, I missed an exit. This was before GPS navigation. We looked at our map and then detoured through the small town of Goshen, Indiana. We corrected as we made a few turns in town. We were driving past an alleyway between old buildings, maybe thirty miles an hour, as my truck led the convoy of other vehicles.

In the stillness of the morning, I saw a flash, then a boom followed - this unmistakable sound of a gunshot from my left, coming from an alleyway between two buildings. Immediately, my driver's door window exploded into a thousand pieces! I was shocked, stunned at what happened, and felt pain in my left shoulder! I sped up momentarily to get away, then pulled over with the rest of our trucks.

The bullet hit and shattered my window, then hit my shoulder. Fortunately, the bullet lost some of its energy smashing through the glass. I removed my shirt to look at the damage. Thankfully, the bullet didn't penetrate my skin. My shoulder looked and felt like I was hit with a baseball bat swung by a Major leaguer! Had the window been down, I could have been killed. My safety was the result of prayers of protection.

Part Five

**NOT EVERYTHING IS A SPIRITUAL ATTACK.
WE MUST TAKE RESPONSIBILITY
FOR OUR ACTIONS AND DECISIONS.
POOR DECISIONS WILL LEAD TO DIFFICULTIES.
TAKE THE TIME TO THINK THINGS
THROUGH. ALWAYS PRAY DILIGENTLY.**

Another Trip, Another Time:

My travel schedule was firmly in place. I was going to leave for a few days on the road after my men's 'Reload Bible Study' Tuesday morning. Robins' days and my days are covered in prayer; that's who we are, and that's how our marriage works. Every night, when either of us is away from home, we make the time to pray for each other, even in remote hunting camps in West Texas or other places on the road. I simply excuse myself from the group, go into a parking lot or wherever, and call home to pray. Although not always convenient, we have made this a priority for each other and our marriage. Sometimes, it is inconvenient.

I was heading for West-central Illinois, and my GPS took me away from the major highways to traveling on primarily two-lane routes. I missed one of the turns that day, so I turned around and made the correction. I was driving at the posted speed of fifty-five miles an hour, going through relatively flat farmlands. The farmers were working the fields, so my peripheral vision was excellent. I had 'clear sailing' as I proceeded down the highway.

I noticed a pickup truck on a side road approaching from my left about a quarter mile ahead of me. I thought the truck looked like it was driving way too fast. I watched the pickup truck blow through a stop sign at what I estimated to be at least seventy miles an hour. I hit my brakes hard and then yelled out, "Oh God!" as my truck missed a broadside collision by mere inches. The other truck never braked. It was a miracle that both of us were not killed!

Hair-raising near misses are all around us! The 'prayers of covering and protection' were visibly seen and felt that day. I prayed for the safety and alertness of the other driver.

1 Peter 2:19-23 (NIV)
"It is commendable if someone bears up the pain of unjust suffering because they are conscious of God. But how is it to your credit if you receive a beating for doing wrong and endure it? But if you suffer for doing good and endure it, this is commendable before God. To this, you were called because Christ suffered for you, leaving you an example that you should follow in his steps." - Peter

Part Six

CONFRONTING EVIL FACE TO FACE

My heart loves to serve in the inner city. I have referenced these many times in the previous chapters. Another ministry lunch in the park was winding up on a hot summer afternoon. Pastor Moses and I reviewed some of the details of the day's event. The food line was down to the last twenty-five or so people. Pastor Moses and I enjoyed some light conversation when the Holy Spirit 'pointed out' a man standing in line. I told the Pastor I would go over and carry this man's plate of food. The man was pulling a small suitcase containing his possessions and a couple of bags.

WHEN THE HOLY SPIRIT SPEAKS, KNOW HIS VOICE. WITHOUT HESITATION ACT ON HIS LEADING.

I introduced myself, and he responded, "I'm Steve." To my eyes, Steve looked like he could die within a week and maybe looked thirty years older than his age. Steve continued, "I am an evil man; I have always been evil. You will never meet a more evil person than me. When I die, I want to go to the deepest, darkest place in Hell there is. I want to go where the 'worst of the worst' people in Hell are. That's what will make me happy." I didn't call Steve evil. Steve introduced himself as, "I am evil." I took half a step backward... I did not retreat, but quickly asked the Holy Spirit for wisdom.

There's no safer place to be than in the center of His will - and no more meaningful message than the Gospel of His Son! Even when you are face to face with pure evil, I am reminded that God's children are the 'light' in a very dark place.

It was then I realized the forces that we, as Christians, are up against. The details of evil have no boundaries, nor are they guided by any sense of moral code. Never have I heard someone speak this way with such deep conviction. Steve was not just an unbeliever. He was a full-fledged satanist. Steve was unashamed and told it like it was (for him). Steve looked evil. This was not an act to shock our group; Steve was the 'real deal'.

Pastor Moses looked Steve in the eye and spoke. "Steve, I want to pray with you. I want to change the trajectory of your eternity." Pastor explained the plan for salvation saying, "Would you like to make Jesus the Lord of your life?" Steve answered, "Yes, I will pray with you." Pastor Moses led the prayer of salvation, and Steve and I repeated the prayer together. We finished the prayer. Steve turned his head, looked at us, smiled, and said, "Cool." I then excused myself. Pastor Moses and Steve continued having some conversation while Steve ate his meal.

Before leaving my home, Robin prayed for a 'covering' over me. In addition, Robin prayed for a 'fortress' of protection over our event and for the safety of the volunteers. But unfortunately, evil was all around us. This was one of the most severe spiritual warfare battles I have ever witnessed.

Part Seven

TAKE AUTHORITY OVER WHAT WE HAVE BEEN GIVEN. WE NEED TO TAKE AUTHORITY OVER EVERY IMPURE THOUGHT. OUR THOUGHTS AND IDEAS MUST BE ALIGNED WITH GOD'S WORD.

The Bible says that the devil uses malicious strategies to accomplish his goals. He will stop at nothing to fulfill his plan and destroy your faith. The adversary's goal is to move the child of God toward doubting the goodness or truthfulness of Him. Like any good strategist, his plans are several steps ahead of our knowing - strategically planned temptations that will steer you away from God and ultimately take you out.

I must be consciously aware of my circumstances, thoughts, and choices. Do my views, preferences, and decisions align with the entire Word of God? As previously written in an earlier chapter, the compass always points to the truth, and the truth is the whole Word of God. Without question, without compromise, and without any cultural influence, know and understand what you are up against. The victory has been written, and the devil is defeated, but we will still face challenges.

Throughout this book, I have written much about the sensitivity to the Holy Spirit's voice. I find it challenging to put hearing His voice into words, but I know it when I listen. Without question, I know it. Unfortunately, on this day, the voice I heard was NOT of the Lord. I can say this with complete certainty: the attack was full-on from the adversary.

Like every Wednesday throughout the year, this day will find me working on my farm. An endless list of chores year-round that need to be worked on. Our farm is a working maple syrup operation, so we are organizing and trimming trails in our area of Michigan. From December to when the maple sap begins to flow around the third week of February, there is much to do. It is seven days a week from February through early April, with all 'hands-on deck' to maximize our production. But, as the saying goes, you must 'make hay' while the sun shines!

BEING FAITHFUL IN SERVICE FOR THE CAUSE OF CHRIST WILL ALWAYS COME AT A COST.

The other aspect of our farm is typically working the ground for small crop areas called "food plots." This is a month-long process that deer and turkeys use for food throughout the year. These are small areas of a few acres throughout the farm. The farm life allows time for a lot of thinking and praying, seeking God's will for the days ahead. There is something special about driving a tractor and breaking your ground. Life's problems can sort themselves out while working the farm. There is a lot of time to think, listen and pray.

THE VOICE OF THE ENEMY

The Spiritual Gift of Discernment

Discerning of Spirits - This is the supernatural ability to distinguish between good and evil, truthful, or deceiving, prophetic versus satanic spirits. The Holy Spirit gives the gift of discernment to enable certain Christians to recognize and distinguish between the influence of God, Satan, the world, and the flesh. The church needs those with this gift to guide believers away from spiritual danger.

Acts 5:3-6; 16:16-18 (NIV)

Then Peter said, "Ananias, how is it that Satan has so filled your heart that you have lied to the Holy Spirit and have kept for yourself some of the money you received for the land? Didn't it belong to you before it was sold? And after it was sold, wasn't the money at your disposal? What made you think of doing such a thing? You have not lied just to human beings but to God." When Ananias heard this, he fell down and died. And great fear seized all who heard what had happened. Then, some young men came forward, wrapped up his body, carried him out, and buried him.

STAYING ALERT!
STAYING ON GUARD AGAINST THE ATTACKS OF SATAN KEEPS US ON COURSE TO BE FAITHFUL AND EFFECTIVE IN GOD'S WORK.

In the anointing of His wisdom, you will discern good from evil, right from wrong, angels and demons, and wise people from foolish ones. But above all, get the Spirit's wisdom and understanding. "Wisdom is principal; therefore, get wisdom. And with all your getting, get understanding." (King Solomon's wise words)

RESISTING THE POWERS OF DARKNESS

James 4:7 reminds us - "Resist the devil, and he will flee from you."

As powerful as he is, the devil is forced to leave when we call on the name of Jesus. When the circumstances of life seem so impossible, call on the name above all names, just say, "Jesus!" God has given us the power and authority over the devil. God has given each of us these tools to use as needed.

Always recognize the attack at hand. Sometimes, it is camouflaged in goodness, masquerading as truth and good works. Other times, it's an outright temptation to steer your eyes and heart away from God and His will for your life.

On this day, I am driving a little blue tractor. Nothing unusual, just driving down one of the roads through the woods. As I went downhill, I heard a voice tell me, "This day, your life will be required of you." It was not the voice of the Holy Spirit or the voice of God. I immediately rebuked the voice repeatedly. I rejected the message and prayed that Satan would get behind me, get under my feet. I claimed the power of Jesus over the whole matter. Over and over, I prayed the 'Power of the Blood of Jesus' over the voice. To stomp out the enemy right there, I prayed a prayer of covering and protection around me and my family. Finally, I resisted the devil, and he fled from me!

1 Peter 5:8-9 (NIV)
"Be alert and of a sober mind. Your enemy, the devil prowls around like a roaring lion looking for someone to devour. Resist him, standing firm in the faith, because you know that the family of believers throughout the world is undergoing the same kind of suffering." - Peter

Learning to control and capture our thoughts is of utmost importance. The thoughts we willingly entertain have the potential to either pave the way for our triumphs and fortify our faith or provide an opportunity for the adversary to gain influence over us. It is crucial to recognize falsehood the moment you hear it; it only empowers the one spreading deceit.

God always provides refuge to those who trust Him and seek His face. I am covered with God's presence. I am protected because of my wife's prayers. I am covered because we prayerfully asked for His 'covering'. I am covered because I am His. I am reminded that God does not promise us a world without danger. Instead, He promises help and covering when we face a threat. I continued to pray for a covering over our health, finances, home, children's lives, and grandchildren. Their professions, their jobs, and businesses all covered under the blood of Christ. There would be no harm, no danger to come into their lives.

Farming is dangerous work. Every aspect of tractors, plows, disks, and bulldozers is an opportunity to get hurt. If you use these implements carefully, the risk is minimized. The voice of the enemy has nothing to do with riding a tractor downhill that day or changing out a piece of equipment. It threatened to make me run and cower, then be afraid to move. The point is this: understand who the enemy is. Always pray for your marriage, and ask for a 'covering' over you, your children, and your grandchildren so that you are covered and protected from any unforeseen danger.

My time at the farm ended that day. I went home, showered, and cleaned up for dinner. I shared the day's events with Robin and how I rebuked the enemy. We agreed to continue the prayers of covering and safety for our family. I refuse to live in fear. Fear often masquerades itself as wisdom. As always, I turn to the written Word of God. I know and understand the imposter's voice. It cleverly twists the truth to make it sound natural and true.

I am bought with a price paid in full on the cross of Calvary. I know who I am. I am a child of the King of Kings and Lords of Lords. I know where my help comes from!

Amid the 'storm', we are so concerned about our issues that we might not understand how this attack might affect other people. We are simply trying to make it through ourselves. However, the difficult trials that life throws our way often involve others we are unaware of. Our experiences dealing with these attacks may impact others' salvation and faith.

Much like the coyote, the adversary's first order of business is to 'cut you from the herd', then take you out and separate you from others and God. He will try to drown out the truth in your life.

A few hours after the tractor incident, the Holy Spirit 'spoke' into my life. This threat was intended for two other families as well. I called my friend Doug and explained the events of the day: the tractor, the voice, and now the other families. The threat was for my family, Doug and Sandy's family, and another friend's family - Don and Lisa's family. It sounds "far out" to warn two other families of the adversary's threat against them! One family lives in Mississippi, and the other family lives in Illinois. When I finished explaining to Doug, we prayed for all the families involved.

MINISTERING ANGELS

As the days passed, our families were united in prayer, lifting each other up, and asking for the Lord's covering in all our lives. Don and Lisa's church in west central Illinois, along with Doug and Sandy, planned three block parties three days in a row. Doug and Sandy brought up about twenty volunteers to help at these meetings, plus Don's volunteer group from his local church assisted as well.

The weather forecast wasn't looking good. The weather service predicted rain one hundred percent of the time all weekend long, washing out all of Pastor Don's planned events. When people travel from several states, there is no "Plan B" or rescheduling of any events. The groups brought the volunteers together at Doug's hunting camp for an evening meal and a praise and worship prayer meeting. It was said to be a "mighty moving of the Holy Spirit." The group prayed for clear skies and God's will to 'pull off' the town-to-town events.

The group was leaving Doug's lodge. Don and Lisa left in their pickup truck. They live about eight miles from Doug's lodge. Don was beginning to slow down as he and Lisa were on the outskirts of town. As Don slowed, he looked into his rearview mirror and saw a vehicle coming up behind them at a high rate of speed. Don estimates he was slowing to about thirty-five miles per hour when, out of nowhere, they were struck from the rear by a suspected drunk driver driving approximately eighty miles an hour!

Don's truck was hit hard, and he fought to control it. They were obviously shaken with bumps and bruises. His truck was wrecked. Stepping out of their vehicle, Don and Lisa walked out onto the road in time to see the drunk driver's car hitting a tree head-on and almost hitting a house! The drunk driver then fled the scene. Doug called me with the news. We prayed for Don and Lisa who thankfully walked away with just bumps and bruises. Nothing was broken nor were there any other serious injuries.

Doug and I agreed this was an attack from the enemy to hurt Don and Lisa and "take them out."

The Holy Spirit revealed this to me in my prayer time, not specifically the truck accident, but something that would significantly harm Don and Lisa's lives. The importance of couples, friends, and families praying for a hedge, or a fortress of protection cannot be overstated! I believe God has His surrounding angels fending off these daily attacks throughout our lives. Praise God for the hand of protection over their lives that day!

The following day had a horrible weather forecast: one hundred percent chance of rain, heavy rain, and thunderstorms. Doug and Don gathered their volunteer group together and asked that the skies would part, and the Holy Spirit would bring the people from the small town to hear the word and participate in the day's events. The volunteer groups began to set up for the activities. "The sky looked horrible," Don said. The black clouds and rumbles of thunder threatened their block parties.

That morning, Doug received a phone call that any business owner would want to avoid receiving. Doug's call came from his secretary several states away. Doug's business had been cyber-attacked, and four hundred thousand dollars had been stolen. The money was removed from his corporate bank account and was missing. This was devastating news. These accounts pay for employee salaries, inventories, and other operating expenses.

Doug gathered his thoughts and called his bank to 'freeze' all accounts immediately. Next, the bank notified the local authorities, right up to the FBI. The authorities would do separate investigations that could take four to six weeks. Then, they would meet to discuss the details of their findings.

Like a punch to the gut, another attack occurred in less than forty-eight hours! Again, it is precisely like what the Holy Spirit revealed to me during my prayer time. There was nothing specific that this would be a financial attack, but the battle was full on. The adversary will stop at nothing to disrupt and distract the ministry and the people involved. Doug shared his dilemma with the group. The group began to pray for a 'move' of the Holy Spirit in the hearts of the local townspeople. They prayed for souls to come into the kingdom and hearts to be changed for eternity, for good weather as they served the community, and for the quick resolution of Doug's business situation.

Doug described the skies when you looked to the west. "You could see the clouds separating, moving to the left and the right, leaving their revival space dry with glimpses of the sun from time to time." The volunteers served, testimonies were spoken, and lives were changed to the glory of God. The event ended with everything packed up, then on to the next small town to do it again. Leaving their event, the rains began to fall as forecasted...

The small-town events ended that weekend with some who might have doubted the weather forecast. But that is the power of prayer wherever two or more are gathered in His name. God is in it. We continued to pray against the cyber-attack on Doug's business. Very specifically, that the money would be recovered, and no harm would come to his business. Periodically, Doug would ask for any updates from the authorities. They always responded that there would be "no information released until all investigations were completed."

Everyone continued to pray for the money to be fully recovered. Doug said he believed the money was safe and locked into an account, and he said the Holy Spirit revealed it to him during his and Sandy's prayer time. The investigations continued for many weeks, going into months. Finally, Doug received a call from his bank President with the news the money was safe and in his account! Through several security measures that were in place, the money was never moved, though it looked like it was. Glory be to God in the highest.

This is how our 'prayers of protection' work. So, we are often protected from the many attacks we face daily. Thank you, Jesus, for Your divine hand of protection. May we always thank You for being our loving Father; our lives are in your hands.

Part Eight

THE CAR CAME OUT OF NOWHERE.

The evening was winding down from our home Bible study group. The meal had been served, and there was great fellowship and conversations around the dinner table. Of the many topics we discuss as we eat, it is often asked, - "What is God doing in your life?"

With joy, the group tells of the different encounters they have experienced, sharing Christ, and praying for people. I enjoy hearing of these "Divine" appointments where lives came together that could only be from the Holy Spirit.

Robin prides herself in serving others and being a gracious host. Aside from serving incredible meals, she works hard on the weekly studies, developing the curriculum for her teaching. As the discussions ended, I needed to excuse myself from the group. I was going to be leaving for an event before our study concluded. So, the group gathered around me laid hands on me to pray for my safety and my that Christian witness would open the door for any opportunity to share Christ.

When my brother arrived, we packed my truck while Robin continued the Bible study. We then drove up to the little town of Newaygo. We checked into our hotel. We drove up the night before to be fresh in the morning because about ten guests were scheduled to meet us in the morning. Every year, we host a fishing event in the fall. The steelhead (rainbow trout) begin to follow the salmon up the rivers from Lake Michigan. Steelheads can weigh as much as twenty pounds, while most weigh in the six to twelve-pound range. Steelhead are a fantastic freshwater game fish. They are highly sought after for the thrill of the catch, not to mention for the dinner table, as well! Like many others, our guests come in from around the country. Our business perspective here is to appreciate our suppliers and associates for making our business possible. There has never been a clever, manipulative sales pitch, just simply thanking our guests for helping in our success.

The planning of these trips takes place a year in advance. I work with my friend and guide Kris, who aligns the fishing guides and boats. So early on, we send out invitations for our guests to have this time reserved on their calendars.

We plan this as a 'family' event. We aim to deepen our relationships with suppliers and help everyone catch some steelhead.

We meet early at a local town restaurant for a big breakfast and do some introductions, followed by a short presentation. I thank them for taking time out of their busy schedules and traveling to this location. I briefly explain how we appreciate their partnerships and business with my company. We assign guides with fishermen and then we are off.

THE ATTACKS OF ENEMY COME QUICKLY
AND OUT OF NOWHERE...

After checking into our hotel, we went downtown to a local restaurant. My brother needed dinner. We paid for our meals and then walked outside onto the sidewalk. The next few moments felt like I was frozen in time. As I stepped into the street, I looked both ways twice. The posted speed limit downtown is twenty-five miles an hour. With no cars coming from either direction, I walked into the street. I didn't look behind me, but I thought my brother was walking behind me.

I had just stepped over the center lines painted on the street and was just a few steps from my truck when I heard a car squealing around a sharp curve. The car was going so fast that it rounded the corner sideways. My first thought was that it was traveling at least sixty miles an hour. The car was skidding across the center lines on the road and was about to hit me! The car didn't brake or swerve to miss me; it aimed to hit and run me over! I had only one reaction: lunge forward and try to jump out of the way. This happened so fast that the car missed me by four or five inches.

In the momentum from my lunging out of the way, my right leg was turned very far to my left, with my body going to the right. As I landed on my right foot, I felt my right knee explode. The pain was indescribable! I immediately realized I was severely hurt. The car sped away, continuing through the downtown street. I looked back and noticed my brother hadn't crossed the road with me. He was safe. He ran to my aid and helped me up from the sidewalk.

We made it back to our hotel rooms. I waited to see how my knee would be in the morning. Unfortunately, I was unable to be with our guests later that day. I drove back toward home, met my wife at the hospital, and later had surgery to repair the damaged knee.

The praying for my safety before I left our Bible study kept going through my mind. The Holy Spirit knew what lay ahead, and through the prayers of our study group, I had remained safe and not killed on that downtown street. I prayed for the driver of that car, I forgave him quickly, then asked the Holy Spirit to surround that person with His love and bring him unto Himself.

Part Nine

I have emphasized the importance of being covered in prayer. When I met Steve in the food line in the city park, I could sense he was a different kind of guy when I introduced myself and Pastor Moses. This was one of the most extreme cases of evil I have ever encountered.

Steve said, "I am an evil man, and when I die, I want to go to Hell's deepest, darkest place. That's what will make me happy." The only way to minister in such moments is to have others praying for you and your 'covering'. This day, evil was face to face. Understandably, not everyone is tormented like this.

Steve was indeed in a very 'dark' place. It is where he was choosing to be. Regardless of the situation, we, as believers are the 'light', and the light displaces the darkness. I have written about the importance of prayer before ministry in the downtown park. We ask God that the "atmosphere changes with the presence of the Holy Spirit" and that the Holy Spirit goes before us. God knows the encounters we will have in the park. He also knows the encounters we will have daily in our work and interactions. Pray for His presence to go before you.

Conclusion

The Lord hates evil.

Recognize evil and temptations.

Keep your focus on Christ.

Change begins when God is first place in your lives and home, and in couples' and family lives. Christianity is not just for church or one or two days a week, but all the time and everywhere we find ourselves.

SMALL GROUP MINISTRY IS ESSENTIAL – WE NEED TO BE IN THE COMPANY OF OTHER BELIEVERS WHO SHARPEN YOU AS YOU SHARPEN OTHERS.

I remember changing from a church attendee to starting my journey to intimacy with the Father. As a family, we learned and grew together. Small group ministry is essential to be in the company of other believers who 'sharpen' you as you 'sharpen' others. This growth began as a desire to want more, so much more of Him. What better way to learn and grow in Christ than in the company of like-minded believers? This group is always available - no matter the need, anytime, day or night. As you read this, my hope is that you will also develop your groups.

The attacks from the enemy come quickly and out of nowhere. The prayers of my wife, friends, and family are priceless in covering our lives. I will repeat this statement from earlier in this chapter: "Unfortunately, only two percent of church-going Christian couples pray together daily." This is a challenge for teams to be united in prayer every day, everywhere. Continue in your group and grow within your group. May your group study be healthy enough to produce more and more study groups. Above all, stay connected with other believers who challenge you, sharpen and hone you. Be the Everyday Believer you are called to be.

The challenges of life will come. The greatest weapon against the enemy's attacks is to be covered in prayer. Quickly recognize temptations and pray against anything that comes into your ungodly thought process. Dismiss anything negative that is seen or heard by accident.

Lastly, we have the victory! God is our Source and Shield. He has won the battle for every one of us. Call on Him, asking for a hedge and a fortress of protection over all aspects of your life, health, finances, children, and grandchildren's lives. He is our protector in times of trouble and difficult circumstances.

Walk out this day in the strength and power of the Lord, covered and loved by the King of Kings and the Lord of Lords. You are His and His alone. Nothing can come against the covering of our God. Go, go into the world, for this is your mission field. Share Jesus!

WE MAY NEVER KNOW WHEN THE HAND OF GOD STEPPED INTO OUR LIVES, AND A DEADLY ACCIDENT WAS AVOIDED.

Thoughts and Footnotes......

Life is protected when covered in prayer. Marriage commitments grow closer when husbands and wives prayerfully enter a relationship that includes God in every aspect of their lives. The Holy Spirit walks alongside us as the great Comforter, in loss and challenging times - and as the great Comforter, restoring joy and peace to our situations.

Ephesians 6:18 NIV
"And pray in the Spirit on all occasions with all kinds of prayers and requests. With this in mind, be alert and always keep on praying for all the Lord's people." -Apostle Paul

Don't welcome the enemy into your house. Guard your heart, eyes, and ears on what you see, hear, and listen to. Sometimes, it's impossible to walk through life without the negative influence of others. In your spirit, quickly discern Godly vs. ungodly behaviors, determine them, and promptly walk away from any negative impact or interaction.

With today's technology, we are bombarded with images, temptations, and information that will steer us away from our walk with Christ. Above all else, guard your heart and never compromise your values.

Not everything is a spiritual attack. We must take responsibility for our actions and decisions. Poor decisions will lead to difficulties. Take the time to think things through.

Always pray diligently!

Never look to blame a spiritual attack on poor decision-making.

2 Corinthians 2:11(NIV)
"In order that Satan might not outwit us. For we are not unaware of his schemes."
Apostle Paul

We place ourselves in great danger when we do not heed the warnings. God has given us guidelines and instructions that mark the difference between good and evil - or another way between God and the devil. It should not be surprising how Satan tries to hurt or tempt us. God has pointed them out. Paul reminds us that we are supposed to understand how the devil works. In other words, "Do not open your door a crack and then allow a locomotive to come in and run you over."

Lastly, we are never alone. God is omnipresent throughout the world with every one of us. So be sensitive to the Holy Spirit's voice. God is moving all around us, listen, and follow His voice. Obedience always starts in the heart, and if what is inside is not correct, eventually, it will become apparent on the outside.

MAIN TAKEAWAYS:

Spiritual Attacks

Mike's Knee Injury: Viewed as a satanic attempt to hinder his ministry. The truck almost hit me and exploded my knee!

Satan's Fears: Insight on how the enemy's attacks reveal fears about your potential.

Daily Prayer: Emphasizing the importance of spiritual 'covering' for family. Always, always pray for your family.

Chapter 8 Study Guide Questions

The devil wants to enter your life or your marriage. He will use any means possible to compromise, bend, or manipulate the truth. This can be achieved in the most innocent of ways.

Individuals and couples must be on guard constantly. The most significant defense against the devil's evil schemes is to be in the Word of God and in prayer throughout the day. Everyone is in his crosshairs. This chapter has just a few examples of my real-life encounters. The devil hates God-loving followers of Jesus. Guard your heart and what you see and hear. Never open the door to a crack to sin or sinful behavior. Spiritual warfare is all around you.

I have written about having a sensitivity to the Holy Spirit. Through your prayer time, ask God to show you the world through His eyes; to see what He sees. I want to be available to be used for the kingdom, but more specifically, I want to do exactly what he wants me to do.

Do you see yourself as a person sensitive to the Holy Spirit?

It has been said that compromising your values may look enticing initially; however, sin will take you further away than you ever thought possible. It leads many down the road to destruction and possibly eventual death.

The 'prayer of covering' for couples is essential for marriages and families. It is always possible to begin to pray together as a family.

Praying for your family is asking God for protection and favor. This is one of the most important things you can do for your family.

Can you think of a time when you can say with certainty God protected you from a spiritual attack?

There is risk and danger when someone is isolated. Reflect upon my above example of the coyotes and the deer in my backyard,

Do you know of someone who is alone that you could invite to church or to become part of a small group?

God will never leave you or forsake you.

In times of spiritual attacks, explain how you resolved the conflict.

When in spiritual conflict, do you have to go to Bible verses? What are your thoughts?

CHAPTER NINE

OBEDIENCE

Part One

1 John 4 (NIV)
**"Dear friends, let us love one another, for love comes from God.
Everyone who loves has been born of God and knows God. No
one has ever seen God, but if we love one another, God lives in
us, and his love is made complete in us. We know that we live in
Him and He in us because He has given us His Spirit." - John**

Living a life of significance finds its perfection in serving others. It becomes most valued when faith is shared and at the center of our motivation. The Bible is an amazing treasure for each of us to share. It is available to bring hope and healing to everyone.

God values how we serve Him just as much as the outcomes or results we achieve. It is not enough for us to carry out tasks or achieve success; God is equally interested in how we serve Him. He looks at our attitudes, motivations, and how we treat others as we do His work.

The Bible shows many examples of God's concern for the process. For instance, in the story of Cain and Abel, God looked at the heart and motives behind their offerings, not just the offerings themselves. Similarly, Jesus praised the widow who gave her last two coins as an offering, highlighting her sacrificial heart rather than the amount she gave.

Genesis 4: 3-5 (NIV)
**Over time Cain brought some of the fruits of the soil as an offering
to the Lord. And Abel also brought an offering—fat portions from
some of the firstborn of his flock. The Lord looked with favor on**

Abel and his offering, but on Cain and his offering He did not look with favor. So, Cain was very angry and his face was downcast.

This perspective reminds us that our relationship with God is not solely based on accomplishments or results. It is about our willingness to follow His lead, love and serve others, along with having the right attitudes and motives in all we do. Whether we are serving in a ministry, at our workplace, or within our families, God cares about how we go about it - with humility, love, integrity, and a genuine desire to honor Him.

I think God also thinks about our work life. Do I honor Him in the way I work? Do I count it a joy to work in unfair circumstances? Is my attitude one of being disgruntled and complaining? My Christian witness is always on display for others to see. Living an authentic life is my goal. I want my process to reflect God's goodness, especially under challenging circumstances. Indeed, I have fallen short in this perspective. I confess this to you, but more importantly, to Him.

Ultimately, God's concern for the process reflects His desire for a deep and authentic relationship with us. He wants us to grow in character, to reflect His image, and to experience transformation as we serve Him. So, as we strive to serve God, let us remember that He values the process just as much as the product, and let us look to serve Him with all our heart, mind, and strength.

Luke 21:1-4 (NIV)
As Jesus looked up, he saw the rich putting their gifts into the temple treasury. He also saw a poor widow put in two very small copper coins. "Truly I tell you, "He said, "this poor widow has put in more than all the others. All these people gave their gifts out of their wealth, but she, out of her poverty, put in all she had to live on."

Seeking intimacy with God in everyday living is encouraging and challenging. It requires dedication, commitment, and a genuine desire to connect with Him deeply. However, the rewards of such intimacy are limitless. Intimacy with God allows us to profoundly experience His love, grace, and wisdom. It opens the door to a more meaningful and purposeful life. When we seek intimacy with God, we invite Him to transform us from the inside out, molding us into who He created us to be. I want to be firm but soft also. I want to be bold but have sensitivity. I want to teach but also be teachable. This can only happen with my submission to Him daily.

Seeking intimacy with God does not come without challenges. It requires us to prioritize our relationship with Him above all else. It means setting aside time each day to spend in His presence through prayer and studying His Word. It means intentionally seeking His will and aligning our desires with His.

It also means being vulnerable and transparent before God, allowing Him into the deepest parts of our hearts. This can be uncomfortable and even painful as He reveals areas in our lives that need His healing and transformation. But it is through this vulnerability that true intimacy with God is achieved.

As we seek intimacy with God daily, we may face distractions, doubts, and temptations that try to pull us away from Him. Our commitment to seek Him becomes even more purposeful in these moments. We must persevere, trusting God is always there, waiting for us to draw near to Him.

So, let me encourage and challenge everyone to seek intimacy with God daily. May we prioritize our relationship with Him above all else, dedicating time and effort to grow closer to Him. And may we be open to the necessary changes He wants to make in our lives - knowing that true intimacy with God is worth every challenge we face.

Part Two

NOT EVERYONE IS CALLED TO BE A PREACHER. HOWEVER, EVERYONE CAN SHOW HIS LOVE THROUGH SIMPLE ACTS OF KINDNESS SHARING THE MESSAGE OF HOPE IN JESUS.

2 Corinthians 9:13-15 (NIV)
"Because of the service by which you have proved yourselves, others will praise God for the obedience that accompanies your confession of the gospel of Christ and for your generosity in sharing with them and with everyone else. And in their prayers for you, their hearts

will go out to you because of the surpassing grace God has given you. Thanks be to God for his indescribable gift!" - Apostle Paul

We had a dinner party with a few couples from our church the other night. A late September evening with perfect weather and close friends as daytime turned into nighttime under our lighted patio canopy. The food was fantastic as everyone brought a dish to pass. The main course was fried perch with all the side dishes. Listening to our group, I can't help but think how blessed we are to be in a community with other like-minded believers. These are 'our people', people in close fellowship, people we go into prayer battle with, and people who have our back, and we have theirs.

GODLY MENTORS ARE PRICELESS. SURROUND YOURSELF WITH PEOPLE YOU CAN LEARN FROM.

Surround yourselves with good, Godly company. Your growth is possibly determined by the people you surround yourselves with - not to seek the approval of others - but to serve together in unity and to 'lift up' each other and carry one another's burdens. Conversations quite often lead to what God is doing in our lives. This group of friends lives out their faith, speaking of 'God-used' moments. Some of our groups are highly sensitive to the voice of the Holy Spirit, while others are less. Some are bold in their faith, while others are more reserved. But together, we are moved with the conviction that God has us on this earth to use us, to share our faith, and to live out our destiny in what and who He has called us to be.

I love being in a group that I call "fluid" Christians. We understand that no one has arrived at their ultimate destination, but we all see our lives in motion, being sensitive to the Holy Spirit throughout our days and weeks. Our group sees divine appointments as those moments where our faith is shared with others or to bless others. "Iron sharpens iron" together, and we are made stronger through the spiritual gifts He has uniquely gifted us.

I remember making a conscious effort to connect with other couples some years back. At the time, we were swamped in business and honestly quite tired. Investing in our friends' lives weaves the fabric of close relationships rooted deeply in Christ. Early on, we had to get out of our comfort zone and out of our daily routines to make this happen. Years later, we have many close brothers and sisters in Christ - strong prayer partners that can be counted on in times of need or crisis. Being intentional was the key to this growth in our lives. Looking back, I see this was pivotal in our growth and development as believers.

Our friend Dave graciously offered to drive us to the airport for an early morning flight and we gladly accepted his offer. Earlier in the morning, I prayed that God would use Robin and me today as we readied our bags and attended to some last-minute details before leaving home. The prayer I use is always unique and never a 'safe' prayer. It can go in a thousand different directions and is usually well out of my comfort zone! But God IS God, and today, I surrendered myself to Him. Using us would take on some unexpected turns...

II Peter 1:10-11 (Amplified)
"Therefore, believers, be all the more diligent to make certain about His calling and choosing you be sure that your behavior reflects and confirms your relationship with God, for by doing these things actively developing these virtues, you will never stumble in your spiritual growth and will live a life that leads others away from sin; for in this way entry into the eternal kingdom of our Lord and Savior Jesus Christ will be abundantly provided to you." - Peter

With that surrender - today, like every day, is a 'mission' trip. Every encounter is a moment to share Christ with someone.

I had a friend whose mom was in her nineties, and her life's goal was to win at least one person for the kingdom daily. She lived out her purpose until she passed away. What an example of her faith, knowing the importance, and understanding her gift of leading others to Christ.

We arrived at our gate after checking in and going through the security lines. We found some seats in the waiting area. As the boarding time neared, we stood and listened during the usual pre-board announcements. I felt we still had five minutes, so I walked to the end of the concourse. (My wife thinks I'm a little bit hyper). I just like to keep moving! I walked to the end of the concourse. There was a woman with her head down seemingly in distress. I asked her, "Are you okay? Can I help you?" She replied, "I'm having severe cramps." closed her eyes, and turned away. I continued to walk and began to pray for her that the cramps would release, and the pain would be gone—just a quick, simple prayer for a stranger who was not feeling good.

I returned to the gate, and we continued to wait. The crowd of travelers had grown to a couple hundred people as we waited to board our flight. Then, walking through the group was the woman I had just prayed for. She looked right at me. I walked to her and asked whether she was feeling better. She said "Yes", and I told her I had been praying for her. I introduced myself, and she said, "My name is Gena". I asked her if I could pray for her again. Right among a couple hundred people, we joined hands as strangers and prayed for complete healing of her cramps and that God would do amazing things in her life. Gena then remarked that the cramps were gone! She was healed of the annoying cramps that were a miserable distraction to her all morning. Gena continued to her gate. I stepped back in line to wait with Robin. She asked me what had happened. I responded that God had 'moved'. I explained, "I prayed for Gena's healing, and He healed her." I was simply the 'vehicle' that the Holy Spirit chose to use.

In earlier chapters, I have written about encouraging others. One of the aspects of the Christian life is to be an encouragement to others. It costs me nothing to help and to add value to someone's life. People want and need to feel valued. From family members to strangers, being interested in their lives opens the door to ministry opportunities. I love the Holy Spirit. I love the 'inner sensing' I feel when He prompts me to do something unexpected and unplanned. For Gena, God showed up and removed the misery of cramps, but it's so much bigger than that. Gena felt loved and cared for not only by me, but by the God of the universe. He used me in a most unexpected moment. Through this sensitivity and His prompting, and by my obedience and boldness - she was healed in Jesus' name. Some might ask, could you have led her to Jesus right there in the crowd of hundreds? My answer is I did exactly what God 'called' me to do. In my prayer with Gena, an overwhelming peace came over me. I prayed as the Holy Spirit led me to pray, which was good. It was just what Gena needed.

CARING FOR ANOTHER IS AN OPEN DOOR FOR MINISTRY

Recognizing that Gena was in some form of distress didn't take any act of courage; it just simply showed I recognized her discomfort and cared enough to ask if I could do anything to help. Caring for another is an 'open door' for ministry. The Bible says you will know Me (Jesus) by how you love others - nothing in return, not expecting anything - just moving in the flow of the Holy Spirit. Caring for another person doesn't come with any special qualifications. We care because we recognize someone in need. The simple offer to help amid someone's distress comes from the heart. God has placed that in all of us. Seeing these opportunities around us is an open door to ministry. Helping another person is often the first step in what God calls you to do.

Sometimes, it can be scary to witness to others in a public place. It is much easier within a community of believers. Other times, we do it alone in a crowded space. However, stepping out in obedience is, much of the time, precisely what another person needs. If you feel nervous about witnessing, that's natural – but, understand that the Holy Spirit is already moving ahead of you in the conversation!

Confess your insecurity to Him. The reward in all of this is that someone may be in Heaven because of you. The possibility of changing the trajectory of someone's eternity is always worth the risk!

This act of boldness took place when I joined hands with her among a couple hundred people watching. I - a tall middle-aged guy with white hair, and Gena - a younger, shorter, African American woman, uniting in prayer for her healing. God's moments are all around us. We simply need to be made aware by asking God to 'use' us. Use us for His glory wherever we may be. Gena's healing was remarkable. I prayed for her to live out her destiny and grow into the woman God created her to be. The moment was filled with praying into Gena's life that God's destiny would be fulfilled - a powerful, focused prayer for Gena's life. The morning ministry in the airport terminal was yet another opportunity for me to be ready to be used as the Holy Spirit leads.

Part Three

OUR FAITH IS NEVER MEANT TO BE KEPT TO OURSELVES

I waited for God to 'speak' to me rather than for myself to move ahead of His timing. As I said in earlier chapters, the right word at the wrong time is the wrong word. So, the question is - when to speak and move into the ministry set before me. I have been welcomed by my offer to pray for someone and share my faith, but also, I have been rejected by others. Was it a matter of timing where I jumped ahead of the Holy Spirit's leading? The answer to this is mostly no. Some people simply reject you for reasons of their own.

The act of obedience and discernment answers the question. The discipline is to listen and not shoot back with rapid-fire answers. I need to pray for discernment before entering and during these conversations. I might just be the vehicle God uses to plant the seeds of faith in someone's life. Again, it's always God's timing for His cause and purpose. God knows the timing, plan, and purpose for everyone in our lives. When He moves, am I ready, and did I prepare? Being willing is being aware of the world around us. Think of it as situational awareness—the ability to look and see things ahead of a situation and be sensitive to others' needs. Being prepared comes by reading the Bible, knowing the 'word' regarding the world around us, and its application. Be in prayer about everything. The needs are all around us. Be ready to answer with love, kindness, and respect.

Being in a relationship with Christ sharpens our sensitivity to the world. There is no more incredible feeling in the world than being used by God. Nothing can compare to walking out of obedience and doing what God has called you to do. God will use each one of us to manifest the spiritual gifts He has promised us. Pray, study your gift, ask God to use you, and develop your talents. Find a friend or group of friends with similar strengths who can mentor you. Grow into maturity and minister to others' lives.

God is not a casual observer of our circumstances, but actively working on our behalf. It is crucial for us to avoid resignation and instead remain vigilant, constantly seeking the power of God to bring breakthroughs in our lives.

We must resist the temptation to simply accept our situation as it is and instead adopt a mindset of expectancy. We should eagerly expect and actively seek the intervention of God in every aspect of our lives. He is not distant or disinterested; He wants to come alongside us, offering His strength and guidance in every situation.

Our faith in God's ability to bring about change should fuel our determination to seek His intervention. We should not settle for mediocrity or succumb to hopelessness. Instead, we should persistently seek God's power to bring transformation and breakthrough in our circumstances.

This requires an active and intentional pursuit of God. We must pray, seek His will, and align our desires with His. We should immerse ourselves in His Word, allowing it to shape our thoughts, attitudes, and actions. Additionally, we should surround ourselves with a community of believers who can uplift and support us in our journey.

We must not be discouraged by obstacles, challenges, and setbacks. Instead, we should remain steadfast in our faith, knowing that God is aware of our circumstances and actively working to bring about positive change.

So, let us reject passivity and complacency, always embracing expectancy and hope. Let us continually seek the power of God to break through our limitations, knowing He is always ready to intervene on our behalf. With this mindset, we can confidently navigate life's challenges, knowing that God's active involvement will lead us to breakthroughs and victory.

Part Four

One of our favorite Western United States trips is visiting Arches National Park in Moab, Utah. The drive through Arches and nearby Canyonlands National Parks is breathtaking, and the ability to do some hiking makes this trip spectacular! The natural stone formations rise out of the earth uniquely around every corner, almost as an opposite to the deep carved draws and ravines that lead downward into massive cannons that go on for miles. The sunrises and sunsets are exceptional in their natural beauty as the look of the landscape changes from morning to evening as the daylight changes and diminishes throughout the day.

When we arrived in town on this trip, it was late in the evening when we checked into our room. I saw a young lady working in the hotel, and the Lord spoke to me and told me to tell her that God loves her. That was unique as I wanted to verify with the Lord whether I heard Him correctly before speaking into the young lady's life. I turned around, and she was gone. We thought we would probably cross paths with her in the next few days during our stay. I will surely see her and tell her that God loves her.

Proverbs. 16:9 (NIV)
"In their hearts, humans plan their course,
but the Lord establishes their steps."

WHEN LED BY THE HOLY SPIRIT, IT IS ALWAYS WORTH THE RISK

The 'voice' of the Holy Spirit was heard deeply in my heart as I shared with Robin what God said to me. I could not shake the feeling of the message - to simply tell her that God loves her. Over the next couple of days, as we went to dinner, or went into or out of the National Parks, we had yet to see her. The Holy Spirit was deep at work within my heart, and deeper was the inner desire to share the message of God's love with her. On our last evening, we would go to dinner, pack up, leave early in the morning, and continue our trip's itinerary.

I sought more profound clarity on this situation, but trusted God for the opportunity. Sometimes, these moments become difficult while discerning the exact message. I must deny my thoughts of what I can do, patiently waiting on the Holy Spirit and waiting on and finding the word given to me for the exact time.

We ate breakfast in the hotel restaurant and still had not seen the young lady. I prayed to the Lord, "we've looked for her, and she's nowhere to be found." With nothing else to do, we took the elevator to our room to get our bags and check out. Standing on the fifth floor in front of the elevator, waiting to enter, she walked by. I left my luggage with Robin and caught up to the young lady. In my mind, I thought this was going to be awkward, but I knew this was precisely what the Holy Spirit was calling me to do.

John 13:34 (NIV)
"A new command I give you: Love one another. ... As I have loved you, you must love one another." - Jesus

So, I introduced myself to her. She seemed pleasant and polite. After all, she is a hotel employee, and I am a hotel guest. I confidently said, "I am a man of prayer and deep conviction and want to share this with you. I want you to know that God loves you. This is a message He wants you to know - that He loves you." To understand this moment, I am six feet four inches tall, she is about five feet tall, and weighs about one hundred pounds. Thoughts began to run through my head as I shared this message - "God loves you."

You never know completely what someone's past is. We never see the full impact of hurt and heartache someone has endured. Maybe perhaps her earthly father or some other trusted adult male in her life walked out on her. I felt confident in that. She was deeply hurt and had a general discord toward men as she looked up at me. These were simple and obvious observations, not any form of judgment on my part. The pain in her eyes was as bad as I had seen as she spoke these words to me...

She pointed her finger at my face and said, "I don't want anything to do with your God. I will never submit to Him or any other man for that matter! I don't want anything to do with Him!" I said, "I understand," to which she replied, "no you don't!" After two days of prayer leading up to this meeting, this was her reaction to me. I told her I would pray for her in the coming days and weeks. I wished her my best and turned and walked towards the elevator.

My message was to convey God's love to her, not to argue or quote scriptures. My spiritual maturity allowed me to understand the mission. No last words, no 'hitting' back. I'm just the messenger to tell her that God loves her. I would have said more IF the Holy Spirit prompted me to do it. He didn't. I left it in God's hands. She is His child, and He will plan the next steps for her life. I took the position to share Christ's love, to give favor and blessing to her. She stood her ground as I walked away. She chose not to accept God's message for her.

Proverbs 15:1 (NIV)
"A gentle answer turns away wrath,
But a harsh word stirs up anger." - King Solomon

WE HAVE A CHOICE - TO PRESS ON AND PUSH, OR TO LET THE HOLY SPIRIT DO WHAT THE HOLY SPIRIT DOES.

Life as we know it is difficult. When we meet someone along our travels or even a coworker, we never know the backstory of their lives. Our lives can sometimes reflect our past. Our personalities may show everything from hurt to happiness. Pain and troubled times can transform you if you 'wait on' the Lord and work through the process. Pain is a constant reminder that it might seemingly never leave you. It is a continual reminder of a difficult time. However, you can choose to do nothing as you watch the pain 'marinate' into anger and bitterness, or you can choose to have it transformed into healing for your testimonial story for God's glory and goodness. Our trials can bring us nearer to God rather than away from Him, hardening our hearts and hatred toward Him. We can choose to grow in Godly character and the healing it provides or accept the consequences of our choice.

One might think this young woman's reaction defeated me, but I wasn't defeated. I completed what the Holy Spirit called me to do. Just give her the message that God loves her. I would have chosen for this encounter to go differently and much better in my heart. I was the messenger that God used that day. She may have been waiting to hear from a mature adult male her entire life that the God of the universe loves her.

I continue to pray for the softening of her heart and that the Holy Spirit does what He does best: to bring her into the woman of faith and relationship she was created to be.

There was no salvation, no forgiveness, and certainly not the reaction I had hoped for. But I was walking out my obedience in love with kindness and respect. I pray for the best in her life - that she finds healing and forgiveness, and trusts God the Father, Jesus the Son, and the Holy Spirit. So, in my heart, there is some slight form of disappointment, but I recognize that God is at work and still good. With the 'seed' planted, I believe it will grow and develop as the next person is chosen to share God's love with her. In my humanness, I wanted more. I wanted to see a breakthrough for her. However, it's not my plan, but His plan that it will be done.

I trusted the Holy Spirit. I never wavered or became nervous that I would not see the young lady before leaving the Hotel. I prayed for the opportunity and waited. Interestingly, she came by as we entered the elevator just moments before leaving the hotel. Maybe the adversary was involved in keeping her busy from meeting me. I don't know. As always, this was God's perfect timing to tell her that God loves her. The message was delivered, though she was less than receptive. I left it in God's hands, and that is always the good and right thing to do!

The path to forgiveness is a process. Again, we never know what someone has gone through in their lives. The hurts and heartaches of a life cut deeply into one's soul. Without God, one's identity is an accumulation of scars along the way. When she said, "I don't want anything to do with your God", and she said it with such conviction, I backed off and allowed her to speak. Not in surrender to her but in surrender to the Holy Spirit. She is His. I'm just the messenger, and I fulfilled the message of speaking, "God loves you. He loves you." And He does. Walking away from the conversation was leaving her 'arm-wrestling match' in God's hands, trusting Him to soften her heart and surrender her pain to Him.

The apostle Paul reminds us we are "created in Christ Jesus for good works that God prepared beforehand so we can do them."

Part Five

Ephesians 2:10 (NIV)
"For we are God's handiwork, created in Christ Jesus to do good works, which God prepared in advance for us to do." - Apostle Paul

A Tale of Two Ladies

On this winter morning, I was trying to decide whether to travel to the northern Michigan town of Cheboygan to look at a work project. I usually schedule my work projects weeks in advance, but today was different. This specific morning was in January 2014. The weather was rough, even considering Michigan's often harsh winter weather conditions. My morning began as usual: reading the Word, studying devotions, and praying.

I was 'on the fence' about whether I should travel. It was early, around five in the morning. A quick look out the window toward the streetlights showed horizontal snow blowing at about 30 miles an hour. Driving on a northbound highway with wind and snow blowing from the west will make the roads treacherous! I could reschedule, but that backs up other projects and then makes for having to rearrange travel plans and schedules. I have some almost knee-high winter boots that are great for hunting that I could take along but would be less than proper to wear for making sales calls and visiting construction sites.

For some reason, I chose to go forth with this day trip with the tall boots and packed emergency bag that I call my "lifeline" packed with snow pants, hand warmers, extra gloves, etc. In my mind, I figured I could turn around if conditions were too dangerous. This is what the winter season is like in Michigan. I have lived here my entire life. Work must be done at every company level, even in extreme weather conditions. I left the house with my truck in four-wheel drive and began the drive north. The highway looked like a two-track with snow blowing horizontally across it with twenty-five to thirty-below-zero wind chills. The visibility was about one to two hundred yards ahead.

About one hour into my trip, I was still committed to completing my task when the van I was following caught a gust of wind and blew it sideways. The driver tried to correct the van as it slid over a few inches of snow-covered white ice. The van drove off the highway and began to barrel roll several times, landing upside down on its roof. All four wheels were up in the air. I carefully slowed, turned on my emergency flashers, and stopped. I called the Michigan State Police to report the accident. They replied they would try to assist as soon as possible as they reported back to me, "There are about thirty accidents ahead of you!"

I grabbed a work shovel and walked down the embankment in the knee-deep snow. The van was a commercial phone company vehicle. When I knocked on the window, the driver wasn't hurt, but badly shaken up. The snow was deep, so I began to dig through an area to allow the door to open. As I shoveled for about fifteen minutes to get the female driver out, the snow from around the roof caused much difficulty because the door wouldn't open. The driver assured me she was not injured, so I unbuckled her from hanging upside down, being careful as to not hurt her, she dropped into my arms. Within a few minutes, SUV was freed from the wrecked van, and I walked her to my truck. I had left it running to keep the truck warm. After she climbed inside, she used my phone to call her relatives to report that she was okay. I poured her some hot coffee while we waited for the State Police to arrive.

Back then, I always traveled with a couple of books to give away when prompted by the Holy Spirit. The book *Jesus Calling,* by Sarah Young, was a soft devotional with a written message for every day of the year. As we waited for assistance, it soon became obvious to me that this woman was not a happy person. As I tried to be the voice of calm, she let out more cuss words than a drunken sailor! I tried to point out things like "I'm glad you didn't get hurt," but she continued to voice how angry she was.

I reached into my console, pulled out a book, and said, "I would like to give you this book. It has helped me in difficult times. It's a devotional with scriptures and thorough content for each day." She thanked me, although I could sense she was still a very angry and unhappy person. I held her hands, and we prayed together in my truck. She seemed thankful that I stopped to help her in her time of need.

At last, the state trooper pulled up behind my truck. I walked her back to his police car. I said goodbye and wished her a better rest of her day.

I gathered my thoughts as I drove and continued my way north toward Cheboygan. Slowly, the weather began to get better. I eventually made it to my destination. A few hours later, I did my work and turned toward home. The day was brutally cold, and the sun had begun to break through the heavy cloud cover throughout the afternoon. The highway department's road crews had been busy clearing some areas down to wet, bare asphalt with their large county plows.

Michigan weather and road conditions can change quickly. Winds can produce 'white-out' conditions that instantly blow snow cover over the plowed roads, making the roads go from wet to icy conditions in a matter of seconds. As I continued south, a person in an SUV right in front of me hit one of the icy spots at highway speed. Like in the morning, the SUV rolled several times, ending up on its roof with all four wheels in the air.

I pulled off the highway again, grabbed my work shovel, and approached the vehicle to help.

Once again, the lady was hanging upside down, being held up by her seatbelt. She assured me that she wasn't hurt. So, after doing some digging, I was able to get the door open. I lay on my stomach in the snow, trying to cradle her in my arms while trying to release her seatbelt. This was very hard to do, considering everything was upside down, and finding the seat belt release button was difficult. I slowly let her down into my arms and pulled her out of her SUV. I then carried her with her arms around my neck, one of my arms around her waist, and my other arm under her knees, through the knee-deep snow up the snowbank where other bystanders were standing along the highway's edge ready to help.

She was sweet and thankful for the help. Her only concern was she was on her way to get chemotherapy treatment. The accident was going to make her late. Many others were there to help. I spoke to the state police trooper who responded to this accident and explained the circumstances of her needing to get to her doctor's appointment. He assured me he would hasten the process of getting her to her appointment as soon as possible. I hugged her and told her I would be praying for her. Another bystander stepped up to take her to her chemotherapy appointment. God is so good that His hand of protection was upon her. She was not hurt, but only delayed, as the right people at the right time helped with her needs.

Driving back south on the highway, I couldn't believe how the Holy Spirit arranged everything so that I could help these two ladies. One was very angry as a hornet, and the other was among the most thankful people I have ever met! I was so happy as we stood on the side of the highway on a frigid winter afternoon. Another stranger stepped up and cared enough to get her to her cancer treatment appointment.

God positions us at the right time and place to help and share our faith. Sometimes faith is shared through the written word and prayer, and other times through acts of kindness and caring for people in their time of greatest need. God calls us to be the 'light' wherever we are. Most importantly, we are called to 'walk out' our obedience as led by the Holy Spirit. There is an immense sense of well-being 'walking out' your faith and serving others. Some people are grateful, others not so much. There is a need within each of us to help others. There is no greater way to do this than through our faith.

Conclusion

ETERNITY IS FOREVER

**Galatians 6:2 (NIV)
"Carry each other's burdens, and in this way, you
will fulfill the law of Christ." Apostle Paul**

Answering the call to help someone doesn't place us in the position of choosing who we will serve, but simply to do it by offering to help. God ordains our steps and places us in these moments to respond. Living with the mindset of Christ, we have the inward ability and the desire to help in all circumstances. With this understanding, helping, and ministering have a unique and close relationship to the everyday believer. You see, God laid the plan before us, and we choose to follow the plan He has laid before us.

These instances become the story of our lives. This is where our stories are brought forth, our actions reveal His glory, and our testimonies are developed. This is not what we did, but where God did things through our lives. To God be the glory!

**Jesus said,
"You will be my witnesses, telling people about me everywhere."
(Acts 1:8 NLT)**

How we treat others is an unmistakable and undeniable proof of our love for God. Our decisions today will have eternal consequences, with or without God, for eternity. Eternity will last forever. Choose whom you will serve today because your choices will affect where you will spend eternity. Live with a Godly purpose by your example every day.

As I have written in earlier chapters, helping, or doing ministry in these true-life examples didn't take superhuman courage. I saw the needs of others and did my best to help. Caring for one another is being used by God. It is extending ourselves to meet the needs of others, sometimes in moments of crisis and other times just telling someone that God loves them.

There is no greater time to be alive than today! Today is a gift; use it for God's glory. In everything, give Him praise. God will trust you with the 'scars' from your stories' pain and heartbreak. Allow Him to use those scars of your life from your story, but most importantly - for His glory.

In everything you do, tell the world about Jesus. Your voice may be the only sermon someone might hear in their lifetime. Be bold, be sensitive, go to be the church!

Thoughts and Footnotes...

SURROUND YOURSELF WITH PEOPLE YOU CAN LEARN FROM. GODLY MENTORS ARE PRICELESS!

Surround yourselves with good, Godly company.

Your growth is possibly determined by the people you surround yourselves with, not to seek the approval of others but to serve together in unity and to raise each other up and to help carry one another's burdens for the cause of Christ.

CARING FOR ANOTHER IS AN OPEN DOOR FOR MINISTRY

Helping begins with the perspective of caring for people, to help carry and bear one another's burdens. Caring for others can be a part of your small group Bible study. The world will praise those who seek fame and recognition for their acts of service. Christ set the example for us to serve others, not to gain fame or recognition, but to walk humbly, not seeking attention or self-promotion. Seek God's will, look around, and be aware of others' needs. If you care and show love, the ministry will follow.

Recognizing that Gena was in some form of distress didn't take any act of courage; it just simply showed I recognized her discomfort and cared enough to ask if I could do anything to help. Caring for another is an open door for ministry. The Bible says "you will know Me by how you love others" - sometimes saying nothing and not expecting anything in return. Moving 'in the flow' of the Holy Spirit and at that moment with Gena, it was God, and it was good.

The Holy Spirit knew the plans for those days in the early morning hours - to care for Gena, who was sick at the airport, to be in the right place at the right time. I was as blessed as she was by reaching out to a stranger to share and receive God's love.

The Holy Spirit's message was as strong as ever. He spoke to me in the Utah hotel. I knew I was to deliver a message of hope. I didn't know or understand how the message would be received. Evil forces, abuses, and neglect run deep in a victim's soul. The pain of abuse is never forgotten, no matter how traumatic the hurt or type of abuse, or when it occurred. Neglected victims are hurt equally as badly, compounded by the never-ending feelings of being unwanted and unloved.

With some people, hearing the message that God loves them is like a drink of cold water on a hot day. It is as refreshing as any message ever received! In comparison, others will continue to reject any Godly message preserving self-sustainability that they have carved out for themselves for decades. The thought of fending for yourself overrides the message of hope.

To meet a young lady in a western mountain town who rejected the message of God's love - she heard the message of God's love when I stepped out in obedience and spoke to her. I was sent to bring her that message, which was fine.

TO HELP SOMEONE IN THEIR MOST SIGNIFICANT TIME OF NEED IS A PLEASURE AND NOT AN INCONVENIENCE.

For me to get up and travel on a horrible winter day, to wear knee-high boots made helping these ladies possible. To lay on my stomach in the snow, unbuckle their seatbelts while they hung upside down, and pull them out to safety was considered a joy because I was able to help and serve them in their time of need. To help someone in their most significant time of immediate need is a pleasure and not an inconvenience. God knows the impact that we will leave on others' lives. As Christians, these are seeds of faith planted along life's way in a stranger's life.

In retrospect, I said and did exactly what the Holy Spirit wanted me to do and speak. I hope and pray these men and the women were able to grow closer to the Lord through the meeting of a stranger in some challenging circumstances. No preaching, lectures, or quoting scriptures at someone, just simply caring enough to help. When caring for someone, the ministry comes naturally. Being aware and available to the Holy Spirit's voice makes the life of the "Everyday Believer" very special.

MAIN TAKEAWAYS:

Significance in Service

Living a Life of Significance: Serving others as the essence of a significant life.

Obedience to the Holy Spirit: Following through despite rejection. We all play a small part in sharing our faith. Some accept this while others do not.

Chapter 9 Study Guide Questions

Living a life of significance finds its perfection in serving others. It becomes most valued when faith is shared and at the center of our motivation. The Word of God is an amazing treasure for each of us to share. It's available to bring hope and healing to everyone.

Living a life of significance brings a deeper meaning to our everyday lives.

Can you describe your motivations in serving the Lord in how you share your faith?

God values how we serve Him just as much as the outcomes or results we achieve. It is not enough for us to carry out tasks or achieve success; God is equally interested in how we serve Him. He looks at our attitudes, motivations, and how we treat others as we do His work.

The statement above speaks of the process being as important as the outcome.

In what ways do you serve Him where you can see or recognize the process as being as vital and necessary as the outcome?

Understand that seeking intimacy with God does not come without challenges. It requires us to prioritize our relationship with Him above all else. It means setting aside time each day to spend in His presence through prayer and studying His Word. It means intentionally seeking His will and aligning our desires with His.

How do you prioritize your day with the Lord?

List your study habits, prayer time, and devotional time.

(It is unnecessary to discuss this with anyone unless, of course, you are okay with sharing).

Being vulnerable and transparent before God and allowing Him into the deepest parts of our heart can be uncomfortable and even painful as He reveals areas of our lives that need His healing and transformation. But it is through this vulnerability that true intimacy with God is achieved.

Have you surrendered everything to God?

Sometimes, we hold on to something from our past. Is there anything you are holding on to that is keeping you from being completely transparent with God?

Surround yourselves with good, Godly company.

Your growth can be decided by the people you surround yourselves with - not to seek the approval of others, but to serve together in unity. We are called to lift each other up and carry one another's burdens.

Caring for another is an open door for ministry. The Bible says you will know Jesus by how you love others, expecting nothing in return, just moving in the flow of the Holy Spirit, and at that moment, it was good, and it was right.

What is your approach to serving?

Serving can come at an inconvenient time. How do you respond to this inconvenience and keep your integrity?

Seeing these opportunities around us is an open door to ministry. Helping another person is often the first step in what God calls you to do.

How do you see the correlation between being kind and actual ministry?

Is it the same or different?

The young lady at the Utah hotel had been deeply hurt and had a general discord toward men which I sensed as she looked up at me. The pain in her eyes was as bad as I had seen as she said those angry words to me. These were simple and obvious observations, not any form of judgment on my part.

She pointed her finger at my face and said, "I don't want anything to do with your God. I will never submit to Him or any man for that matter! I don't want anything to do with Him!" I said, "I understand", and she said, "No, you don't!" After two days of prayer leading up to this meeting, this was her reaction to me.

I could withdraw from this conflict. The young lady was upset with me.

How would you have reacted in this situation?

How would you have handled a rejection of this nature?

Driving back south on the highway, I couldn't believe how the Holy Spirit arranged everything so that I could help these two ladies. One was very "angry as a hornet", and the other was among the most thankful people I have ever met. She was so happy as we stood on the side of the highway on a frigid winter afternoon. Another kind-hearted stranger stepped up and cared enough to get her to her cancer treatment appointment.

Would you describe this as a ministry?

I was equally happy to have helped both women. One, a very angry lady, the other, SO grateful for the help. I helped them because of their need.

In retrospect, it's always nice to help someone who's truly thankful. However, both ladies were equally ministered to. In life, we may never know the rest of their story.

If you had to choose, which lady would you first help?

If you decided to help the more likable lady first, are you helping someone to be rewarded with a "thank you" or "much appreciated?"

Which lady do you think was most ministered to?

Is there a difference?

CHAPTER TEN

LOST

Part One

Luke 15:5-7 (NIV)
**"And when he finds it, he joyfully puts it on his shoulders
and goes home. Then he calls his friends and neighbors and
says, 'Rejoice with me; I have found my lost sheep'. I tell
you that in the same way, there will be more rejoicing in
Heaven over one sinner who repents than over ninety-nine
righteous persons who do not need to repent." - Jesus**

I have been an avid outdoorsman my entire life. I can think of a few times
when I was "turned around." That's a macho way of saying "you're lost!"
Years ago, I was helping a friend who had taken a buck on our farm deep
in the swamp. We walked into the swamp in the late afternoon while we
still had daylight. As the light faded, we tagged the buck, and my friend
field-dressed the animal. Swamps lay in the lowest parts of the land. High
hillsides surround the lowland swamp. Thus, no lights from neighboring
farms help guide us in the darkness. The wetland goes on for several miles,
so walking out the wrong way in this area would be devastating.

My flashlight batteries lost power after completing the necessary
tagging and field dressing duties. The heavy cloud cover made everything
pitch dark – no moon or stars to be seen in the dark night sky. Now, realize
that I have spent most of my life on this farm, and yet, I could not see my
hand in front of my face! I thought this was embarrassing as we began
pulling the buck in knee-deep muck amidst twelve-foot-tall cattails, never
knowing if we were going in the right direction...

Those who have been 'turned around' or lost know the feeling in the pit of your stomach. There are moments of panic and hopelessness that quickly set in. We were wet and sweating and needed to know which way to go. The feeling of panic makes you want to hurry and accentuates tripping and falling face forward into the muddy abyss. We were turned around for an hour or two, most likely walking in circles, wondering if we were walking in a straight line. Pulling a big buck only compounded the difficulty. It's hard enough in the daylight, but much more difficult in the complete darkness.

GOD HELP ME!

I prayed a simple prayer my friend John had taught me. Through the years, we needed a quick resolution to an immediate situation—nothing fancy or long and drawn out. Just "God help me!" Just a full-on surrender of myself to Him, "God help me." I have prayed that simple prayer lots of times in my life. I have had some medical crises and business circumstances that were out of my control and called on Jesus for an instant dose of wisdom, knowledge, and direction.

After some time had passed, our eyes began to adjust to the surroundings, and we could see the outline of one of the hillsides. We used that as a waypoint and eventually made our way out to dry, familiar ground. What a feeling of relief to find one of the farm roads and then just walk on out! Tired, thirsty, and embarrassed are the best ways to describe the moment. Thinking back on this time is almost laughable; I am thankful that 'cooler heads' prevailed as we worked together as a team that night, and my simple prayers were answered.

Some lessons learned from this adventure: Carry a fresh set of flashlight batteries and compass and flag your way in to follow your flags back out. The only thing that hurt was my pride and feeling foolish for not being better prepared.

Being lost easily leads to feelings of despair fueled by fears. The unknown or the uncertainty of the following situation feels hopeless. As you have read, being lost in the physical dimension, even on a familiar farm, can be somewhat frightening and frustrating.

Sometimes, being 'lost' can be experienced with your feet firmly planted on the ground in a place where you're familiar. Choosing what decisions to make can be overwhelming and confusing at the same time. Being lost in the woods or overwhelmed by your circumstances has many similarities and can stir up the same emotions and fears.

Life can change instantly, from a medical diagnosis to losing a job or an accident to losing a friend or a loved one. The feeling of time standing still leaves us stunned as we pause and reflect, giving way to shock, hopelessness, and sometimes despair. The words "heart disease" or "cancer" leave the world spinning around you. The plans and the dreams for the future are hampered in the moment, where the mind shifts to wondering, "Can I, or will I survive?" This is the feeling of being 'lost in the moment' while waiting for our mind to absorb the changes, or perhaps even processing a season of grief that has settled into our lives as we once knew it.

Part Two:

Fear becomes powerless in the presence of faith.

One powerful method to overcome fear is to shift our focus toward cultivating faith. By redirecting our attention toward faith, we can effectively silence the grip of fear.

Feeling 'lost' produces panic of not knowing which way to turn, thus, creating a feeling of being frozen in place. The wrong decision can make us fearful and uncertain of the outcome. Then worry and anxiety take over and we begin thinking there is no way out of this situation. It's no different than being backed into a corner with no way to turn and no way out.

Back in Chapter Five of this book, I was out of options. My doctor sat me down and decided to end my life-sustaining medical treatment plan. It felt like my world was spinning out of control as I sat there with my head in my hands. My doctor's words honestly shook me to the core. "Mike, without these treatments, you have about thirty days to live. Choose now where you will pass away. Each day will become more complex until you succumb to your terminal disease". I then looked at the calendar and thought to myself, "I will not even live to the end of the month!"

WE HAVE the POWER to REJECT FEAR - and instead direct our attention to

> Jesus, who is eagerly awaiting to 'light up the
> darkness', dispelling every ounce of fear!
> Fear masquerades itself as wisdom, perhaps through a sense of
> pride or in our weakness. Pray against fear and pray for God's
> wisdom in all situations. Step back momentarily and seek the
> Father in everything you do and always in times of crisis.

Thankfully, I had the Lord in my life. I prayed along with an army of others for my healing. I can only tell you that God carried me through a tough time.

THE WAY WE SPEND OUR LIVES IS THE MOST UNAMBIGUOUS INDICATION OF OUR PRIORITIES AND WHAT WE VALUE MOST.

Another way of being 'lost' is spiritually lost. We live in a culture where we can demand our way. The world will tell you, "If it feels good, do it! Choose what you want - without any worry or responsibility for your actions."

Without faith, we are hoping for the best in life's circumstances. Being 'spiritually lost' is living life by your own set of rules without any regard or consequences for the future.

Man's ways are not God's ways. Men and women, in general, thrive in charting their course. People in today's culture derive their identities from being self-sustaining and making their way. Our culture creates its own rules for living and in many ways those rules are well outside of biblical standards. The way we spend our lives is the most unambiguous indication of our priorities and what we value most. Much of the time, people will work themselves into a frenzy to get what they want.

As believers in Christ, we are each given the vital task of being ambassadors for reconciliation. It is our divine calling to break down the walls that divide us and foster relationships that mirror the love and grace of our Savior. By embracing unity, we have the incredible opportunity to showcase the life-changing power of Christ's love to the world. This love goes beyond human divisions and can heal those who are hurting. Christ's love is meant to bring unity to the body without compromising the word of God.

Part Three

HOPE FOR
THE HURTING

Each of us needs to look deep within ourselves. Ask yourself this question: "Can I continue to carry this 'load' of life by myself?" God wants to turn your hurt into healing. Then, He wants to use you in the lives of other people. He's just waiting for you to surrender your will to Him.

In chapter seven, I asked myself, "Do I seize the moment?" Meaning, do I step forward, freeze in place, or turn away? The same can be said for having the courage to change. Changing is shifting from a lifetime of sinful habits into a relationship with Jesus Christ, resulting in His forgiveness and the salvation He provides. Every person will be faced with the question of life - "Have I accepted Jesus Christ as my Lord and Savior? Are my sins forgiven?"

Jeremiah 1:4-5 (NIV)
The word of the Lord came to me, saying,
"Before I formed you in the womb, I knew you,
before you were born, I set you apart.
I appointed you as a prophet to the nations." - Jeremiah

HOPE FOR ETERNITY

THE CHOICES WE MAKE THROUGH OUR
OBEDIENCE WILL DEFINE THE CLOSENESS OF
OUR RELASHIONSHIP WITH THE FATHER.

God wants our hearts, and through our obedience, our lives can be lived out in love for Him. The choices we make through obedience will define the closeness of our relationship with the Father. He wants you to love Him enough that you gladly choose the life and relationship it provides. God knows everything about our lives, and nothing is hidden from Him. Our thoughts, actions, and conversations are all known.

TRUTH ALWAYS LEADS TO FREEDOM.

As we now see, being 'lost' can mean many things. Being lost raises all kinds of questions, insecurities, and doubts. However, lost is when there is uncertainty about what to do or where to go next. You know when you are 'lost', you are out of options. 'Spirituality lost' is living your life without Christ.

When someone is in the hospital, and things are uncertain, they don't call out to the devil! You would never hear, "Oh devil, oh devil, help me!" Everyone cries out to God whether they know Him or not. They cry out to the God of the universe: "God help me, help me!" In their heart, they know what is right and Who to call on.

I shared my story about being lost as an analogy so everyone can relate that we are 'spiritually lost' without a relationship with God. You are wandering through your life without a Savior. My hope is that throughout these chapters, I have clearly explained and shared with you about my life in Christ. Life is never easy. It can be filled with difficulties and many disappointments. God is by your side in the good times and in dire circumstances.

LIVE YOUR LIFE IN OBEDIENCE TO CHRIST BECAUSE WHILE SIN MAY SATISFY YOU FOR A MOMENT, THE CONSEQUENCES WILL DRAW YOU IN FURTHER THAN YOU COULD IMAGINE. THOSE DECISIONS WILL OFTEN LEAD TO DEATH.

Think about eternity. Eternity is forever, either with God in Heaven or without God in the miry pit of Hell. We are sealed at our death, either knowing Jesus as Lord and Savior or not knowing Christ and separated from God for eternity.

Psalm 46:1 (KJV)

"God is our refuge and strength, an ever-present help in trouble." - King David

The Bible says to "Seek the Lord while He may be found." I can ask God for help in my current situation because He is always here with me – an ever-present help.

Think of truth like a compass. The needle on a compass always points to the true north. Whether walking in circles on my farm in the dark or turning to the left or the right, the needle's point never moves off from true north. The truth will always point to the Word of God; it does not deviate or have any gray areas. The truth is unchanging, always supported in the Bible or the Word of God, and always up-to-date and relevant. A compassionate and uncompromising stand for the truth is essential in our walk with Christ.

God has supplied us with a life plan, which is found in the Bible. When we read the Bible, we can apply its wisdom and knowledge to our lives. The Bible is our reference book. The Word directs our lives to navigate the questions and issues we face every day. The Bible does not deviate or change. It is 'rock steady' and can be counted on to guide you through life's circumstances. Unfortunately, we live in a culture that is increasingly hostile to the truth of God's Word.

My writing this book is an example of my relationship with God. My relationship with God is a beautiful journey. My journey has been full of wonderful experiences of marriage, children, and grandchildren.

Through each season of my life, God has led me as I have celebrated life's joys and worked through its heartaches. As you have read, I have been at the edge of death. Only by God's grace and the fulfillment of His plan for my life am I here today to write this book. God has been faithful, and for that, I am truly grateful.

Part Four

SALVATION IS FREE FOR EVERYONE

Psalm 139:13-18 (NIV)
"For you created my inmost being you knit me together in my mother's womb.

I praise you because I am fearfully and wonderfully made; your works are wonderful. I know that full well. My frame was not hidden from you when I was made in the secret place and woven together in the depths of the earth. Your eyes saw my unformed body; all the days ordained for me were written in your book before one of them came to be. How precious to me are your thoughts, God! How vast is the sum of them! Were I to count them, they would outnumber the grains of sand—When I awake, I am still with you." - King David

God sees your heart. We begin to understand our Savior and ourselves better in moments like this. Our faith journey is a marathon, not a sprint. Let Christ sanctify you daily, and let your maturity produce steadfastness, perseverance, and endurance, all to be used by Him.

Your choice is being 'born again', 'dying to the old self', and dedicating your life to Christ. By asking for forgiveness of your sins, being cleansed from every mistake you have ever made, and walking free from the shame and guilt of your past, you begin your new life in Christ. The slate is wiped clean, and Jesus is your Lord and Savior. This changes your outlook on life as a believer. Short and long-term goals and aspirations in life take on a whole new meaning. The trajectory of your eternity will now be secured in Heaven, and every day, your life is walking in a relationship with the world's Creator.

John 4:14 (NIV)
"...but whoever drinks the water I give them will never thirst. Indeed, the water I give them will become in them a spring of water welling up to eternal life." - Jesus

There comes a time when we must look within ourselves and ask whether there is more. Is there more to life than material possessions and superficial relationships? There is a wanting and desire for something deeper and more substantial. God desires all your heart.

The Lord picked you and me to be His very own.

1 Peter 2-9 (NIV)
"But you are a chosen people, a royal priesthood, a holy nation, God's special possession, that you may declare the praises of him who called you out of darkness into his wonderful light." - Peter

God, help me when I am lost in the darkness.

"God, help me to trust you when I fear the worst in life's circumstances. God, help me amid my medical diagnosis. God, help me to submit from my ways to your ways. God, help me to see the world through your eyes. God, help me be the person you created me to be in living a life of significance. God, show me who I am in You. God, reveal my identity in Christ." - A prayer for anyone seeking God's deliverance and direction.

God looks at us as His beloved sons and daughters.

Maybe you've been running from God for years, perhaps even decades. This is your moment to come to Him, be forgiven by Him, and have a relationship with the God who loves you. He loves you so much that He sent His only Son, Jesus Christ, to earth for you and me. Jesus died on the cross for your sins and rose from the dead. And now He 'stands at the door of your heart' and knocks. If you hear His voice and open the door, He will come into your life. Are you tired and worn out? Are you filled with sadness and depression? There is hope! This is not about religion or rules and regulations. It's hope that Jesus Christ will come to live inside you. He can pardon you of every sin you've ever committed. You don't have to be controlled or crippled by the shame of your past. You can become a new person in Jesus Christ.

PREPARE

According to the Bible, the path to Heaven teaches that we can attain eternal salvation by simply accepting the incredible sacrifice made for us by Jesus on the cross. All the necessary steps to reach Heaven have already been taken care of. Jesus, out of pure love, accomplished everything on our behalf. This divine act is bestowed upon us as a gift without cost or obligation. Your role in salvation is openly confessing your sins and embracing Jesus as your Lord and Savior. You receive God's boundless grace by acknowledging and appreciating what he has done for you. It is truly a precious gift given to you by God himself!

Jesus replied, "Very truly, I tell you, no one can see the kingdom of God unless they are born again." "How can someone be born when they are old?" Nicodemus asked. "Surely, they cannot enter a second time into their mother's womb to be born!" Jesus answered, "Very truly I tell you, no one can enter the kingdom of God unless they are born of water and the Spirit. Flesh gives birth to flesh, but the Spirit gives birth to spirit. You should not be surprised at my saying, 'You must be born again'. The wind blows wherever it pleases. You hear its sound, but you cannot tell where it comes from or where it is going. So, it is with everyone born of the Spirit."

Accepting Christ as your Lord and your Savior begins here. Ask for forgiveness, make Jesus the Lord of your life, and turn from your sinful ways. Everything you have read in this book is because I chose Jesus many years ago. When I surrendered my heart to Jesus, I decided to live intentionally and committed to Him. Honestly, my life has never been the same!

Maybe you committed to God once, but somehow, you became 'lost' and 'turned around' along life's travels. You once loved Him but are now falling away and backsliding. The good news is that it is never too late to change direction! Confess your sins to God, your Father in Heaven. HE WILL HEAR YOUR PRAYERS. Today is the day of salvation. Make today a brand-new start. Ask Jesus into your heart today.

Philippians 2:9-11 (NIV)
"Therefore, God exalted him to the highest place and gave him the name that is above every name, that at the name of Jesus, every knee should bow, in Heaven and on earth and under the earth, and every tongue acknowledge that Jesus Christ is Lord, to the glory of God the Father." - Apostle Paul

THE PRAYER OF SALVATION

"Dear God, I am a sinner. I repent of my sins; I want to turn from my sins and ask for Your forgiveness. I believe that Jesus Christ is Your Son. I believe Jesus died for my sins and that You raised Jesus to life. I want Jesus to come into my heart and take control of my life. I want to trust Jesus as my Savior and follow Him as my Lord and Savior from this day forward. In Jesus' Name, amen."

Conclusion

FOUNDATIONS FOR GROWTH

Talk to God and pray throughout the day.
Read your Bible. This is foundational to grow.
Find a church that teaches the unchanged (Bible) Word of God.
Get water baptized at your first opportunity.
Find a mentor and small group Bible study.

As you fully surrender your life to Jesus Christ - know that this is a life-changing moment - where your eternal destination has been changed from Hell to Heaven. Find a group of believers and a Bible-based church to participate in. Learn and grow into the person God has created you to be.

Romans 8:15-17 (NIV)
"The Spirit you received does not make you slaves, so that you live in fear again; rather, the Spirit you received brought about your adoption to sonship. And by him we cry, *"Abba,* Father". The Spirit himself testifies with our spirit that we are God's children. Now if we are children, then we are heirs—heirs of God and co-heirs with Christ, if indeed we share in his sufferings in order that we may also share in his glory." Apostle Paul

You received God's Spirit when He adopted you as His children. Now we call Him "Abba, Father". His Spirit joins with our spirit to affirm that we are God's children.

Thoughts and footnotes

I wrote the analogy of being lost in the swamp on my farm in the dark. I had yet to decide which way to turn to find the way out. Being lost creates fear, then panic and hopelessness.

Being 'lost' can come in many ways and circumstances. One of the examples I used was a life-changing medical diagnosis. Nothing in life will get your attention like heart disease, cancer, or other severe medical conditions! These changes happen quickly and can alter the trajectory of your life.

Living life without God is an example of being 'spiritually lost'. God desires relationships with His children. Accepting Jesus Christ as your Lord and Savior and asking for the forgiveness of your sins brings our hearts into unity with God.

My life exemplifies how God has changed me from a self-centered man into the man God created me to be. My life has never been the same.

MAIN TAKEAWAYS:

Salvation Message: The core Christian doctrine is about leading others to Christ, sometimes through our words but also by our example.

Chapter 10 Study Guide Questions

Today, I live an amazing life. My life is full of purpose as God designs every step. I see the hand of God throughout my days. My days are filled with intentionality, and the reward is His blessing and favor.

Reflecting on a time BEFORE you surrendered your life to Christ...

NOW, since you are in Christ, God says you're "adopted into His family."

Can you describe what this means?

Can you identify a particular moment when you needed to change your heart and submit your life to Christ?

Some people fight to surrender their lives to Christ.

Can you explain when you resisted the call of Jesus in your life? Why do you think you resisted Him?

One of the most significant parts of our salvation is forgiveness - Knowing you are forgiven of every mistake, every wrong decision. The 'slate has been wiped clean'. Along with forgiveness, it removes the guilt and shame of your past.

One of the most effective ways of sharing your faith is your testimony. Your story has a powerful message because of the transformation that has taken place in your life.

Can you write down some of the details of your life and compile them into a story form that exemplifies how God has changed your life?

Can you describe your life as being free of guilt and shame?

How does that make you feel?

How would you describe your daily outlook on life?

Have you found a church and group of other believers or a small group to be involved with?

CHAPTER ELEVEN

GOING THE DISTANCE

Part One

2 Chronicles 15:7 NIV
"But as for you, be strong and do not give up,
for your work will be rewarded."

In September 2022, my wife and I were in the Grand Lake, Colorado, area. We had just completed a ride through Rocky Mountain National Park, starting in Estes Park. The ride through the park takes you to altitudes in the twelve thousand plus feet high in the mountain range. The beauty is exceptional in some areas, with year-round snow on the peaks.

After lunch in Grand Lake, I sought cold mountain streams to throw a spinner and catch a personal best, Brook Trout. My largest "Brookie" is twelve and one-half inches. These trout are some of the most beautiful of all the fish species in the world.

The rays of sunlight on the stream looked magnificent as the water ran fast from the steep mountain hillsides. In the mountains, the vertical elevation drops where boulders are as huge as vehicles, creating white water rapids and deep plunge pools for trout of all varieties to seek shelter. Behind the boulders, the water's current swirls and forms the eddies, becoming a haven for aquatic life.

As I walked along an unnamed stream, the mountain waters were as clear as ever. I stopped to breathe in the beauty of the snow-covered mountain peaks in all directions. The beauty of this place makes you feel alive! I recognized that only our God can create such splendor. As I continued down a narrow trail, I saw two men walking toward me. As the men approached, I realized they were hunters hiking with oversized backpacks. Their look and their demeanor showed they were utterly exhausted. Their packs contained large hindquarters of elk. They stopped and chatted in the shade. They were two friends who planned an archery elk hunt. Several days prior, they had taken multiple trips packing in their camp and provisions. Finally, both friends harvested their bull elk. Their difficulty was evident in that these were very large animals. Therefore, you must carry everything in your backpack.

NEVER GIVE UP!

To keep the meat from spoiling, these men had already made several trips daily and nightly hiking the meat out of the wilderness. One of the men said it was nine miles to reach their base camp. After their second-round trip, their feet burned and were covered in massive blisters. The next trip in, the blisters popped, and they had no skin on the bottoms of their feet. Every step was like walking on fire! So much pain, and they still had three more round trips to remove the remaining meat and camp provisions altogether.

The reason I shared the details of these elk hunters' dilemma and hard work is simple: You must see it through and complete the job once committed to the project or task.

I was only with these elk hunters for a few minutes; they seemed to be men of their word. I am sure they retrieved every ounce of this organic, high-protein meat to feed their families throughout the winter, rather than being tempted to take the easy way out and leave something behind. What makes some people see things through while others simply quit?

The elk hunters reminded me of an elk hunting story of my own. Some years back, my brother and I harvested two bull elk standing next to each other at an altitude of eleven thousand plus feet. Eleven thousand feet high is also called rim rock, which is the line on a mountain where vegetation cannot grow due to the lack of oxygen. It was a twenty-eight-mile day between quartering the elk and making trips back to camp. The physical exertion rendered us completely exhausted. Nevertheless, we stuck it out, taking every piece of meat off the mountain and returning to camp well after dark.

Reflecting on section one and the story about Fred's six-year prayer journey to come into faith, it might seem like a long time, and it was. When God has called you to do something you must see it through, and you can't quit. I committed to praying for Fred, and it was a long time but well worth the journey.

I have decided to share one of the stories from my book, *The Power of Forgiveness*. This story of prayer was a forty-two-year journey. The Holy Spirit 'walked' with my brother Phil and me through ministering to James and other difficulties, but when God puts something in your heart, you stay the course, knowing God is working and revealing His plan. At times, we were "plunging through the wilderness" and at other times, it was easy to "read the script." In the end, God's timing is His timing. The Word says the enemy comes to steal, kill, and destroy. That's what we are up against. We are reminded God has the final word, and everything will bow at His feet, even the adversary.

John 3:16 KJV
"For God so loved the world, that He gave his only Son, that whoever believes in Him should not perish but have eternal life." - John

Compassionate living is all around us. It breaks down to investing in others' lives. Once the formalities are removed, the real person's personality is revealed over time, and the Holy Spirit prompts deeper conversations. This is the heart of ministry.

Part Two

A Lifetime of Pain Meets Forgiveness

Jeremiah 29:11 NIV
"For I know the plans I have for you, declares the LORD plans to prosper you and not to harm you, plans to give you hope and a future." - Jeremiah

I needed forgiveness for my sins and to submit my heart to God. Therefore, I gave my life to Him. First, I needed to have my heart made right with Him. Then, the Holy Spirit began working inside of me so that I could forgive those who hurt me, just as Christ has forgiven me.

God used an old story for His glory to bring love to a man with a broken heart. This story and testimony represent a forty-two-year relationship between a farmer and two brothers. Slowly, ever so slowly, this farmer's heart was softened by the Holy Spirit and changed. Make no mistake about it - this was a battle. But, like climbing a mountain and gasping for air, you never lose sight of your goal. You never give up.

When I was fifteen, my brother Phil, and friend Mark packed our bow-hunting gear so that after school, we could drive outside of town and find a place to hunt. I was in the back seat of Mark's 1971 red Ford Fairlane as we drove the country roads, looking for a place to hunt. I said, "that's the place", pointing to a farm. I jumped out, asked permission, and we hunted until dark. That day began a forty-two-year relationship with the farmer. His name was James. James was the most hardened and calloused man I have ever met.

Most of his sentences were full of negativity and often filled with profanity. As the years passed, my brother and I would cut, split, and stack 6-8 cords of firewood to heat his home throughout the cold Michigan winters. This is back-breaking work. After knowing James for about ten years, he slowly began to trust us and opened about his past.

During a wood-cutting break, he shared that he lost a son at eight years old to a childhood illness. He spoke about the painful hospital stays and the boy passing away. The hurt was evident in his eyes as he recalled this time of great sadness. As James continued to open up, he shared more of the painful episodes of his life with us.

Another one of his sons was 25 years old, riding his motorcycle, and was hit broadside and killed instantly. The son was married with two daughters at the time of his death.

Brother Phil and I found ourselves in this place of ministry. We were the 'light' in a very dark place. Upon further reflection on when Phil and I came to this farm to hunt in our youth - Phil and I had not yet given our hearts to Christ. We attended church and were raised in a Christian home - just ordinary kids placed by God in a position to be used for His destiny. God knows the plan and will do whatever is necessary to see it through!

James did not respond when my brother and I tried to witness to him about God. Instead, he asked why didn't God protect his family? *(Does anybody have the answers to these kinds of questions?)*

James's internal pain was real and deep within his soul and often came out through his rough language. James also shared the story of his two granddaughters, and he cherished these girls! You see, their dad was James's son, who died in the motorcycle accident.

This was the most painful story for him to share. His words were almost impossible for him to speak. "The oldest granddaughter had just received her driver's license. She took her younger sister for a ride on some country roads. Maybe she was driving too fast or lacked experience. The skid marks on the pavement showed where she lost control of the car, then rolled the vehicle several times and both girls were killed instantly."

"One granddaughter was…. sixteen, and the other granddaughter was…..... twelve."

This heartache was lived out in the everyday reality of James' life…. when dreams are broken …and lives full of promise are cut short…. leaving James with a deep heartache. It was hard, if not impossible, for James to be thankful or happy for anything. James carried lifetimes of grief, unable to think past the losses in his family. We prayed, showed love, and cared for James year after year. He was consistent in his rejection of our efforts and in the sharing of our faith. We didn't accept the rejection personally. This was our mission. James had the hardest of 'walls' built around his heart.

My thoughts go back to the mountain where the friends hiked and carried hundreds of pounds of elk meat off the mountain in complete exhaustion. James must have figuratively 'walked up that mountain' thousands of times, gasping for air, hoping the nightmare of losing his family members would disappear. Then, the re-occurring nightmare invades his sleep yet again, where the police come to the door to relay the tragic news, again. Quickly jolted awake in the middle of the night with the stark reality - that his loved ones are gone. The pain was as natural for him decades later as if it had just recently happened. James did everything he could in all these cases, then blamed himself for not doing enough. In these moments, I'm sure he was confused in not knowing or understanding what to do next. One constant throughout our forty-two years together is that James was angry and blamed God for everything.

The thought of blaming God was perhaps the only logical conclusion

James could make to reconcile the losses in his family. He hurt so deeply he couldn't even smile. These losses hardened his heart, which were full of hardship and difficulties. Yet, the elk hunters continued to stay the course throughout their pain, because once the shots hit their marks, the rules of responsibility had changed. Fortunately, my brother Phil is a very patient man, and his patience steadied the path for us throughout this forty-two-year journey. James was determined to continue his career until retirement. Yet, he took every step with constant pain and reminders of what could have been. James's pain differed from the elk hunter's blistered and skinless feet as they trudged ahead to retrieve their meat and provisions. James's pain was heartache from within and exacerbated through the negative words and constant profanity he became accustomed to speaking. His losses had hardened his heart. Callousness became a way of life and his way of coping.

Brother Phil and I continued to show James love, and we cared as Jesus would care for a friend. It wouldn't be fair to judge James. Virtually no one can relate to the pain and heartache in his life. Phil and I didn't give up, though. We stayed consistent in our efforts to lead him to Christ. Our efforts were met with constant rejection as we continued to pray for him.

The Holy Spirit is gentle, consistent, and true.

Our prayers were, *"God, we ask that James would not perish without knowing You as his Lord and Savior."*

We can all reflect on the difficult people we know in life. I encourage you to keep praying and never give up; keep believing in a breakthrough for the 'walls' to come down around broken and calloused hearts.

The lines on his face had decades of unimaginable pain and grief buried deep within them. No words had to be spoken to understand the pain that turned into anger, and the anger turned into outright bitterness. The collateral damage in James' life was a 55-year marriage that ended in divorce, and other family relationships were broken and shattered well beyond repair.

James blamed God for all his troubles. As the years passed into decades, James was now in his eighties. Brother Phil and I took him to doctor appointments and grocery stores, had him over for holiday meals, and helped care for him.

God had a plan of Redemption.

In the months before his eventual death, we prayed with James as he surrendered his heart to the King of Kings and the Lord of Lords. It was hard for James to surrender his soul from the decades of pain. His pain had become his identity. The pain of his identity came out negatively, with profanity and a very deeply wounded heart.

The heaviness of everyday living weighed on James's life like the thought of making another trip up the mountain to retrieve hundreds of pounds of meat and carry it on our backs. Every day was more challenging, like the previous days, months, and years. James' time had come. He had fought decades of pain, heartache, hard times, and disappointments long enough. And finally, he surrendered it all to the Lord.

He held to the truth that his life was hard, but there was a "new day on the horizon" that every one of us will see. This day will come when we take our last breath on earth and our first breath in Heaven. Until then, we will live fully in God's goodness and presence each day. Believers know this day is coming. Heaven is our reward. Ultimately, until then, we live in relationship to Him every day.

Where the enemy came to rob, steal, and destroy a man, The Holy Spirit took this very hardened man suffering a lifetime of pain, and in the end, healed his broken heart.

The Holy Spirit brought his life into peace, forgiveness, and salvation.

Late on a Friday evening, the call came from the nursing facility. James passed from his life on earth into eternity and into the arms of Jesus. From the fifteen-year-old boy who said from the back seat, *"That's the place"*, this was no surprise to God. Sometimes, forgiveness is a decades-long journey. It's incredible to be used by God and see how a life was changed for eternity!

Conclusion

It's amazing how the Lord works in mysterious ways. Even though we may not fully understand or anticipate how things will unfold, if we stay faithful and seek the guidance of the Holy Spirit, God can bring together testimonies that span decades. He sees the 'bigger picture' and knows the significance of divine appointments, even before we come to faith.

Throughout life's journey, there will be moments when we feel like giving up. However, it's important to persevere and keep pushing forward, like "keeping our shoulders to the plow." Life is not easy. It's not a sprint, but a long-distance marathon that requires endurance and determination to reach the finish line.

Our journey with James began as acquaintances, and then we became friends over the next several decades. Phil and I were consistent in our love and caring for James. Over time, James's heart began to soften – And that's exactly what the Holy Spirit does with every one of us. He brings us unto Himself.

Thoughts and Footnotes

An elk hunt can sometimes take years to plan, involving not only the participants' chemistry, but also ensuring the memories of the hunt last a lifetime. However, friendships are forged in the wilderness regardless of whether their shots hit their mark. I believe James' life was, to some degree, a type of 'wandering' in the wilderness. Brother Phil and I began this friendship with James that started to bring his life into balance. Over a long period of time, we introduced James to the loving-kindness of our Lord.

As you have read, life changes quickly. For the hunters in this chapter, their success changed the immediate plans for the next several days. The losses in James's life had dramatic changes over about a ten-year period.

The hunters planned for their success, and their success completely changed the outcome of their hunt and the days to follow. James needed to adapt to the tragic circumstances in his family, one death at a time. Change in his life was inevitable.

We know and understand that death is permanent, and eternity is forever. There are no more goodbyes, holidays, or other important dates. Life, as James knew it, abruptly changed forever.

The perspective on navigating these changes had determined our lives for decades. Yet, again, I have no idea how a family walks through these tragedies without the Lord. James held his feelings deep within his soul and blamed God every day.

Whatever God has for you today - perhaps it is to be a good listener – realize that He has placed you exactly where He wants you to be. God uses your experiences and unique character in "the right place at the right time" to make a difference for Him through your words and actions. Be an encouragement to those around you.

God was working on His plan when my brother Phil and I found James's farm based on His divine plan. As high schoolers, that day began a forty-two-year journey in finding and praying for James. To put this in perspective, I was fifteen when I met James, and when he passed away, I was fifty-seven. That is a long time to pray for someone. So, when God put this calling in our lives, we continued through many highs and lows that life doled out to us.

As those years turned into decades, our mission was the same: witness our faith in Him and ask the Holy Spirit to lead James to Christ. Phil and I had compassion for James, but in the end, it was James' decision. I am thankful God used two brothers to see His plan through. It was our pleasure to be kind and caring where God worked His plan through to salvation.

MAIN TAKEAWAYS:

Divine Strength in Action

Persistence with James: Story of persistence in ministry.

Divine Empowerment: When called to action, God provides strength and endurance to see it through.

Chapter 11 Study Guide Questions

To better understand the magnitude of this story. Brother Phil and I had not given our hearts to Christ when we first met James as high school kids. God's plan was multifaceted in how this testimony worked its way out. Honestly, we were into this for the long haul. I encourage you, the reader, to NEVER GIVE UP on your friends or family coming to the Lord.

When you have been praying for someone for years, believe that God is working all things for His glory. He loves everyone and wants to see them in a relationship with Him. Never give up, even as months go on to be years, and years become decades.

Who have you been praying for that you might think is hopeless or refuses to change?

What does it mean to be 'called to prayer'?

This chapter talks about going the distance. Sometimes, the finish line changes. Other times, we cannot see the end. The elk hunters pushed themselves beyond their capacity to retrieve their meat and camp provisions and fought not to give up. Their responsibilities changed once they were successful. Life is hard for everyone, just in different ways.

How can you stay committed to the task when you are exhausted?

My brother Phil and I stayed committed to our prayers for decades that James would surrender his life to Christ. First, for his salvation, and the other for a sense of peace to come into his life.

Can you go the distance for someone by praying, believing, and trusting that God will see this through?

What motivates you to pray continually for someone when you do not see any results?

Write down your mission-based prayers.

Can you commit to praying and believing to 'see it through' or until you are released from the burden?

CHAPTER TWELVE

PERSONAL LOSS

Part One

Matthew 5:4 (NIV)
"Blessed are those who mourn, for they will be comforted." - Jesus

God grants us a peace that surpasses all understanding, and to receive this peace, I willingly surrender my need for complete comprehension. Life is filled with various challenges, and we often face 'storms' daily. Jesus foretold this reality, urging us to be prepared. Our faith is firmly rooted in withstanding these storms, not solely through knowledge but by actively living out God's word.

John 16:33 (NIV)
"I have told you these things so that in me you may
have peace. In this world you will have trouble. But
take heart! I have overcome the world." - Jesus

When the news came - it was not the news I wanted to hear, but we were trusting God for the greater good in our situation. One of the secrets of joy is learning to trust God, even while walking through a 'valley' amid heartache and loss. Even in these moments, God is ever-present. His strength is excellent, much, much more significant than our pain. I don't know what I would do without Him!

I took this news hard. Months afterward, my eyes still well up in tears when I read this.

This is about a life that left us far too soon...

I am the protector of my family. I stand on guard as the elder statesman and prayer warrior for my tribe. When an issue comes, I support my family in every way possible. I want them to know that. This is just one of the many ways our Father in Heaven does the same for each one of us.

The enemy is not concerned about your discomfort or any hardship that he may cause you. He is out there, ready to take from you and tempt you into compromising your values, character, or your integrity. We pray for protection and covering, as previously stated. These prayers are so vital to our family's well-being. For years, we have been praying for another grandchild. We stood with my son and daughter-in-law in prayer for their second child. They wanted to add a second child for our grandson, who would have another sibling close in age.

The effort to make this happen was more challenging than expected. We prayed as months turned into years with nothing happening. God's timing is His timing. We were mature about that in our thinking and so was their mindset even with many months of disappointments.

The news came, and the pregnancy happened, and we were overjoyed! After a month and a half or so, some problems began to surface. My daughter-in-law shared the news with others by writing this note:

"This year, we have had many ups and downs for us. In our last card, we shared with many of you that we anxiously awaited and prayed for another baby. Our prayers were quickly answered, and in January 2021, we discovered we were pregnant. Sadly, our sweet babe only stayed with us a short time and went into the loving arms of Jesus. While we never held our babe in our arms, we'll always have our babe in our hearts. We continue to pray about how to grow our family and would love to be kept in your prayers."

We supported my son and daughter-in-law and shared this news with close family members and friends. We grieved the loss of our grandchild privately. We trusted the Lord was providing healing and provision for another child.

The only lesson was to stay diligent in our prayers, to be surrounded with prayer for complete protection to cover our family and grandchildren's health. And one day, we will be reunited with our grandchild.

The loss of this child was hard on me. My thoughts at the time were that there would be no tractor rides, walking on the farm, reading books, or little league games. Instead, I grieved inside for losing a young child growing into a mighty man or woman of God, wondering where their interests might lie. How would their life's destiny be lived out? Would this grandchild be a teacher like his parents, a writer, or a musician like his dad? God only knows. Whenever I reach the limits of my understanding, I keep my focus by relying on Jesus.

I trust Jesus with all my heart instead of leaning on my own understanding. We can never change the past, but I can start now by seeking His guidance to move me forward into the future.

IN TIMES LIKE THIS HOW DO WE REACT?

FINDING GRATITUDE AMIDST SADNESS IS CRUCIAL FOR CULTIVATING HOPE.

With practice, it can become our instinctive reaction. Regardless of unchanging circumstances, we praise God because He is our dependable Savior. We trust that He is in control.

By doing this, we unlock the Holy Spirit's influence within us, allowing the "Fruits of the Spirit" to abound even during challenging moments. This includes love, joy, peace, patience, kindness, goodness, faithfulness, gentleness, and self-control. It is a supernatural way of living that is accessible to us now.

My only reaction was to trust Jesus. We just simply trusted Jesus. His ways are more significant and higher than our ways. We can't even begin to comprehend His understanding of the big picture. Jesus was once a human like us; our Savior truly understands and feels compassion for our situation. I don't question God. I trust Him in everything, in sad times like this and when life hurts.

SATAN HATES GOD.
SATAN HATES THOSE WHO FOLLOW GOD.
SATAN HATES THOSE WHO EVANGELIZE FOR GOD.

The devil loves insulting God's people for their work in His name. We recognize and can agree that every person who did anything for God also suffered persecution and difficulties on His behalf.

The loss of my grandchild is something I cannot explain. This was so deeply personal. I decided not to waste time on my pain and kept it deep within me. My purpose is to please God and live faithfully, declaring His message to those around us, even when it hurts.

Millions will read this and relate to my loss. Was it an attack of the adversary, or did God step in and bring this baby to Him? I do not know how to answer the loss of a grandchild. Life can be full of heartache, emotional drain, and difficulty. I accepted God's plan, but the grief continued to cause pain and hurt.

WHATEVER THE CAUSE OF OUR HARDSHIPS, THE BIBLE SAYS THEY HAVE A GODLY PURPOSE.

The goal is for us to become more like Christ. Difficulties and trials cultivate our endurance, shape our character, and give us a sense of hope—a hope that serves as the rock-steady anchor for our souls. It is through the process of enduring suffering that a unique kind of maturity and compassion can be achieved.

Part Two

Asking The Hard Questions

1 John 4:21(NIV)
"And he has given us this command: 'Anyone who loves God must also love their brother and sister." - John

A friend, who will take us "as we are" is priceless - but leaves us better than before. A friend can lift us with a word of encouragement or be a shoulder to lean on—the one who can remain steady through time.

I developed close relationships with some of my employees in my business life. Our business took men all over the country every week. During that period, I worked with some, roomed with others, and sat down and had dinners together for over twenty years.

Mark had a "loner" personality; however, he was a strong man in his convictions and beliefs. Mark could be counted on and that is a great character trait of his. In our conversations, I learned that Mark had few friendships. Mark mostly cared for his aging mother, where he lived with his neighborhood friend Gabe, his children, and one granddaughter. Mark was proud of his children. I remember watching them grow up from attending our company's yearly Christmas parties.

Some years ago, we started a maple syrup operation on our farm. Mark had lots of suggestions as we began our start-up and had some experience helping others. We would gather at our local breakfast spot to discuss our plans. Mark loved to give input.

Our group included grandchildren, friends, and family. This was a "family-time" event. Those who participated were paid by receiving maple syrup products. We carefully kept track of everyone's hours logged into a book, and when the season was over, they received their allotment of finished syrup. This was a family event led by men and women working hard and setting forth good work-ethic examples amid wholesome farm work experience.

Throughout the years, Mark and I had solid conversations about life. Like most people, he had lots of opinions and questions. Mark had a hard time with forgiveness. He said he had someone that had been disloyal to him and "could not forgive them." I encouraged him to forgive those who had hurt him. He just simply said, "I don't know that I can." I gave him a copy of *The Power of Forgiveness* book that I had written. Mark was the most loyal reader of that book I have ever heard of! He said he read several pages every night at bedtime, then continued reading the book repeatedly.

I knew he had read the book close to ten times!

These conversations led me to ask Mark, "Where is your heart with Jesus?" Mark replied that he had "publicly confessed his faith" earlier in his life. He assured me that his life was 'right' before the Lord. I accepted his statement. Each of our lives has taken us through many twists and turns. Sometimes, we have made mistakes; other times, we've done great.

Early on a Monday morning, I received a phone call that would shake a person to their soul. My friend and former employee Mark was found dead in his backyard, suffering a fatal heart attack after cutting his grass. Mark was fifty years old.

I found it very difficult to speak at his funeral service. I shared times of laughter, hard work, and lots of other memories. I spoke of his commitment to the Lord and what God meant to him. When attending a funeral, a great peace comes over the attendees when they are assured that their friend or loved one was 'right' with the Lord.

I reflected to a time when Mark called me into his office a year and a half after I retired from our company. Mark handed me a small box with this note. I read this note at his funeral service: "You were so much more than an employer to me. You are my family." The box contained a handcrafted hunting knife he had made for me in Germany. With deep conviction - I miss Mark, our conversations, and our friendship.

Death is never easy and never comes at a convenient time. But it is an appointed time in all our lives.

Each of us is given a certain number of days. Some are few, and some stretch into long numbers of years. From my own life experience, I treat each day as a gift to be used for God's glory and His purpose. I am thankful that Mark and I were friends. I am grateful that I had the boldness to ask the hard questions like, "Is your heart 'right' with Jesus?" Mark's answers made dealing with his death much more manageable knowing he was with his Almighty God.

It's not up for debate whether he or someone else is living according to my standards. We will stand before the Lord and give an account of our lives. Had I not asked Mark, I might have wondered and regretted not knowing about his salvation. Asking where someone's 'heart is' an incredible moment to possibly share your testimony of how you gave your life to Christ and what He has done for you. These can be moments of great encouragement. Everyone needs to be encouraged from time to time.

Part Three:

PRAYING FOR A FRIEND IN THE NIGHT

Several years ago, I woke in the night. The Holy Spirit put it on my heart to pray for my men's ministry friend, Don. I didn't understand it, but Don was so profoundly 'on my heart' that I needed to pray for him. The Holy Spirit only revealed to me that Don needed to be comforted and that his heart was hurting. So, I prayed sincerely for Don that whatever the need was, God would 'see him through' the night.

I asked the Holy Spirit to meet Don right where he was. In some instances, like this, I am still determining the need for clarity, but I was sure of the Holy Spirit leading me to 'lift up' my friend in prayer, whatever the circumstances. I don't need to know the circumstances. The Holy Spirit knows, and I am encouraged to pray and intercede on my friend's behalf. This was late Monday night or very early Tuesday morning. (Tuesday mornings were my men's group meetings around five-thirty A.M.)

As the men gathered for the Tuesday morning meeting, I saw Don from across the room. Don looked a bit troubled. I approached him and asked, "Don, can I talk with you privately?" He replied "Yes." I said, "You have been on my heart throughout the night. The Holy Spirit woke me, and I prayed for you." Don replied with tears in his eyes, "Today is the first anniversary of my son Chad's death."

Chad's life was full of purpose. He was a thriving, vibrant young man with a world of opportunity ahead of him. Chad developed his own IT business and because of his success, a larger company purchased it. Chad was the eldest of three children and was well on his way to a very successful life. Chad had also developed a serious relationship with his girlfriend with the possibility of marriage soon.

Chad was excelling in his job and his relationships in life - and then the call came that no parent would ever want to receive... "Unfortunately, your son Chad has been in a terrible accident, and I'm sorry to tell you that he has passed away from his injuries."

Time stops. No more goodbyes, handshakes, high fives, or, most importantly - the hugs, and the words, "I love you." The word 'death' is final and leaves an unmistakable pain that radiates in a father's heart that never goes away. To those like Don, who are left behind, the shock is so real you need to be told to breathe.

Chad was driving on a typical January winter mid-afternoon day with clear roads when his car slowly drifted across two lanes of oncoming traffic, then off the road, where he hit a tree head-on. The medical report from the autopsy revealed that this healthy young man had a "medical incident" while driving to see a business client. Witnesses from the scene said Chad appeared "slumped over in his seat, looking like he had passed out."

With death comes the aspect of faith and the eternal life that follows. Chad chose to give his life to Christ and wanted others to know and live in the freedom it provides.

Don can live confidently knowing Chad's heart was 'right' with God and is in Heaven today. No middle-of-the-night insecurities or worries, just simply, Chad is with Jesus - safely home with his Lord and Savior whom he loved and cherished.

It has been said the first year after a death is the "year of firsts" - the first time spending a birthday without your loved one, the first Thanksgiving meal, or Christmas morning without them. Every one of these special days brings the detailed reality that death in this life is permanent, but eternity goes on forever. Eternity with God is the reality of our lives for those who have chosen the forgiveness of our sins and accepting Jesus as Lord and Savior. For those, the transition from this life to the next will be in an instant, and they will live on with the Father in Heaven forever.

To those lives left behind, there is comfort and peace in knowing their loved ones are in Heaven. It is the basis of our faith when we understand death is permanent and eternity is forever. The hope we hold on to is that we will be reunited in Heaven one day.

THE GOD OF ALL CREATION IS THE ONLY ONE WHO CAN SEND HIS PEACE, LOVE, AND UNDERSTANDING TO COMFORT HIS HURTING CHILDREN.

The pain of Chad's death was evident in Don's heart a year later. I am unsure how one recovers from the news of such a tragic accident. Yet, Don felt a unique peace and understanding throughout these difficult circumstances knowing that God was in control.

The heart is broken beyond understanding, so the God of the universe awakens a fellow believer to pray for the hurting. The God of all creation can send His peace, love, and understanding to comfort His children in the middle of the night. The possibility of connecting the dots for this to happen is not possible. It was nothing other than the love of the Holy Spirit touching Don's life.

John 3:16 (NIV)
"For God so loved the world that he gave his one
and only Son, that whoever believes in him shall
not perish but have eternal life." - John

The ache in a father's heart goes beyond our understanding or comprehension. God the Father, must have felt the difficulty when the plan of Jesus' life was being fulfilled, as Jesus prayed, "Not my will, but Your will be done." When Jesus died a gruesome death on the cross for all of humankind, for the sins of the world - it was (and is) a painful reminder of a Father losing His Son – and, in this case, for the more significant gain of the world. There can be no greater sacrifice to the world than the story of Calvary, where Jesus took the sins of the world on His shoulders and died for you and me.

One of my favorite contemporary Christian groups is Mercy Me. I have seen them several times in concert, and every time, we have been ministered to and enjoyed the entertainment. Don commented on the Mercy Me song 'The Hurt & the Healer' and how much it ministered deep into his soul. If you have lost a loved one, I hope you can gain peace and comfort from our Heavenly Father through this song. You can search on social media for the lyrics it if you need to familiarize yourself with the song. (Mercy Me, The Hurt and The Healer)

Conclusion

While the sudden loss of a friend or a loved one hurts, and life seems to stop in its place after a tragedy happens - the shock of it turns into a dull numbness - like living out the moments of a bad dream where our subconscious tries to make sense of horrible news:

"This can't be real. It feels like I'm drowning and gasping for air. I need to tell myself to breathe." Your mind processes over and over, eventually accepting the news that life has changed permanently. In these few examples, life changes where one-story ends and the new story begins.

I make it a priority to pray for those who have lost loved ones. My prayer is that God's peace and comfort will be with them. Even when we have difficulty understanding the loss, surrounding others with a love that only the King of Kings can bring can be encouraging during times of loss. God is with us on every step of our journey. The journey might take place within our own pain and suffering, or as God leads you to 'stand in the gap' by loving and supporting others who have lost loved ones.

There is no greater question to ask someone other than - "Is your heart 'right' with Jesus?"

My thoughts go to Mark and Don on how quickly or instantly life changes, from life to death to eternity. Some people gladly accept Jesus, His forgiveness, and salvation. Sadly, others reject the 'message of hope' and ignore any relationship with Christ.

God is enough. In trying times and facing the challenges of my grief, my God is enough. God will supply all my needs according to His riches and glory. I will rest in Him.

Gratitude for the undeserved things God gives us helps maintain a spirit of contentment.

Thoughts and Footnotes

We do not get to choose when or how to deal with the pain that comes from loss; sometimes, it comes swiftly and often in our lives. We only get to choose the journey of going through it.

In the depths of our trials and losses, we can experience His goodness and love, comfort, and compassion in the storms of life.

This is where we return to our 'childlike faith' not to bargain with God, but to trust Him.

These 'small steps' in life are often necessary and often moment by moment. God puts His arm around you and helps you to breathe again.

When walking through the phases of grief, our healing begins. Where healing begins, rejoicing follows on the road to wellness.

There are difficulties in life. I shared my loss of our unborn baby grandson. It was tough on me. There is no way I could understand God's plan in this loss. My only thought was to trust God in these trying circumstances. There were no 'middle-of-the-night answers', just trusting God.

MAIN TAKEAWAYS:

Loss and Grieving

Personal Loss: Dealing with the death of a grandchild.
Reliance on Jesus: Maintaining focus during times of deep sadness and loss.

Chapter 12 Study Guide Questions

Can you explain 'peace and comfort' in the middle of a season of grief?

What are some examples of how you have ministered to a grieving person?

We are told, "Be a good listener when being with a grieving person."

Many times, the bereaved will tell their stories repeatedly.

Are you able to just sit and listen to simple conversations?

We do not have the ability to 'fix' another person and make them better.

What can you do as a friend or family member to help ease their pain?

CHAPTER THIRTEEN

WHERE WE GO FROM HERE....

Part One

Go and live the message of Jesus.
Then go out and tell the world about Him.

Psalm 107:43 (KJV)
"Whoever is wise will observe these things, and they will understand the loving kindness of the Lord." - King David

When individuals wholeheartedly dedicate themselves to God's purposes, remarkable things unfold for His Kingdom. As you've discovered in the preceding chapters of this book, God desires to utilize your potential to make a significant impact in the world in His name. By fully committing yourself to His divine purpose for your life, you will witness the incredible ways He works through you. Stay open and available to His guidance and be prepared for the amazing journey ahead. To God be the Glory!

YOU HAVE TO PREPARE FOR OPPORTUNITY - AND THEN EXPECT IT TO HAPPEN.

The journey through the last Twelve chapters has been a sampling of my faith-walk. It is God working through me. The stories in this book compile a small percentage of my Holy Spirit 'encounters'.

There is nothing like 'hearing' the voice of the Holy Spirit and then being 'led' by Him in an act of service! I encourage every reader to step out in faith when directed and follow His lead.

My son and I were in the first row on a recent flight to Dallas.

Throughout the journey, we engaged in some small talk with the flight attendants. I was writing this book regarding forgiveness in Chapter Five. The two front cabin flight attendants began talking about forgiveness. I shared with them a few instances where I chose to forgive others.

I will use forgiveness as highlights in our walk of faith because that's what they are. When you forgive, you set the captive free. The captive is you and me as we hold onto the infractions of the past. As I meet people along life's way, almost everyone, born-again believers or not, has difficulty with forgiveness. It is refreshing to listen to anyone who understands forgiveness and who has moved on from the past. We can do nothing to change the past - right or wrong.

The exception is to take these wounds and leave them at the cross, then step forward as our response to those who have hurt us. YOU have victory when you can forgive someone for some event from your past!

This began a rather candid conversation with one of the flight attendants. She shared that she and one of her siblings were not getting along. She appeared to be around sixty years old. Disagreements at this age, or any age if not resolved, are devastating. Misunderstandings fester like an abscess deep under the skin if not confronted. The flight attendant gave no specific details, and that was fine. I suggested praying for her and her sibling as we sat in the first row.

We gathered hands at the front of the plane and asked the Lord to intervene in the situation. There was no assigning fault or who was in the wrong; we asked that the Holy Spirit bring them together for a peaceful resolution. Our prayer was one of God being glorified through a sensible conversation. Again, I didn't know the details - which are unimportant - but sometimes, the slightest things can set another person off and sever relationships.

BEING PRESENT WITHOUT DISTRACTIONS

Philippians 2:4 (GNT)
"Look out for one another's interests, not just for your own." - Apostle Paul

As in the conversation with the flight attendants, I showed common interest when we spoke. Simply put, we engaged with each other, listening carefully without "firing a rapid response." I was interested in her story. Being 'present' when others talk is the beginning of any meaningful conversation!

THE IMPORTANT ASPECT OF LISTENING IS 'HEARING' THE HOLY SPIRITS VOICE.

The significance this role plays in the lives of others has yet to be revealed. However, meeting the needs of a hurting person, who is struggling in their most significant time of need, means everything to the one you are desiring to help. Imagine for a moment that you are the one who is in that condition - when a stranger comes up to you and offers to pray with you. There is something special when the Holy Spirit 'moves' with great spontaneity, and everyone is blessed and fascinated at the same time!

I used this story of the flight attendants to say, "I was listening." Listening opened the door to a small ministry opportunity. It's small to me, however, for the flight attendant to share this with strangers might have been a larger problem for her. The important aspect of listening is 'hearing' the Holy Spirit's voice. That 'still, small voice' speaks volumes when mixed with obedience and a bit of boldness! Throughout every testimonial story in this book, I 'heard' the Holy Spirit encouraging me to step forth and act. In these moments, God has brought healing and comfort into others' lives, and as always, glory to God.

Part Two

MAKING THE CONNECTION

I am convinced that when the world stopped talking and started texting, the 'art' of communicating changed from face-to-face conversation to texting each other. I love technology; it is incredible to see the changes in the tech world and how advancements benefit humanity. However, technology comes at a cost as culture has eliminated much of our need for face-to-face communication.

I remember kayaking down a northern Michigan river some years ago with another family and their children. As we started down the river, the entire family inserted their earbuds and began the journey. What they missed were the conversations observing the beauty of nature. These trips, most times, will have bald eagle sightings and hundreds of turtles resting on logs along with deer, salmon, and other wildlife.

The sound of the water spilling over rocks is incredibly peaceful as the current carries your kayak down the river, along with small waterfalls. The moments of discovering nature at its finest as a family and many conversations were missed.

I had no judgment on my part toward them. This was just a simple observation of how they were 'doing' life. We can get so busy with life that we "tune out" others and perhaps even God's voice as He tries to speak to us.

Families need to communicate as openly and freely as possible. Earbuds or not, it's up to them to communicate with each other. I noticed that they did have some reflective conversations at the end of the kayak trip. Perhaps being older makes the difference. I also realize the younger generations do things differently these days.

Part Three:

"Out of our heart, the mouth speaks..."

...but they (our hearts and mouths) can also harm others and ourselves. Sometimes, our past experiences become our default mode.

Reflecting on the importance of being part of a small group or Bible study – it's a beautiful thing because we can learn from others and grow together in our faith in these intimate settings. Standing together in prayer and supporting one another in times of crisis is a powerful way to experience the 'body' of Christ.

As we journey through life, we often find ourselves surrounded by people who stand beside us during difficult times, just as we help others in their hardships. This mutual support and encouragement are crucial to our spiritual growth. The analogy of "iron sharpening iron" from the Bible perfectly captures this concept.

However, it is essential to recognize that the matters of the heart can be profound and sometimes leave scars and wounds. These wounds can shape our vocabulary and lead us to speak words filled with negativity, bitterness, and anger. Not only can these negative comments harm others, but it can also distort our ways of thinking and speaking.

We must address these 'heart issues' in a healthy manner, allowing God to heal and transform us. By dealing with our wounds and negative patterns, we can become better ambassadors for Christ and effectively share His love with others, thus projecting a more positive influence about ourselves to others. Let us strive to build each other up and create an atmosphere of grace and healing within our small groups and Bible studies.

Proverbs 10:9 (NIV)
"Whoever walks in integrity walks securely, but whoever takes crooked paths will be found out." Solomon

Robin and I consciously try socializing with positive and successful people from various backgrounds. Throughout history, there is safety in numbers and wisdom that can be gained within a group. Surrounding ourselves with people with various kinds of knowledge and experiences can, indeed, contribute to our personal growth and learning. Successful individuals often possess a mindset that allows them to move forward and let go of the past which is a valuable trait to learn!

Dwelling on negative experiences from the past serves little purpose in changing what has already happened. It's essential to focus on the present and the future, using our experiences as lessons rather than anchors holding us back.

BY CONSCIOUSLY CHOOSING POSITIVE AND EMPOWERING THOUGHTS, WE CAN CREATE A FOUNDATION FOR PERSONAL DEVELOPMENT AND A MINDSET THAT WELCOMES NEW OPPORTUNITIES AND CHALLENGES.

While it's natural to express negative thoughts or limitations about ourselves at times, it's crucial to be mindful of how these statements' impact our self-perception and overall mindset. We may find ourselves 'stuck' or unfulfilled by continually reinforcing negative beliefs without the desire or intention to challenge and grow beyond our current circumstances.

Instead, replacing those negative statements with empowering and open-minded affirmations can help us cultivate a mindset that embraces growth, possibilities, and self-belief. By consciously choosing positive and empowering thoughts, we can create a foundation for personal development and a mindset that welcomes new opportunities and challenges. Continuing to seek out positive influences and by surrounding ourselves with individuals who inspire us can further support our journey of personal and spiritual growth. Let us remain open to learning from others, embracing new perspectives, and nurturing a mindset that propels us forward toward our goals and aspirations.

Part Three

Colossians 3:12 (NIV)
"Therefore, as God's chosen people, holy and dearly loved, clothe yourselves with compassion, kindness, humility, gentleness, and patience." - Apostle Paul

A POWERFUL EXPRESSION OF LOVE IS MAKING SOMEONE FEEL ACKNOWLEDGED, LISTENED TO AND TRULY UNDERSTOOD. SIMPLY LISTENING IS A SIGNIFICANT GIFT TO OTHERS.

A powerful expression of love makes someone feel acknowledged, listened to, and truly understood. When we take the time to genuinely listen to others and understand their thoughts, feelings, and experiences, we convey a deep level of care and empathy.

Acknowledging someone means recognizing their presence, value, and worth. It involves giving them our full attention, showing interest in what they have to say, and validating their emotions and experiences. This simple act of acknowledgment can make someone feel seen, valued, and respected.

Listening goes beyond hearing words. It involves actively engaging with the person and being attentive to their words, body language, and emotions. By listening, we demonstrate that we value their perspective and that their thoughts and feelings matter to us. It creates a safe space for open and honest communication.

Genuinely understanding someone requires empathy and compassion. It involves putting ourselves "in their shoes", grasping their perspective, and validating their experiences. Understanding others allows us to connect on a deeper level and fosters a sense of trust and intimacy in relationships.

When we make someone feel acknowledged, listened to, and truly understood, we show them love in one of its most potent forms. It creates a bond of trust, strengthens relationships, and nurtures a sense of belonging and emotional well-being.

In life, we find ourselves in various situations for reasons and purposes that God has orchestrated. Take a moment to recognize these opportunities and allow yourself to be led by Him to impact someone's life and have a positive influence. Trust in His perfect timing and fully engage with the people around you and your environment. Sometimes, this happens in very public places.

Being 'present with the Lord' is a fundamental aspect of my faith-walk. It all begins with Him. Then, I surrender myself to Him daily. Again, not my will, but His will be done. I desire to be used for His glory to help someone as He directs my steps and words. The ministry I had with Fred in Chapter One helped me understand the entirety of those conversations. Those were some hard conversations, but to God be the glory - the 'walls' of unbelief were slowly taken down.

Finding a connection point is the start of every relationship. We showed an interest in others and allowed them to talk. I take myself out of the equation, listen to them, and allow the conversation to flow. Our personal experiences can make a lasting impact on those we encounter. God is working through us in our everyday lives, using our lives as a testimony to inspire and encourage others. While not all our stories may be easy or comfortable to share - some parts are profoundly personal and should only be revealed in specific situations or with trained professionals in whom you have complete confidence.

Part Five

YOU ARE CHOSEN TO BE YOUR FAMILY'S PRAYER WARRIOR.

In Chapter Three, "Prayer Warrior," I wrote about the importance of 'covering' your family in prayer. I encourage all parents to do this. Whether you're in a traditional two-parent home or a single-parent home - pray for God's covering over everyone and everything. I encourage every parent and grandparent to pray over all your family's spiritual health, physical health, mental health, and finances. Pray together if you can. Even when I travel, I break away from others to pray with my wife at the end of the day. Differences in time zones and schedules have complicated this, but we have made this a priority and a core value for our family.

I have met people who have told me that they find it difficult to pray for their spouses, families or even at the dinner table before their meals. My response is to try it in unity. We are praying to God, and although others hear it, we are not praying to them. Whether prayers of thanks for our meals or prayers of petition asking God for something significant, our prayers are important. As couples, when we pray before meals or at bedtime with children, we are modeling our relationship with God with our children. Those prayer times should be the standard for our homes. Families should pray together on important issues such as health, finances, or other decisions within proper perspective or topics. We are teaching our reliance on God and learning how He provides for our needs and answers our prayers.

When we have a close relationship with the Holy Spirit and He 'speaks' - we can move into prayer anywhere or at any time. Throughout this book, I have given several examples of when I was bold enough to pray. What's important here is the obedience to the Holy Spirit, to follow as He leads. In Chapter Four, I had several prayer opportunities. These were in public places. The reaction to those prayed for was overwhelmingly positive and added value to their lives. I encourage everyone to be a "Prayer Warrior" in times of crisis - and in times of calm to just say to the Lord, "I love You and thank You for this day."

Part Six:

GOD IS UP TO SOMETHING, AND I AM A PART OF IT.

I reflected on my "story", which is the basis of my book ***The Power of Forgiveness***. I never shared the details with my two sons for twenty-five to thirty years. I locked it up inside of me because I felt shame for not being able to defend myself against the two robbers who tied me up and held me against my will for forty-eight minutes. It was only through the encouragement of my wife that I wrote out the details of my story as a means of personal therapy.

YOUR TESTIMONY IS ONE OF THE MOST POWERFUL MINISTERING AND WITNESSING TOOLS YOU WILL EVER HAVE.

My first book, and its testimonial story, have ministered to people from all walks of life. Throughout the world, people have given their hearts to Christ. We will never know the power of our testimonies and the lives that can be affected until we share them with others. Your testimony is one of the most powerful ministering and witnessing tools you will ever have.

Here's an interesting fact: When we negotiated with my publisher on the book deal, (his name was also Mike), he said, "If your book has some success, the book's life will live on for four to five generations beyond the author's life." Ponder that for a moment. That is an incredible legacy that will live on for possibly hundreds of years after I'm gone!

Our most significant source of joy stems from our unwavering connection with God. When we take the time to acknowledge and appreciate the blessings He has given each of us - and when we reflect on His unfailing goodness in our past experiences - it fills us with renewed encouragement and hope for what lies ahead. Furthermore, as we openly share our testimonies with others, they too, will realize that they can place their trust in God, just as we have, knowing that He will faithfully fulfill all He has promised.

Personal testimonies can bring healing, transformation, and possibly salvation to others. When we share our stories of faith and how we have experienced God's love and grace, it can deeply resonate with others and inspire them on their own spiritual journey. In your pain, don't miss the opportunity for Jesus to make you better - and tell the world what He has done for you!

When our 'stories' impact someone's life in a profound way, it can indeed change their trajectory for eternity. The power of personal testimony lies in its ability to touch hearts, challenge beliefs, and offer hope and encouragement. It can serve as a beacon of light in times of darkness, providing comfort and guidance.

Furthermore, the impact of personal testimonies extends beyond individual lives. When families experience healing and reconciliation through the power of faith, it can have a ripple effect on future generations. As 'broken branches' are mended, the entire family tree becomes stronger and more resilient.

The legacy of faith and transformation can shape the lives of children, grandchildren, and beyond, leaving a lasting impact on the family's faith. The act of accepting Jesus Christ as one's personal Savior brings about everlasting change. It not only transforms individual lives but also has the potential to shape the destiny of families and future generations. When the Christian faith is embraced and lived authentically, it can become the backbone of a family's legacy, providing a solid foundation of values, love, and grace.

Let us recognize the power of our personal testimonies and the potential they hold to impact lives and shape legacies. By sharing our faith journey, we can inspire others, bring healing to brokenness, and lead people toward a relationship with God that can transform their lives for eternity.

We are all called to pass our faith on to others. This must be intentional, and we must be involved in doing our part and acting on opportunities as they present themselves.

Luke 9:62 (MSG)
Jesus said, *"No procrastination. No backward looks. You can't put God's kingdom off till tomorrow. Seize the day!"*

Your testimonial story brings the Bible to life in modern times without changing the Word. We want to influence the world with the Word of God with life-changing, heartfelt moments.

As you know, not all people are called to be writers. The writing process takes many years of discipline to compile a book. Along with the editing, it is a painstakingly long process to get everything exactly right. Ultimately, the effort is a work of art, like clay in a potter's hands. Like the life of a believer as God molds us into the person we are becoming. To become effective in sharing your faith begins with developing your testimony and story of how God has transformed your life.

We should record the works of the Lord, either in daily or weekly journals. Time can pass, and we might forget some of the details of our testimony. These recordings can enable you to reclaim the words of the Lord in times of trouble and difficulties. Nothing is more significant than our witness when we share dynamic examples of His faithfulness and how He carried you through hardship and on into victory. These recordings will allow me to share with others just like I am sharing with you.

Part Six

INTEGRITY MATTERS

My business travels took me to the West Coast for corporate meetings a few years ago. After a day of traveling and connecting flights, I landed at my destination. I went to the rental car counter to sign for my vehicle and drive to my hotel. My conversation with the rental agent was more in-depth than expected as we reviewed the contract. The agent asked me if I wanted the gas fill-up option. I said, "I will fill the car with gas upon the return to the airport." He said, "If you agree to fill it up before returning the vehicle, initial the form here."

The following day, I sat through a challenging, awkward corporate meeting. There were some changes in corporate policies that my company didn't necessarily agree with after some negotiations that didn't go my way. The meeting ended, and I felt defeated. This was a 'high-volume' customer for us. As I walked out to my rental car, I was disappointed that my efforts fell short.

In the car, I called Robin to give her the meeting details. We were both disappointed in the policy changes and what may lie ahead. Non-compliance would mean the possibility of fewer projects and layoffs within our workforce. I drove toward the airport, thinking through the details of the meeting. I stopped for a quick lunch, then on to the airport. A glance at the gas gauge revealed it was still 'full'—no problem.

Still feeling down and, honestly, somewhat upset, I kept driving. The Holy Spirit 'spoke' to me. I signed the rental agreement stating, "I would fill the gas tank." Once again, the gauge was still on 'full'. The round trip from the airport to town to attend meetings was less than seventy miles by car. Full is full, right? I began to think of my character and integrity. Was my word going to be my word? Nobody would know... After all, the gas gauge was still on full...

Philippians 2: 1-2 NIV
"Therefore, if you have any encouragement from being united with Christ, if any comfort from his love, if any common sharing in the Spirit, if any tenderness and compassion, then make my joy complete by being like-minded, having the same love, being one in spirit and of one mind." - Apostle Paul

God is the God of truth - LIVE IT OUT!

God is not interested in simply satisfying my selfishness. I prayed that morning to be used, honest, and available to God. The conditions of prayer are that I have a genuine relationship with God, not on my selfish terms. God is still God, regardless of how a meeting goes. God will use times of disappointment to grow my character and, most of all, glorify Himself. Not filling the gas tank would go unnoticed by everyone, including the rental car company.

I slowed to exit the highway. To the left was the airport; to the right was a corner gas station, and I turned in. I approached the gas pumps, inserted my credit card, and then pumped $2.79 worth of gas, topping off the tank as I said I would. I did the right thing, and I honored my word, which also glorified God in the process. My integrity remained strong, and my character was a building block of who I am today.

All over the world, people are trying to bargain with God. They offer all sorts of deals and justifications for their actions. I could easily justify not filling the gas tank. However, I knew better. I had given my word.

God is in the most significant and major moments in my life as well as the minor ones. My emotions were simple and obvious. I was disappointed, so I could justify my actions by 'taking it out' on a corporation that would never have known the difference. But I knew better, and so did God. All these testimonial stories I have written are based on the foundation of my faith in the Lord. My integrity and character reflect who I am in Christ. Even when I almost blew it!

Part Seven

LASTLY, ALWAYS BE AN ENCOURAGER!

During difficult times, one of God's precious gifts is encouragement. Fellow believers can be supportive and help carry the burden of others. We can be grateful to God for the individuals He has placed in our lives to walk alongside us during these times. Likewise, God can use us to encourage others in troubled times. Your life story and message of faith may be the most crucial message someone is waiting to hear.

I write this book to encourage everyone to step out In faith. Be all you can be by sharing your faith, being an example for others in acts of kindness, and finding your niche in serving. God is good and reveals His fantastic goodness in everyday living. Look for God-filled moments and divine encounters throughout your day.

Ecclesiastes 3:1 (NIV)
**"For everything there is a season, a time for
every activity under Heaven." - Solomon**

As we journey, life changes with our maturity and experiences. Maybe you've grown comfortable in your Christian life and with the people within your 'circle'. My challenge is to think beyond the norm, different from the usual, and find new, fresh, risky ways of serving that are different from your comfort zone.

Suppose you could dream of a big dream of getting out and doing something huge for Jesus. What would that look like? How would you describe your dream or vision?

When I first started serving in the inner city, honestly, I was uncomfortable. After serving, I knew there was no other place I wanted to be. It's not for everyone, but I stepped into an arena beyond what my mind could understand. It's so rewarding to help, feed, and pray with this community!

We will 'grow deeper' in Christ and elevate our spiritual walk by taking more significant risks for the kingdom.

A fearful Christian is a poor testimony to others of the power and love of God. We can be soft and yet, bold, because of His purpose for us.

The Holy Spirit will lead you into many divine appointments. However, some people will never accept the Truth. It isn't because people are necessarily confused or because there are hypocrites in the church. Instead, it's because they don't want to change how they live.

God's plan for our lives is not for us to remain as we are. Instead, He desires to transform us to be more like Jesus. But in that process, it is not enough for us just to turn away from doing what is wrong. We must intentionally and deliberately turn toward what is correct as well.

I never want to enter endless debates, disagreements, or arguments over the gospel. Present it and pray for whom you're speaking with. You're sharing and being led by the Holy Spirit, and then and moving on, as He leads you. Some people will simply reject the message of Christ; ultimately, it's their decision. You and I are the 'vehicles' chosen to convey the message of hope found in Christ. Some people will accept it while others reject it. Once again, along with the gospel message, your life's authenticity, and your testimony of what God has done - as always, this is in God's hands.

May we all always choose love instead of hate.
May we reflect the love of Christ to a world
that desperately needs Him.

"EVERY DAY IS A GIFT." - Bear Bryant
(Former head football coach for the University of Alabama)

Every year, when his football players reported for the first day of training, Bear Bryant would read them a poem he carried in his wallet. He sometimes said it was the most important thing he could teach young men—far more important than anything that happened on the football field.

Every Day is a Gift...

"This is the beginning of a new day.

I can waste it or use it for good.

What I do today is important because I am exchanging a day of my life for it.

When tomorrow comes, this day will be gone forever,

Leaving in its place something I have traded for it.

I want it to be a gain, not a loss;

Good, not evil;

Success, not failure—

In order that I shall not regret the price I paid for it today."

Every day, God gives us the gift of twenty-four hours of time. It is up to us how we spend it, but once it is gone it can never be regained. God instructs us to use that time wisely, investing it in things that matter, not just for this life, but for eternity. The most essential use of our time in our lives is in doing the will of God. We should begin every day with an awareness that our time belongs to God. Ask Him for wisdom in understanding what the will of the Lord is for us for that day.

Make the most of the time and talent God entrusts to you today for it is a day that will never come again. Every one of us is an inspiration and an influence on every person we meet, and when we leave someone, we leave the goodness of God with them.

Thoughts and Footnotes

Philippians 2:4 (GNT)
"Look out for one another's interests, not just for your own." - **Apostle Paul**

As in the conversation with the flight attendants, I showed common interest when we spoke. Simply put, we engaged each other, listening carefully without "firing a rapid response." I was interested in her story.

Being 'present' when others talk is the beginning of any meaningful conversation.

THE MOST POWERFUL EXPRESSION OF LOVE IS MAKING SOMEONE FEEL ACKNOWLEDGED, LISTENED TO, AND TRULY UNDERSTOOD.

I have reflected several times throughout this book regarding being a part of a small group or Bible study. These small groups are where the intimate growth happens. We learn from others and stand together on prayer needs in the body of Christ. As I have journeyed throughout my life, many have stood beside me in times of crisis, and I have helped others in their hardship. It is biblical to say, "iron truly sharpens iron." We can build each other up and make each other better.

'Witnessing' someone along toward a relationship with Christ is an incredibly fulfilling experience for a believer. It is through living out our faith that we can make a difference.

As Corrie ten Boom wisely said, "We don't need to give God instructions, but rather, show up and report for duty." This means bringing our concerns, burdens, and desires before God but also surrendering them to His wisdom and guidance. It is a beautiful invitation to trust in God's sovereignty and allow Him to work in our lives according to His perfect plan.

So go ahead—take significant risks and have bold faith. God can take your most prominent dream. See what He can do with it!

"Father, I thank You for this day. Today is a gift You give to me. I pray I will be able to see the world through Your eyes, and the needs of those around me. Speak into my heart that I may have the boldness to share the truth into someone's life today with kindness and respect. I pray for 'divine appointments' where I can share my faith and pray for someone today. Amen."

MAIN TAKEAWAYS:

Faith Transmission

Family Communication: Stresses the importance of passing on faith amidst life's busyness.

Influencing Believers: The responsibility of shaping the next generation.

Chapter 13 Study Guide Questions

This book is part of a lifelong journey of testimonial stories where God has used me. Like me, God will use you in 'divine' appointments. Sometimes, these are moments of kindness, and other times, praying for a stranger in crisis or a time of need. Take note of these situations. It is uplifting to everyone you meet that God has positioned you to be used by Him.

God Himself has 'gifted' you with stories throughout your life. Some are easily recognizable in the scope and size of His presence. Other times, it may have been His "soft, still voice" in a particular place. My experience has been both in the solitude of a sunrise.

How can you better engage people?

How can you be a better listener?

Are you a part of a small group where you can mentor others along as well as being ministered to?

Explain how you can be a better encourager for others.

In my example of the story, "the rental car" - How did you view my decision and why?

Do you have a testimony story that you can share with others?

REFERENCES

Preface
Mark 5:19 NIV

Chapter 1
Ephesians 1:11 NIV
Numbers 12:6 NIV
Colossians 4:17 NIV
1 Corinthians 12:9 NIV
Hebrews 11:1-3 NIV
Esther 4:14 NIV
Peter 5:8-9 NIV
Ephesians 6:12 NIV
Luke 15:4-7 NIV
Romans 8:28 NIV

Chapter 2
Ephesians 1:15 NIV
John 13:34-35 NIV
Matthew 10:20 NIV
3 John 1:4 NIV
John 8:31-32 NIV Corinthians 13:1-3 NIV
Titus 2:14 ASV
Ephesians 2:10 NASB
Philippians 4:10-18 NIV
Proverbs 11:25 NIV
Deuteronomy 15:11 NASB
Ephesians 6:12-13 NIV
Ephesians 2:8-9 NIV
1 Corinthians 10:13-14 NIV
Romans 2:1-2 NIV

Jude 5:20 NIV
Jeremiah 29:11 NIV
Acts 20:35 NIV

Chapter 3
Ephesians 6:18 NIV
1 Thessalonians 5:16-18 NIV
Acts 6:4 KJV
1 Corinthians 12:8 NIV
Colossians 4:4-5 NIV
2 Peter 3:8-9 NIV
Philippians 4:6 NASB

Chapter 4
Romans 15:5 NIV
Romans 12:8 NIV
Acts 11:23-24 NIV
1 John 4:21 KJV
1 Thessalonians 5:11 NIV
Hebrews 10:24-25 ESV
Romans 12:8 NIV

Chapter 5
Deuteronomy 31:6 NIV
2 Corinthians 1:3-5 NIV
Hebrews 13:5 NIV
Mathew 28:20 NIV
Joshua 1:9 NIV
Ephesians 4:2 ESV
Isaiah 40:31 NKJV
Deuteronomy 31:6 NIV

Chapter 6
Matthew 6:33 NIV
1 Corinthians 12:8 NIV
Romans 12:8 NIV

Chapter 7
1 Corinthians 16:1 NKJV
Esther 4:14 NIV
1 Corinthians 12:9 NIV
Hebrews 11:1-3 NIV
1 Timothy 6:7-8 NIV
Thessalonians 5:17 NIV
Joshua 1:9 NIV
John 15:13 NIV

Chapter 8
John 10:10 NIV
Psalm 97:10 NIV
2 Timothy 1:7 NIV
Psalm 23:1-6 EASY
2 Corinthians 2:11 NIV
1 Corinthians 16:13-14 NIV
Deuteronomy 20::4 NIV
Psalm 121:7 KJV
James 1:2-3 NIV
Joshua 1:9 NIV
1 Peter 2:19-23 NIV
Acts 5:3-6; 16:16-18 NIV
1 Peter 5:8-9 NIV
Ephesians 6:18 NIV
2 Corinthians 2:11 NIV

Chapter 9
1 John 4 NIV
Genesis 4:3-5 NIV
Luke 21:1-4 NIV
2 Corinthians 9:13-15 NIV
II Peter 1:10-11 AMP
Proverbs 16:9 NIV
John 13:34 NIV
Proverbs 15:1 NIV

Ephesians 2:10 NIV
Galatians 6:2 NIV
Acts 1:8 NLT

Chapter 10
Luke15:5-7 NIV
Jeremiah 1:4-5 NIV
Psalm 46:1 KJV
Psalm 139:13-18 NIV
John 4:14 NIV
I Peter 2-9 NIV
Philippians 2:9-11 NIV
Romans 8:15-17 NIV

Chapter 11
2 Chronicles 15:7 NIV
John 3:16 KJV
Jeremiah 29:11 NIV

Chapter 12
Matthew 5:4 NIV
John 16:33 NIV
I John 4:21 NIV
John 3:16 NIV

Chapter 13
Psalm 107:43 KJV
Philippians 2:4 GNT
Proverbs 10:9 NIV
Colossians 3:12 NIV
Luke 9:62 MSG
Philippians 2:1-2 NIV
Ecclesiastes 3:1 NIV
Philippians 2:4 GNT

Printed in the United States
by Baker & Taylor Publisher Services